Linked Data for Libraries, Archives and Museums

Linked Data for Libraries, Archives and Museums

How to Clean, Link and Publish Your Metadata

Seth van Hooland and Ruben Verborgh

An imprint of the American Library Association

Chicago | 2014

© 2014 Seth van Hooland and Ruben Verborgh

First published in the United Kingdom by Facet Publishing, 2014.
This simultaneous U.S. Edition published by ALA Neal-Schuman,
an imprint of the American Library Association, 2014.

18 17 16 15 14   5 4 3 2 1

ISBN: 978-0-8389-1251-5 (paper)

Contents

The authors

Seth van Hooland is an assistant professor at the Université libre de Bruxelles (ULB). After a career in the private sector for a digitization company, he obtained his PhD in information science at ULB in 2009. Following a post-doc position at the University Carlos III of Madrid, Seth joined the Information and Communication Science Department at ULB and became the academic responsible for their Master in Information Science. In the spring semester of 2014, he taught a special course on linked data at the Information School of the University of Washington. He is also active as a consultant in the document and records management domain for both public and private organizations.

Ruben Verborgh is a researcher in semantic hypermedia at Ghent University – iMinds, Belgium, where he obtained his PhD in computer science engineering in 2014. He explores the connection between semantic web technologies and the web's architectural properties, with the ultimate goal of building more intelligent clients. Along the way, he has become fascinated by linked data, REST/hypermedia, web APIs and related technologies. Ruben is the author of a book on the interactive data transformation tool OpenRefine and several publications on web-related topics in international journals.

A word of thanks

A desire to go beyond academic papers and conference presentations drove us in the summer of 2012 to create the Free Your Metadata project. Initially launching it as a gimmick, we were quickly surprised by the uptake of the learning materials that were put online. As failed musicians, we have found the project to be a great alternative way of getting ourselves on tour across the world. It is truly inspiring to see how many people share our passion for metadata, from the World Bank in Washington to information science students in Addis Ababa. So our thanks first of all go out to all the metadata practitioners we have met, and who made us realize the necessity of this handbook. Second, we also want to warmly thank Max De Wilde, our fellow metadata liberator. Without his skills in computational linguistics and his acting talents in our videos, the project and this book would not have been the same.

Seth specifically wants to thank the following people:

Professor Isabelle Boydens has been from the very beginning of my career until now a true mentor. Her critical thinking and quest for perfection in both research and teaching continuously push me forward. I also wish to thank Professor Eva Méndez and Professor Jane Greenberg, who have both been a great source of inspiration. On a personal level, I want to thank Karen Torres, whose Brooklyn home has been a base camp for establishing contacts in the USA over the years. James Lappin, besides being a great friend, provided critical feedback on the book. Lastly, I want to thank my parents for providing me with all the opportunities I could have wished for to develop myself.

Ruben wishes to thank:

The many people I met over the years for several valuable insights on technology and its use in practice. Thanks to fellow researchers and colleagues for lively discussions. My deepest appreciation goes to my wife Anneleen for being so supportive during all those months of writing. Thanks to my parents for encouraging me to follow my dreams and passions. Finally, a tip of the hat to my musician friends Thomas and Steven, secretly hoping that one day we'll do a tour of the world, too.

Foreword

Never before has so much of our global cultural heritage been at our fingertips. Yet as billions have been spent so far on digitization, both public and private, it still feels as though we are in the very earliest stages of what might be possible. Truly usable and intuitive interfaces notwithstanding, there is still much to do in terms of simple search and discovery tools across multiple collections.

Two of the datasets that feature as case studies in this book are from institutions where I've led the teams responsible for their public release. One, the Powerhouse Museum, was a large and comparatively well resourced state institution, with a long history of rigour, excellence and computer-based documentation amongst its cataloguing and registrar departments; and the other, Cooper-Hewitt, a small historic house museum, whose collection still is best documented on cards dating from the mid 20th century. Even when those two institutions held versions of the same object, such as the seminal Aeron office chair, the two corresponding documentary records could not have been more different in detail and perspective. But at the end of the day, the future of both these institutions lies in what they can do with those records and what can be built upon them now and in a hundred years' time. In making these datasets publicly available, downloadable and accessible through simple well designed APIs, both the Powerhouse and Cooper-Hewitt had to embrace an acceptance of the incompleteness of their digitization and cataloguing efforts. I've previously described this as 'institutional *wabi sabi*', referencing the Japanese aesthetic of imperfection as beauty and applying it to organizational strategy and practice.

This book is a much-needed guide to the 'how' of getting more from those collections that form the backbone of libraries, archives and museums, even if the galleries are now being filled with blockbuster 'experiences', and the stacks replaced with internet terminals and comfortable lounges. In fact, as our knowledge institutions increasingly become places of memorable social experiences and interactions, the importance of collections having greater exposure, access and life to those outside the 'building' is ever more critical.

Importantly, this book introduces the means to see the totality of the process of making your collections available, from the arduous processes of cleaning and connecting to publishing it for the world. Along the way there are diversions into controlled vocabularies, crowdsourcing, APIs, data profiling and code. Often inside institutions these tasks, and associated discourses, are still carried out by individuals located on different branches of the organizational tree, and sometimes even in different buildings. This physical and psychological separation has often contributed to an institutional inertia around making collections available, and my hope is that readers will come to a better understanding of the complexity at each stage of the process and begin to collaborate better. Along with a range of useful case studies and code examples, both the budding digital humanist and the long-tenured registrar and cataloguer should be able to quickly start to poke at and experiment with their own datasets.

If my teams had had access to this book when we started making collections data widely available back in 2006, we might have done things a little differently and better.

Sebastian Chan
Director of Digital & Emerging Media
Smithsonian Cooper-Hewitt, National Design Museum, New York

Glossary

AI	Artificial Intelligence
ANSI	American National Standards Institute
API	Application Programming Interface
ASCII	American Standard Code for Information Interchange
ASP	Active Server Pages
BT	Broader Term
CAPTCHA	Completely Automated Public Turing test to tell Computers and Humans Apart
CMS	Content Management System
CSS	Cascading Style Sheets
CSV	Comma-Separated Value
DC	Dublin Core
DDC	Dewey Decimal Classification
DERI	Digital Enterprise Research Institute
DH	Digital Humanities
DNS	Domain Name Server
DPLA	Digital Public Library America
DTD	Document Type Definition
GSC	Gold Standard Corpus
HTML	Hypertext Markup Language
HTTP	Hypertext Transfer Protocol
IANA	Internet Assigned Numbers Authority
IETF	Internet Engineering Task Force
IP	Internet Protocol
IRI	Internationalized Resource Identifier
ISBN	International Standard Book Number
ISO	International Organization for Standardization
JPEG	Joint Photographic Experts Group
JSON	JavaScript Object Notation

LCC	Library of Congress Classification
LCNA	Library of Congress Name Authorities
LCSH	Library of Congress Subject Headings
LD	Linked Data
LIS	Library and Information Science
LOC	Library of Congress
LOD	Linked Open Data
MACS	Multilingual Access to Subjects
MADS	Metadata Authority Description Schema
MARC	Machine Readable Cataloging
MQL	Metaweb Query Language
NER	Named-entity Recognition
NISO	National Information Standards Organization
NLP	Natural Language Processing
NT	Narrower Term
OCLC	Online Computer Library Center
OCR	Optical Character Recognition
OWL	Web Ontology Language
PNG	Portable Network Graphics
PONT	Powerhouse Museum Object Name Thesaurus
QR	Quick Response Code
RAM	Random Access Memory
RAMEAU	Répertoire d'autorité-matière encyclopédique et alphabétique unifié
RDF	Resource Description Framework
RDFS	Resource Description Framework Schema
RDMS	Relational Database Management Software
REST	Representational State Transfer
RT	Related Term
SDBM	Schoenberg Database of Manuscripts
SGML	Standard Generalized Markup Language
SKOS	Simple Knowledge Organization System
SOAP	Simple Object Access Protocol
SPARQL	SPARQL Protocol and RDF Query Language
SQL	Structured Query Language
SRU	Search & Retrieve via URL
SRW	Search & Retrieve Web Service
STITCH	SemanTic Interoperability To access Cultural Heritage
SWD	Schlagwortnormdatei
TEI	Text Encoding Initiative
TMS	The Museum System
TSV	Tab-Separated Value

UC	Universal Classification
UDC	Universal Decimal Classification
UI	User Interface
ULAN	Union List of Artist Names
URI	Uniform Resource Identifier
URL	Uniform Resource Locator
UTF	UCS Transformation Format
VIAF	Virtual International Authority Files
VRA	Visual Resource Association
XML	eXtensible Markup Language

1

Introduction

1 Metadata at the crossroads

While working with metadata practitioners and students over recent years, we often sensed a frustration. Linked data holds the promise to create meaningful links between objects of disparate collections, but the actual implementation tends to be quite complex. According to academics and consultants, RDF triple stores and SPARQL endpoints should bring us a brave new world in which everything is connected in a meaningful manner. Unfortunately, the reality proves to be quite complex and even outright messy. The search for the Holy Grail of data integration can turn into a nightmare, in a world where anyone can state anything about anything. Linked data: the kingdom of structured data to come or an irritating buzzword which we all will have forgotten in a few years?

The ambition of this handbook is to bring a sense of pragmatism to the debate. We will point out the low-hanging fruit currently available, but also identify potential issues and areas where it is uncertain that investments in linked data will deliver benefits. Besides avoiding an uncritical promotion of a hyped technology, the originality of this handbook lies in the positioning of linked data within the broader context of how metadata practices have evolved over the last decades. As many of you may have noticed, the term 'metadata architect' has started to appear on business cards and job descriptions. It is interesting to observe trends in the labelling of professional activities, especially in fields such as information science, which tend to be considered as arcane by the general public. This job title reflects the enthusiasm of the late 1990s and 2000s for the development of metadata standards, application profiles and metadata mappings. The use of the term 'architect' illustrates an almost utopian belief in the design of a global and coherent information architecture which can be implemented consistently across an organization.

Most of us know that the term 'metadata architect' rarely matches the reality. 'Digital landfill manager' sounds less glamorous but reflects the job content more adequately.[1] The implementation of successive technologies over decades has scattered the metadata of our libraries, archives and museums across multiple databases, spreadsheets and even unstructured word processing documents. For business continuity reasons, legacy and newly introduced technologies often co-exist in parallel. Even in cases where a superseded technology is completely abandoned, relics of the former tool can often be found in the content which has been migrated to the new application.

Why does this all matter? This book does not defend a merely technological deterministic view but we do want to emphasize the impact tools have on how we access and use cultural heritage. Throughout different application domains, there is a common belief that the use of new technologies is beneficial. Experience from the terrain has demonstrated that this is unfortunately not always the case. For example, throughout the 1970s and 1980s the first databases were introduced and retro-cataloguing efforts were initiated to convert millions of paper-based cards into database records. Popular database software of that era, such as DBase, ran on hardware with limited storage capacities. Due to this limitation, database administrators restricted the number of characters to be used within fields, leading to a situation where the first databases from the 1980s sometimes contained less detailed information than the paper-based documentation.

As a profession and discipline, we have been working hard over the last two decades to streamline documentation practices in libraries, archives and museums. The rise of the web obliged us to pick up the pace of standardization efforts of metadata schemes and controlled vocabularies, which were initiated after the use of databases for cataloguing and indexing throughout the 1970s and 1980s. At the same time, budget cuts and fast-growing collections are currently obliging information providers to explore automated methods to provide access to resources. We are expected to gain more value out of the metadata patrimony we have been building up over decades. The current hype on linked data seems to offer amazing opportunities to valorize what we already have and to facilitate the creation of new metadata. To what extent can we, as a discipline and a profession, take linked data at face value?

Until recently, metadata practitioners lacked accessible methods and tools to experiment with linked data. In this handbook, we will focus on how freely available tools and services can be used to start evaluating the use of linked data on your own. The quickly evolving landscape of standards and technologies certainly continues to present challenges to non-technical domain experts, but we do want to point out the low-hanging fruit which is currently hanging in front of our noses.

Technology is a means and not an end. Opportunities arise from new tech-nologies, yet never before has it been easier to get lost and trapped within them. Linked data principles are often misunderstood and need to be implemented in a well reflected manner. Linked data present tremendous challenges with regard to the quality of our metadata, and so it is fundamental to develop a critical view and differentiate between what is feasible and what is not.

2 Definition and scope of key concepts

Three concepts define and delimit this handbook: linked data, metadata and cultural heritage institutions. In order to set the expectations right, let us briefly see how these terms are understood within the context of the handbook.

The term **linked data** (often given as 'Linked Data') is often used as if it was a specific, well defined technology. For example, you might have come across technology vendors claiming their products explicitly support linked data. The term does not represent one well defined technology or standard. In the context of this book, linked data is understood as a set of best practices for the publication of structured data on the web. Although a lot of effort is being put into the standardization process of all of the underlying techniques, this set of practices is evolving at a continuous pace. Linked data remains very much a moving target but within this handbook we concentrate on core principles which should remain stable over the years to come.

A linked data handbook with a particular focus on metadata seems to be a tautology, in the sense that linked data as such can be considered metadata. RDF triples are short and simple statements which describe a resource. By doing so, they are data about data and can therefore be considered metadata. This brings up the question of where to draw the line between data and metadata. The short answer is: you cannot. It is the context of the use which decides whether to consider data as metadata or not. You should also not forget one of the basic characteristics of metadata: they are ever-extensible. Just as you can always add an extra Lego piece on top of another, you can always add another layer of metadata to describe metadata. For example, a user review of a book on Amazon can be considered as a form of metadata of the book. By giving users the opportunity to evaluate the usefulness of the review, other users add another level of metadata. The research domain on the issue of provenance and trust on the web is by and large based on this principle. This feature of ever-extensibility comes in very handy but can also turn into a nightmare: every extra layer of metadata adds to the complexity of an application.

Within the context of this handbook, our focus resides on metadata from libraries, archives and museums. Throughout the handbook, we will refer to these as cultural heritage institutions. Each one of these three types of organization has its own deeply rooted traditions regarding metadata. Nevertheless, we think it is useful to synthesize within one handbook common principles and best practices for the management of metadata. When describing practices such as metadata modelling, cleaning, reconciliation, enrichment and publication, the focus of the book will be as much as possible on common needs shared across different types of institutions. However, we do acknowledge the fundamentally different views an archivist, for example, holds when thinking about metadata modelling, compared with those of a librarian or a museum curator. Due to the importance of the notion of the 'fonds', in which the place of an individual document within a larger collection is of central importance, archival collections find a natural fit with the hierarchical tree structure of XML. On the other hand, libraries have worked for decades with the MARC format, which is an electronic file format created in the 1960s to represent flat files containing bibliographic data. These differences have a big impact on metadata practices but throughout the different chapters we have tried as much as possible to develop views and recommendations which are relevant for all three types of institutions.

3 Position and originality of the handbook

Over recent years a wealth of information has been made available on the topic of linked data. In this section we wish to point out the most comprehensive learning resources available but also to emphasize the originality of this handbook when compared to the existing literature.

The computer science community has delivered over the last years specific handbooks on linked data (Heath and Bizer, 2011; Wood, Zaidman and Ruth, 2013). The by now classic semantic web handbook by Allemang and Hendler (2011) is highly relevant for people eager to learn about linked data. Although outdated in some aspects, the practical handbook by Segaran remains a useful resource (Segaran, Evans and Taylor, 2009).

There is to our knowledge no previously published handbook which is aimed specifically at the library and information science (LIS) or the digital humanities (DH) communities. Greenberg and Mendéz published a comprehensive set of chapters on different aspects of the semantic web relevant to the library and information science domain, but the publication remains mainly research-oriented (Greenberg and Mendéz, 2012). People from the LIS community might be surprised by the lack of attention to metadata standardization efforts. Although the topic is relevant in the context of linked data, metadata standards have been abundantly addressed over the last years in other handbooks. Where necessary, we refer to the relevant literature on metadata standards throughout this handbook.

The second chapter of this book is dedicated to metadata quality, which has until now remained under-represented in the linked data literature. The topic of data quality has already attracted attention in other application domains and some handbooks have been devoted to the topic. The most useful book, beyond any doubt, is *Data Quality: the accuracy dimension* by Olson (2003) and is often referred to in this handbook. O'Reilly published an interesting collection of concrete case studies and best practices with the aptly titled *Bad Data Handbook*

(MacCallum, 2012). One of the authors of our book has also published a handbook specifically on the use of OpenRefine, offering readers the opportunity to go into more specific details of all of the functionalities of OpenRefine (Verborgh and De Wilde, 2013).

Compared to other publication formats, handbooks aim to offer a comprehensive introduction to a topic. Within this genre, this handbook specifically has the ambition to:

- lower the technical barrier towards understanding linked data
- propose a critical view of linked data, by not making an abstraction of the challenges and disadvantages involved.

First of all, we wish in this handbook to address the specific needs of people who do not have a technical background in computer science. More particularly, the handbook was written for readers with a background in library and information science and digital humanities. Both communities have shown a strong interest in linked data and hope to leverage through its principles the creation and use of metadata. The two communities have their own tradition and methods with regard to metadata, and it is interesting to bring them together in this book.

Secondly, linked data literature tends to be written by technology evangelists who sometimes hold an almost religious belief in the value of linked data. Unfortunately, technology all too often becomes an end in itself. Based on some of the linked data literature, one might start to think that we will be abandoning our relational databases for triple stores. The reality is that we will continue to use relational databases over the next years (and probably decades), as they excel at managing structured data. Within this handbook, we try to make it very clear what exactly the advantages of linked data are for the publication of your metadata. As with many things in life, advantages often come at a cost. At the end of the day, it is the context of your specific project, with its own needs and resources, that will decide what technology to use. If you can deliver good results with a tool which has existed for over 30 years, then there is absolutely no reason to go along with the most recent technology hype.

4 Structure and learning objectives

In order to achieve the ambitions mentioned above, a lot of effort was put into the structure of the handbook and the combination of theory with practice. This handbook tightly couples the conceptual introduction of technologies with hands-on exercises and experimentation, giving non-IT experts the opportunity to evaluate the practical use of metadata cleaning and reconciliation, named-entity recognition (NER), sustainable publishing and the overall concept of linked data.

Each chapter leads up to a concrete case study with metadata from institutions around the world (USA, Australia and Europe). The accompanying website, http://book.freeyourmetadata.org/, allows you to download the metadata used in the case studies and to repeat the exercises at your own pace.

The chapters and case studies stand on their own and can be read individually. LIS and DH professors and independent trainers can use one of the five core chapters (2–6) to build up a specific class on, for example, metadata cleaning or the use of NER within a more generic metadata or DH-oriented class. One of the biggest incentives to write this handbook was to provide thorough documentation for our own students and workshop participants. We have tested and refined the examples and exercises over the course of three years, with the help of hundreds of students and archivists, librarians and curatorial staff in Europe, the USA and Australia.

Throughout the handbook we have tried to keep as much consistency as possible with regard to the technical skills readers acquire throughout the different chapters. Three out of the five case studies involve the use of OpenRefine. This free and easy-to-use application could be considered as Excel-on-steroids. Visually the interface resembles the popular spreadsheet software, but it offers a host of possibilities for automatically deriving more value out of your existing metadata. Extra functionalities, known as extensions, are constantly being developed for this software. Specifically for the readers of this handbook, we developed an extension which allows the user to apply NER services in a very handy way (see Chapter 5). This extension has been warmly welcomed by the OpenRefine community and is quickly becoming one of the key functionalities for the use of OpenRefine for linked data applications.

Even if the chapters stand on their own, there is a clear logic behind the order in which the chapters are presented. As such, the entire book can also be used as a global handbook on the use of linked data within the humanities. The following list gives a clear outline of the content, learning outcomes and reader profile of each chapter:

- **Chapter 2: Modelling**
  - Overall goal: understand the rationale of linked data through an overview of the major data modelling paradigms.
  - Audience: people in need of a better understanding of the differences and similarities between tabular data, relational databases, XML and RDF.
  - Conceptual insights: impact of data modelling for metadata.
  - Practical skills: construction of queries in graph databases. Readers are made familiar with SPARQL through DBpedia. In order to make use of Freebase, the proprietary Metaweb Query Language is also illustrated with some examples.

- **Chapter 3: Cleaning**
  — Overall goal: understanding that most metadata need to be cleaned.
  — Audience: collection holders who want to understand how to weed out common metadata quality issues and get a better global understanding of metadata quality.
  — Conceptual insights: quality is a fundamentally relative characteristic; 'total quality' therefore does not exist. Instead, focus on how metadata evolve through time.
  — Practical skills: metadata profiling and cleaning operations with the help of the general features of OpenRefine are illustrated with metadata from the Schoenberg Database of Manuscripts.

- **Chapter 4: Reconciling**
  — Overall goal: possibilities and limitations of re-using controlled vocabularies.
  — Audience: practitioners and students who want to understand the differences between classification schemes, subject headings and thesauri, and how they can be represented in a web-accessible format (SKOS, Simple Knowledge Organization System).
  — Conceptual insights: advantages and disadvantages of the use of controlled vocabularies on the web.
  — Practical skills: after an introduction to SKOS through the manual encoding of a mini-thesaurus with a text editor, the use of the RDF extension for OpenRefine is demonstrated. Once the basic functionalities of SKOS and the creation of reconciliation sources is understood, the case study focuses on how the LCSH can be used to reconcile a collection of metadata records from the Powerhouse Museum.

- **Chapter 5: Enriching**
  — Overall goal: possibilities and limitations of applying NER to metadata.
  — Audience: collection holders who want to understand what types of results can be expected from NER technologies.
  — Conceptual insights: introduction to theme of 'Big Metadata' and applying 'distant reading' techniques upon cultural heritage metadata. Overview of the ambiguity of URLs.
  — Practical skills: step-by-step introduction to the use of the NER extension within OpenRefine. Three different NER services (Zemanta, Alchemy and DBpedia Spotlight) are tested upon the descriptive fields of metadata the British Library has provided through Europeana.

- **Chapter 6: Publishing**
  - Overall goal: understanding how to publish your collection in a sustainable manner.
  - Audience: practitioners and students interested in understanding the conceptual and practical benefits of the representational state transfer (REST) architectural style.
  - Conceptual insights: distinguish resources from their representations.
  - Practical skills: through a small prototype with metadata from the Smithsonian Cooper-Hewitt National Design Museum, readers can experiment with how a RESTful application can publish metadata in a sustainable manner. Exercises with the APIs of Europeana and Digital Public Library America (DPLA) allow the reader to better situate the concepts presented in the theoretical part of the chapter.

5 Get in touch!

Throughout the years, we have learned a lot by talking and working with metadata enthusiasts across the world. As a result we have been able to write this handbook, which is very much an outcome of the discussions we have had with practitioners from libraries, archives and museums. We sincerely hope this handbook will offer us the opportunity to get in touch with even more people. The website http://freeyourmetadata.org/ will be updated with case studies and announcements of workshops and seminars. Do not hesitate to contact us – really. If you have a particularly dirty metadata set you want us to have a look at, get in touch. The dirtier your metadata are, the more we will love them. Or if you are busy developing a global institutional strategy for linked data, we'll be happy to share our thoughts with you. Our research and writing needs your input, so we will be happy to hear from you!

Note

1 The term 'digital landfill manager' has been proposed by James Lappin in his article on the evolution of records management (Lappin, 2010).

References

Allemang, D. and Hendler, J. (2011) *Semantic Web for the Working Ontologist*, Morgan Kaufmann.

Greenberg, J. and Mendéz, E. (2012) *Knitting the Semantic Web*, Routledge.

Heath, T. and Bizer, C. (2011) *Linked Data: evolving the web into a global data space*, Morgan & Claypool.

Lappin, J. (2010) What Will be the Next Records Management Orthodoxy?, *Records*

Management Journal, **20** (3), 252–64.

MacCallum, E. (2012) *Bad Data Handbook: mapping the world of data problems*, O'Reilly.

Olson, J. (2003) *Data Quality: the accuracy dimension*, Morgan Kaufmann.

Segaran, T., Evans, C. and Taylor, J. (2009) *Programming the Semantic Web*, O'Reilly.

Verborgh, R. and De Wilde, M. (2013) *Using OpenRefine*, Packt Publishing.

Wood, D., Zaidman, M. and Ruth, L. (2013) *Linked Data: structured data on the web*, Manning.

2

Modelling

Learning outcomes of this chapter

- Putting linked data in a larger context
- Getting out of a hype-driven view on technology
- Understanding the importance of data modelling
- Making sense of data models and their serialization formats

1 Introduction

Metadata managers and the software they use often seem to have a striking resemblance with couples stuck in an unhappy relationship. During coffee breaks at conferences and workshops on metadata within the library and information science domain, it will not take you long to spot a circle of people engaged in what seems to be some form of group therapy. Do not be afraid. Go ahead and stand a bit closer. You will probably overhear typical phrases such as 'We have been struggling to create new metadata fields for years!' or 'My XML export is terrible!' Confronted with these laments, the group members will nod understandingly and express their sympathy. Complaining about one's software is a popular point of discussion across the globe when collection holders come together to discuss metadata. Ironically, just like old couples who think twice about divorce due to the important emotional and economic consequences, metadata managers often persist for years in the abusive relationship with their software. They usually prefer not to move over to another software solution.

How different the ambiance in the digital humanities! Instead of complaining about the difficulties encountered with their database, people active in the digital humanities often are very proud about the information system they built to manage a specific type of resource or collection. Susan Hockey even coined the expression '"Me and my database" papers'. Anyone who has already attended a DH conference is familiar with the phenomenon: a researcher who presents, in tedious detail, how a database was developed to accommodate every peculiar feature of a collection. These speakers tend to be very proud of the database they constructed and radiate love and passion for it.

Why do these two communities have such a different approach to the software they use to manage cultural heritage resources and their metadata? Why do collection holders constantly whine about their database, whereas digital humanists express their satisfaction and even brag about the happiness they found with their database?

These differences relate to the extent to which the *model* used to represent an object and its metadata is deemed adequate or not. When we want to make resources and their metadata available in a structured manner on the web, we first need to decide what characteristics of theirs are the most important to be represented. By doing so, we make an abstraction of the reality through the development of a model.

In the cultural heritage context we mentioned, institutions are forced to work with off-the-shelf software, since the development of a custom-built collection management system is simply not economically feasible. The drawback of working with existing software is that institutions often find themselves limited in how they can describe their objects. Vendors have a commercial incentive to develop generic software that can be sold to as many institutions as possible. This implies that collection management software already prescribes a certain explicit *worldview*, through the use of a pre-established model. It is therefore not always possible to accommodate the specific requirements of an institution and its collections, leading to frustration amongst collection holders.

In contrast, the DH community uses databases for limited and specific research projects, as they tend to focus on the documentation and publication of one specific type of resource or collection. Within these limited research projects with a precise scope, the requirements tend to be so specific that it is not possible to use off-the-shelf software. In this type of context, relational database management software (RDMS) is often used to implement a tailored model. The drawback of meeting all the precise requirements of such a project are the relatively high development costs and the difficulty to maintain the application over time. Investments are made in projects that very often cannot be re-used.

1.1 Deciding where to put the semantics

What does this have to do with linked data? The examples above demonstrate that both the use of a generic, standardized model and of a highly customized, specific model come at a cost. The tremendous amount of effort the LIS community has put into metadata standardization reflects how we have been trying to find a sweet spot between the two approaches. As it will be demonstrated through practical examples, the evolution from an unstructured narrative to a highly structured representation of metadata requires the development of schemas in order to make the metadata interoperable. By slicing up unstructured descriptive narratives into well structured fields, we need to render the meaning of the different fields (also called attributes) explicit by documenting them in a *schema*. By structuring and atomizing metadata fields we make them more machine-interoperable, but we also become more and more reliant on the schemas when needing to interpret our own or someone else's metadata. It is precisely in this context that linked data need to be understood. Through the adoption of a radically simple data model, abstraction can be made of the traditional XML and database schemas we had to use in the past to interpret and re-use data.

1.2 Getting away from a hype-driven view of technology

The adoption of a new technology is often illustrated in the form of the famous Gartner hype cycle (Lynden and Fenn, 2003). The graphical representation of the rise and decline of the popularity of a new technology draws attention to the exaggerated expectations which often accompany its introduction. After the so-called *peak of inflated expectations*, a technology tends to lose most of its appeal on the market a couple of years after its introduction. It is only after an extensive period that the technology reaches a stable level of adoption, based on its genuine added value in a production environment. One of the goals of this book is to teach you how to step away from a hype-driven view on technology by helping you understand not only the exact added value of linked data, but also its weak points.

Where should we situate linked data in this cycle? The recent enthusiasm to connect heterogeneous resources and to draw in new information from external knowledge sources perhaps recalls for some the unbounded enthusiasm the cultural heritage sector had for the eXtensible Markup Language (XML) around 2000 and a couple of years later for web 2.0. In hindsight, we can now safely say that both approaches have been (and continue to be) fundamentally important for how we create and manage our metadata. However, we should also acknowledge that neither XML nor the social web resolved all of the fundamental problems underlying how we can connect resources from various collections.

Despite a major overhaul of the general technological framework, illustrated by other developments, such as the maturing of open-source collection management systems and cloud-based hosting, for example, we are still very much facing the same problems the cultural heritage community was discussing almost five decades ago. For anyone working on the topic of digital cultural heritage, it is a humbling experience to read about the discussions that were taking place in the 1960s and 70s. In parallel with the creation of the Computer

Museum Network in 1967, a project was launched to create a common collection management database that would be used by all participants of the consortium. Numerous other initiatives have since been based on the same fallacy: if we all use the same tool, our metadata will become interoperable. Again and again, projects have demonstrated that even if people and institutions are using the same tools and standards, they implement them in different ways to accommodate the specific nature of their collections.

Are linked data here to break this vicious circle, or are we again confronted with an overhyped technology? Before we answer that question, we need to moderate the inflated expectations surrounding linked data. Practitioners trying to get to grips with linked data principles are frequently frustrated when confronted with the output of large-scale IT research projects. Huge volumes of metadata and controlled vocabularies have been converted over recent years into Resource Description Framework (RDF), producing billions of RDF statements. Unfortunately, these so-called *triple stores* only unlock their value through the use of a complex query language called SPARQL Protocol and RDF Query Language (SPARQL). The purely technology-driven nature of many linked data projects is leaving a bitter aftertaste amongst practitioners, who feel they need a PhD in semantic web technologies in order to take advantage of linked data.

1.3 The world's shortest introduction to data modelling

Let us therefore, in this chapter, step away from the merely hype-driven view of linked data by choosing a more conceptual and historical approach. In order to grasp the potential but also the limits of linked data, we need a better understanding of the different data models which have been used over recent decades to manage metadata. The advantages of RDF, the data model underlying the linked data vision, can only be fully understood in the context of previous data models. At the end of this chapter you will understand that the different data models presented do not supplant one another, but continue to co-exist. The overview of the different models should make it clear that relational databases are here to stay, and will not be disposed of in favour of triple stores. Technology vendors and IT researchers have a tendency to overemphasize the role a new technology has to play. At the height of the popularity of XML, one sometimes got the impression that the back-end of any type of information system would become XML-based. A decade later, XML is criticized more often than not, and new serialization formats such as JSON are often preferred. This chapter will provide the world's shortest introduction to IT fashion, in order to help you see the wood for the trees.

We will specifically focus within the overview offered in this chapter on the management of structured data, but be aware that the traditional barriers between structured and unstructured data are becoming increasingly blurred.

For decades, different communities have been working independently from one another on both topics. Database engineers focus on the optimization of the management of structured data, whereas computational linguists develop methods and tools to manage unstructured natural language in an automated manner. The different traditions and views between the two communities can be illustrated by analysing how both communities make use of XML. Computer engineers see XML as a hierarchical tree in which structured data can be encoded in order to facilitate the communication of data between machines. On the other hand, computational linguists and digital humanists look at XML as a method to insert small pieces of structure into an otherwise unstructured textual document. Indicating where exactly in a full text the names of places or people can be found allows scholars to automate to a certain extent the analysis of an unstructured corpus. We will discuss XML in more detail in the section on meta-markup languages later in the chapter. The traditional distinction between structured and unstructured data is particularly problematic in the context of metadata. For example, within a highly structured metadata record a descriptive field might occur which contains a narrative of several pages of unstructured full text. Should this metadata record be considered structured or unstructured?

The chapter will start with the most intuitive model for structuring data, which is *tabular formats*. Due to the limitations of this approach, the *relational model* was developed in the 1970s, remaining until today the standard to represent and manage complex data. As will be explained over the next sections, the appearance of the web towards the end of the 1990s catalysed the need for *data portability*. Sharing data between different databases is a very tedious process, for reasons which will be explained below. In order to facilitate the exchange of structured data on the web, meta-markup languages, and XML in particular, have been used from 2000 onwards. XML proposes a standardized syntax for the automated exchange of structured data, but the actual use and interpretation of the data can still be troublesome. The meaning of the elements and attributes of the XML files need to be defined in a schema. The interpretation of the schema remains a barrier for an automated consumption of data across information systems on the web. It is exactly here where RDF comes in. By adopting a data model which embodies the meaning of the data in its most essential and stripped down form, there no longer is a need for an outside schema to interpret and re-use the data.

Figure 2.1 compares the different models from a high-level perspective. You could consider this figure as a synthetic overview of Chapter 2. We are conscious that we are covering a lot of ground with this chapter. At times, it might be challenging to understand the interaction and links between the four different data models to be discussed. In order to help you put the individual sections of this chapter into a bigger perspective, Figure 2.1 highlights in an abstract manner the features of each data model. Even though each model has its own properties,

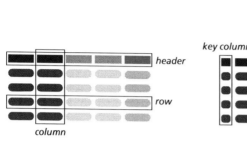

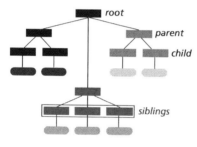

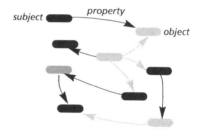

Tabular data
Each data item is structured as a line of field values. Fields are the same for all items; a header line can indicate their name.

Relational model
Data are structured as tables, each of which has its own set of attributes. Records in one table can relate to others by referencing their key column.

Meta-markup languages
XML documents have a hierarchical structure, which gives them a tree-like appearance. Each element can have one or more children; there is exactly one root element.

RDF
Each fact about a data item is expressed as a triple, which connects a subject to an object through a precise relationship. This leads to graph-structured data that can take any shape.

Figure 2.1 Schematic comparison of the four major data models

similarities have been highlighted insofar as possible. For example, rounded shapes represent individual data values; rectangular shapes indicate model-specific ways to add structure (with the exception of RDF, where arrows are used). Different shades indicate data values that semantically belong together, indicating how different models treat them.

1.4 Every advantage has its disadvantage (and vice versa)

Be aware that this chapter explicitly does not represent the different models as a linear succession of increasingly high-performing solutions to manage structured data. In other words: please do not interpret the following sections of this chapter as a story of how we have gone from an inadequate approach towards the perfect solution. As with many things in life, advantages offered by a data model often imply disadvantages (and vice versa). For example, the schema-neutral feature of RDF comes at a big cost. Whether a data model (and the methods, technologies and tools it comes with) is suited for you entirely depends on the context of the problem you want to solve. To make things as clear as possible, every model will be illustrated with the help of small examples of metadata in relation to the work of Pablo Picasso.[1]

1.5 Data models and their serialization formats

Before we proceed to the overview of data modelling, it is important to clearly distinguish each model conceptually from the formats that have been developed to *serialize* the data model. The serialization process converts data structures into a *format*. The format allows the translation of the information you are representing into a stream of bits that can be manipulated by software, communicated over a network, etc. The format allows a conversion from the bit level back into the original data.

The difference between a model and a serialization can be compared to a dish and its recipe. The in-memory model is the thing itself and is accessible for manipulation – or is immediately ready to be eaten, like a prepared dish. A serialization contains all necessary elements to construct the in-memory model, just as a recipe contains all the information you need to prepare the dish. Table 2.1 gives an overview of the different data models and their serialization formats which will be discussed over the next sections.

Table 2.1 Data models and their serialization formats	
data model	**serialization formats**
tabular data	CSV, TSV
relational model	*proprietary binary files*
meta-markup languages	XML, SGML
RDF	Turtle, N-Triples, RDF-XML

2 Tabular data

Suppose you were given a collection of resources, such as photographs, books or DVDs, and were asked to describe the collection. What would be the most intuitive and natural thing to do? Chances are high that you would take a sheet of paper, or create a spreadsheet on your computer, and create columns in which you will aggregate the most important metadata of the resources, such as title, creator, date, etc.

2.1 Model

Conceptually, the world view you create with tabular data is comprised of columns and rows. The intersection of a column with a row gives meaning to the data contained in the particular cell. Figure 2.1 illustrates this data model on an abstract level. There is only one modelling dimension, consisting of the fields in the first header row. Each row contains data from different semantic entities, which we can also refer to as *records*. This is why tabular data are often referred to as *flat files*. Coming back to our concrete example, it is an intuitive act to use this model and to draw up a list as presented in Table 2.2, illustrating how you might develop a tabular overview of your resources.

Table 2.2 Example of metadata encoded as tabular data			
title	creator	date	collection
Guernica	Pablo Picasso	1937	Museo Reina Sofia
First Communion	Picasso	1895	Museo Picasso
Puppy	Koons, Jeff	1992	Guggenheim
...	...	...	...

Over centuries, catalogues and indexes were encoded in this tabulated form. The list, as most people would call tabular data, can probably be considered as the oldest information technology. Drawing up lists organized in columns is still often the first step taken when brainstorming and developing ideas about what metadata elements should be used to document a resource. Why is this such an intuitive data model? Tabular data offer the big advantage that they are almost self-explanatory. When reading a catalogue or an index in this format, you have a natural tendency to read in a horizontal manner by focusing on one line of the catalogue and reading from left to right the information gathered in the different 'boxes'. This allows you to get an immediate overview of all the different metadata elements (in our table: *title*, *creator* and *date*) concerning one specific object. Semiologists or linguists would refer to the importance of the *syntagmatic* relations. Through the combination of different elements, meaning is created in the sense that we understand what an object is, when it was created and by whom. A vertical reading, gazing up and down the columns, allows you to get a sense of the different values of one specific metadata element. On this level, the so-called *paradigmatic* relations operate. These relations cluster members of the same category.

The difference and interaction between syntagmatic and paradigmatic relations might seem like a pedantic academy side note. Keep in mind that they play an important role in understanding the difference between the use of unstructured descriptions, which we can refer to as narratives, and structured metadata fields, which have been sliced up to make them more machine-processable. Lev Manovich drew attention to the fundamental difference between these two forms of presenting information:

As a cultural form, a database represents the world as a list of items and it refuses to order this list. In contrast, a narrative creates a cause-and-effect trajectory of seemingly unordered items. Competing for the same territory of human culture, each claims an exclusive right to make meaning out of the world. The database (the paradigm) is given material existence, while the narrative (the syntagm) is dematerialized. Paradigm is privileged, syntagm is downplayed. Paradigm is real, syntagm is virtual.

Manovich, 2001, 231

Traditionally, people have privileged the form of narrative when communicating information, but the massive presence of database-driven applications on the web is reversing the situation. This evolution is very much embodied in how our metadata practices have evolved. From the beginning of the 20th century, our cultural heritage institutions have started to decompose the lengthy narrative descriptions drawn up by curators and transferred them to card catalogues and database records. This evolution drastically helped to facilitate search and retrieval, but actually making sense of a complex object is still based on the unstructured description. Manovich goes too far when presenting the two forms as exclusive and competing. It is the introduction of database-driven websites that made the advent of web 2.0 applications possible. As Chapter 5 will demonstrate, user comments can offer a valuable enrichment of the limited metadata an institution can provide, whereas named-entity recognition (NER) can currently be applied to facilitate complex search and retrieval procedures based on unstructured full text in natural language.

2.2 Serialization

The most popular serialization formats of tabular data are comma-separated values (CSV) and tab-separated values (TSV). The only, but important, difference between these two formats are the characters, appropriately called delimiters, used to indicate the separation between values. As their name indicates, CSV files use a comma as a delimiter, and TSV tabs. Please note that any type of character can be used as a delimiter. The CSV data from Table 2.2 are separated by a *comma* and rows are ended with a *line break* as follows:

```
title,creator,date,collection
Guernica,Pablo Picasso,1937,Museo Reina Sofia
First Communion,Picasso,1895,Museo Picasso
Puppy,"Koons, Jeff",1992,Guggenheim
```

The TSV version would look exactly the same, but the commas would be replaced by tab characters. And strictly speaking, the quotes around Koons, Jeff would not be necessary because the comma has no special meaning. If, however, a value needs to contain an actual tab character, quotes would be necessary.

2.3 Search and retrieval

What are the implications of this data model for search and retrieval of metadata? A quick look at the metadata in Table 2.2 gives an overview of the limitations of the tabular file approach. For example, the name of the creator is expressed in different manners ('Pablo Picasso' and 'Picasso'), as we encode the same reality every time when describing a new object this artist made. For a human being, it is straightforward to map these two different representations to the same reality. You have probably also noted the presence of "Koons, Jeff", in which quotes are used to protect the comma separating the family and the first name.

When performing a full-text search on a string of characters, an algorithm will have more problems to deliver good search results. Let us therefore suppose that you want to update your metadata and encode the name of the creator in a uniform manner. Now imagine you do not have three records (as it is the case in our example) but a couple of hundred thousand . . . Managing your metadata in a tabular list would imply that you would need to go through all these records to see where one of the different spellings of the creator's name appears and update it if needed to the preferred spelling. This working method is bound to introduce *inconsistencies* in your metadata. On a computational level, search and retrieval is very inefficient with this approach, as again the totality of your metadata records have to be checked to see whether they contain a specific value. Neither do tabular files offer the right tools to impose rules on how we encode values, resulting in inconsistencies in the way we encode metadata.

Problems only become worse when you start to think about searching across multiple files in this format. Another institution might have its own tabular data which contains relevant information for you, but how could you possibly perform a query across independent flat files in a consistent manner? Proficient users of Microsoft Excel could make use of macros and look-up tables to create links across multiple independent files, but these functionalities cannot be used outside Excel. This implies that you no longer have a platform- and application-independent format.

2.4 Change

How can tabular data evolve through time? The structure of catalogues and inventories does not change every month, but we could easily imagine at some point that we need to encode extra information, such as the technique (oil painting, aquarelle, etc.). Within the context of tabular data, we can simply add an extra column describing this new feature of the resources we are documenting. If for some reason a column is no longer used or no longer contains relevant information, it can be deleted without any consequences for the rest of the data. Adding or deleting a column does not require you to make any modifications in the structure of the file. In this regard, an information system based on tabular data is resilient to change.

2.5 Implementation

Tabular data is one of the easiest conceptual formats, and as such, any software package will offer support. The most common form are *spreadsheet* applications such as Microsoft Excel, which in essence offer one giant table that can be modified. All spreadsheet software offers the possibility to export to TSV or CSV, albeit of course with the loss of formulas (cells that are calculated based on other cells), formatting (such as colour and borders) and functionalities such as macros, which we mentioned previously. Data types are also lost: all cell contents are stored as text.

Even with the simplest data model, a lot can go wrong in practice. Several elements are noteworthy here:

- Data can be separated by a *comma* but depending on a system's local settings, this might actually be a semicolon! For instance, in many European languages, a comma instead of a dot is used as decimal separator in numbers (so 1,5 is actually 1½). On these systems, it would thus be impractical to use a comma as column separator, hence the choice of a semicolon – so CSV is not always true to its name. In practice, CSV has come to stand for any separator-delimited type, which confusingly also includes TSV.
- Rows end with a *line break*. Unfortunately, different systems can produce different results. For instance, on Windows systems, a line break actually consists of two characters (a *carriage return* followed by a *newline*), whereas on Linux-based systems, it is just a single character (only a *newline*). Additionally, Linux-based systems might expect the last line to end with a line break, while this is not necessary on Windows.
- There is no way to indicate the difference between the *header row* and the rest of the data. This means that we will have to tell this explicitly to the parser.
- If the field value itself contains a comma or a line break, such as Koons, Jeff here, the value is typically enclosed in *double quotes*, so it can be parsed correctly as a single value and not as multiple rows or columns. Note that not all parsers support both cases; line breaks, especially, might be confusing. In general, enclosing any field with double quotes is allowed, even if no special characters occur within the value.
- Another dangerous issue is *character encoding*. Different systems use

different byte codes to represent characters, in particular if these characters lie outside the traditional ASCII alphabet, such as accented letters or Japanese characters. If one system has written a file in a certain encoding, it is important for another system to use the same encoding to read the file. Otherwise, an accented character in one encoding might accidentally be transformed into one or more other characters in a different encoding. This phenomenon is called *mojibake*, the incorrect presentation of characters due to an encoding mismatch. Chapter 3 will explore how the above-mentioned issues impact metadata quality and what can be done to mitigate them.

- What if the field value contains a double quote? This is solved by *escaping* the quote, adding a character in front of it that signals the next character has no special meaning. In the case of CSV, this escaping is done by doubling the quote. For instance, the value `width: 7", height: 5"` is encoded as `"width: 7"", height: 5"""`, wherein each literal quote is preceded by another.
- The main problem with CSV is that there are many ways to *encode* a file. The Internet Engineering Task Force (IETF) proposed a standard way of serializing CSV (Shafranovich, 2005), and this format can be read by most parsers. However, this by no means implies that all generators will follow this standard. Fortunately, most parsers are *adaptive*: they apply a heuristic on the file in question to determine which conventions were used. For instance, if every line in the file contains an equal number of semicolons, it is likely to assume that the delimiter is a semicolon. Also, if the third column always consists of decimal digits, except the first row (as in our example), then it can be assumed that the first line contains header data. Of course, none of these strategies are perfect; in practice, human verification is necessary for correct parsing.

3 Relational model

The relational model was developed to deal with the issues related to redundancies and inconsistencies as described above. Developed at the end of the 1970s, the relational model has been by far the most successful approach for managing structured data, and will continue to be used in the decades to come.

3.1 Model

The model asks you to take a step back from the individual metadata recorded in the tabular format and to identify on a higher level what the different *entities* are in the reality that you want to represent. We may define an entity as the 'type of information that varies independently of another' (Ramsay, 2004). Each entity is characterized through the use of *attributes*. As depicted in Figure 2.1, entities are connected through *relations* to one another. Every record contains a unique *key* per table, which other records can use to refer to it in a relation.

3.2 Design methodology

Building a relational model is a difficult task that requires a lot of experience. Nonetheless, there are some guiding principles that you can use:

- The first task is to discover the *entity types* that the database will contain. Typically, entities correspond to independent concepts in the world of which there will be many, and each one has properties of its own. In our example, it is certain that 'Work' will be an entity type, as the database will contain several works. It is also likely that 'Creator' will be an entity type, as it is independent from Work and there will be many of them. However, an entity type of 'Country' will probably not be necessary, as we will only need the country's name and no other properties. However, for other use cases, it might be meaningful to encode 'Country' as an entity type.
- For every entity type, a table will be created in the database. Each row in the table will have a unique identifier, often a numeric value that is automatically generated. Each property of the entity will be a column in the table, and each column can have a value type. Our 'Work' table might have a textual field for the title and a date field for the creation date (or a four-digit field if we only plan to store the year).
- Next, *one-to-many relationships* must be modelled. They provide a mechanism for a record in a table to link to one record in another table, and the record in the second table can receive several such incoming links. As each entity has a unique identifier, we can add a column to the first table that will contain this identifier. That way, the objects in the first table can point to an item in the second table. For instance, the 'Work' table should contain a 'Creator' column that stores the identifier of the creator. That way, each work can be associated with one creator, and each creator can then be associated with several works.
- Finally, many-to-many relationships should be described. As fields in databases are traditionally not multi-valued, we must find another way for a record in a table to point to several records in another table. This is done by having a third relationship table, which has one column for identifiers of the first table and one column for identifiers of the second table. That way, we can find all items that belong together by traversing the rows of this table. Additional columns might describe properties of the relationship. In case works are authored by many creators, we could opt to represent them as a

many-to-many relationship. Then, we would have a third table called 'Creatorship' with columns 'work' and 'creator' that store the respective identifiers. We might add a textual column 'role' describing how the person was involved in the creation of the work.

The above points are merely guidelines. In practice, there are many possible motivations behind the choice for a certain design decision. There will always be trade-offs between optimal modelling flexibility, performance and simplicity. This is well illustrated by the option of whether to allow multiple creators for a work. This might allow you to describe the reality more closely, at the expense of a more complex (and possibly slower) data model.

Let us come back to our example. In order to have a sufficiently complex scheme, extra attributes, such as style, were added, as in Figure 2.2. It should be clear that there is no such thing as one unique and perfectly adequate model, as the same reality can be interpreted in multiple ways.

Creator

ID	first name	surname	birth year	death year
(43)	Pablo	Picasso	1881	1973
57	Jeff	Koons	1955	*null*
...	...	...	...	...

Work

ID	title	creator	collection	year	style
5	Guernica	(43)	20	1937	cubism
7	First Communion	43	(22)	1895	realism
16	Puppy	57	18	1992	conceptual
...	...	...	...	...	...

Collection

ID	name	address
18	Guggenheim	Bilbao
20	Museo Reina Sofia	Madrid
(22)	Museo Picasso	Barcelona
...	...	...

Figure 2.2 An example entity relation model with the relationships highlighted

Depending on the importance you give to an aspect of the reality you are modelling, you either decide to consider it as an entity or as an attribute. Despite the simplicity of the scheme in Figure 2.2, many readers of this book probably would come up with different versions of the scheme. For example, one could decide to reduce the entity Collection to an attribute of the entity Work, if you do not consider the address as an independent aspect that needs to be documented. The process of placing separate entities in separate tables is called *normalization*. Unfortunately, the more tables that need to be accessed to reconstruct the related metadata of an item, the slower operations will become. Therefore, a meaningful balance should be found between what data will be stored in a single table and what data is stored as a relationship.

The added complexity on the modelling level is made up for by the advantages offered by having a single record for an entity, that can be referred to with a unique ID. For example, every time you need to refer to the fact that an object is housed in a specific collection, you do not have to re-encode the metadata in relation to the address of where the collection is managed and other attributes of the entity Collection. You simply refer to the ID of the collection, and the same applies to other entities such as Creator. This approach ensures a lot more consistency. Those IDs are typically *indexed* to ensure the corresponding rows can be fetched in a fast way without traversing the entire table.

3.3 Implementation

Software built on top of this model, referred to as *relational database management software* (RDMS), has been extensively developed over the last decades and is currently at a very mature stage. Everyone has probably heard at some point about MySQL, the most popular open-source RDMS used for web applications, or MS-SQL, a proprietary RDMS developed by Microsoft. Another well known manufacturer is Oracle. Collection management systems, archival inventories and library catalogues are all built on top of a RDMS.

Most database systems work in a client-server set-up, where the server runs a RDMS and the client interacts with it using SQL statements. Consumer and small business applications, such as Microsoft Access, simplify the structure by offering a graphical user interface that works directly on top of a local database file. For regular RDMS, graphical interfaces for clients exist as well, but the communication underneath is done in SQL.

For instance, a table in MySQL can be created with:

```
CREATE TABLE Work (
  id INT AUTO_INCREMENT PRIMARY KEY,
  title VARCHAR(100),
  creator INT,
  collection INT,
  year CHAR(4),
  style VARCHAR(40)
);
```

This makes a new table called Work with an integer id column (INT), a textual title column (VARCHAR(100), meaning a string of characters with variable length, maximum 100), and integer creator and collection columns a 4-character year column, and a 40-character style column. The id column is special, since it should provide a unique identifier for each record. Therefore, it has the labels AUTO_INCREMENT (so new numbers are assigned automatically) and PRIMARY KEY (so the database knows that this is a unique field).

To insert data in this table, we can use:

```
INSERT INTO Work (title, creator, collection, year, style)
        VALUES ('Guernica', 43, 20, 1937, 'Cubism');
```

We supply the table name, followed by the names of the fields and then the values for these fields. Strings are surrounded by single quotes (and single quotes within strings are escaped by a backslash). Note how we did not supply a value for the id field, as this value is automatically generated (and will default to 1, 2, 3, … on an empty table).

3.4 Search and retrieval

After several records have been inserted, we can retrieve them with SELECT queries. For instance:

```
SELECT * FROM Work;
```

will select all records in the Work table. If we only want the titles of works by Picasso (assuming he has identifier 43 in the Creator table), we can do:

```
SELECT title FROM Work WHERE creator=43;
```

This is only a basic introduction to SQL, as end-users are only confronted with predefined SQL queries accessible through a graphical interface of a collection management system. However, it is important to understand through the example the logic behind the SQL query language. Section 5 will build further on this example to illustrate how the SPARQL query language works.

3.5 Change

The previous section on the tabular format described how little impact change has on the structure of a flat file. Adding new columns or deleting existing ones does not fundamentally alter how the tabular data can be used. The situation could not be more different with relational databases. Adding an extra table requires the database manager to rethink the entire schema of the database, as adding an extra table might imply a degrading of the normalization process.

Let us come back to our example. Imagine we want to add an entity *ArchivalItem* which describes the archival holdings of an artist that the institution possesses, such as correspondence, notes, personal photographs, historical press clippings, etc. How do we update our database with minimal effort? We can create a table *ArchivalItem* with the attributes *ID*, *document type*, *year*, *creator*, and *collection*. Then the change can happen by just adding this single table. However, that table would carry a considerable overlap with *Work*, as both have a creator, collection, and year. This information spread becomes difficult to manage in the end. If we want to respect the normalization requirements, we cannot just add extra tables, but we also need to modify the existing tables. Figure 2.3 shows a better integrated solution: the common attributes of *Work* and *ArchivalItem* are placed into a separate *Asset* table. However, this means that the existing table and data structure has to be modified.

Apart from ensuring the normalization of the new database schema, the

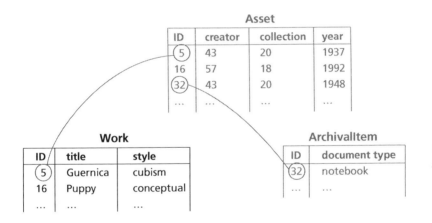

Figure 2.3 To support archival items in a consistent way, the *creator*, *collection*, and *year* fields must move from the *Work* table into a shared *Asset* table

modifications also impact external systems, such as the public front-end built to give access to the data on the web. Performing these types of updates and modifications every couple of months can be very cumbersome. In practice, these modifications are often avoided, as there is no time to fundamentally rethink the structure of the database. In this context, people often rely on lightweight and ad hoc solutions, such as creating a standalone spreadsheet. This type of short-term decision causes, over a period of years, tremendous issues with data consistency, as reference data are scattered across different applications. We can therefore conclude that it is not a trivial matter to update and maintain a database, due to the complexity of modifying the database schema.

3.6 Sharing

As referred to in the beginning of this chapter, institutions already thought about interoperability between collections right from the start when RDMS were implemented in some pioneering cultural heritage institutions. There was (and there still is) a strong belief that acquiring the same collection management system provides the needed basis for interoperability. However, the customization of these software tools to accommodate specific requirements of each institution more often than not resulted in different approaches regarding the use of metadata elements. This made the exchange of records between institutions, which might have been using exactly the same software, problematic. Letting databases talk to one another and share their content is a complex matter, regardless of the application domain.

At this stage, it is important to point out the difference between *binary* and *non-binary* files. The previous section illustrated how tabular file formats make use of text files, allowing you to open a .tsv or .csv file with any standard text editor or spreadsheet software, making the exchange of metadata very straightforward. Databases, however, are stored in binary files which introduce a dependency on a specific software application. If you wanted for example to re-use a database of an institution, you would be obliged to use the same RDMS. Licences for proprietary RDMS easily cost around US$10,000 and you could potentially run into compatibility problems if you used different versions of the same software. You could also create a Structured Query Language (SQL) query, allowing you to create a data dump, and to import it afterwards in another application. But even if a standardized version of SQL exists, be aware that vendors implement the standard in varying ways. Certain RDMS have their own proprietary extensions, for example for column types, leading again to potential data compatibility problems.

We can therefore conclude that the interoperability of databases is quite problematic. Fortunately, methods have been developed to facilitate the export and import of structured data from and into different databases.

4 Meta-markup languages

Before we get into the details of how XML is used to facilitate the exchange of structured data, this section will make quite an extensive detour to the origins of markup and meta-markup languages. XML is probably the most abused and incorrectly used acronym (apart from RDF) at meetings in the cultural heritage sector. Some people consider it a programming language, others think it will automatically make their metadata *smart* and *semantic*. A broader view on the origins of XML will allow you to understand the tremendously important difference between applying *markup* and *makeup*. Understanding the difference between a *data-* and a *narrative-centric* view of XML will also allow you to better understand why tool or standard A is better than tool or standard B, depending on whether you are managing text or data. Moreover, the evolution of XML is very much intertwined with the development and the future of HTML. The relevance of initiatives such as Schema.org or the OpenGraph protocol will also be better apprehended with a good understanding of the global context of meta-markup languages.

4.1 Adding structure to content

In parallel with the work on the development of relational databases for the management of structured data, producers of large volumes of unstructured texts, such as the pharmaceutical or aeronautics industry, developed the concept of a meta-markup language throughout the 1970s and 1980s. These industries are confronted with the need to manage complex and voluminous documentation of production and safety guidelines. In order to streamline the typesetting of these complex text documents, the idea was developed to make use of *markup* to indicate the presence of *structural elements* (title, subtitle, paragraph, etc.) inside a document.

Markup can be thought of as *annotations* added to a document. A manuscript would be annotated with signs indicating how specific parts of the text should be displayed. Through the use of *delimiters* (remember the role these play within the tabular model), such as angle (<>) or square brackets ([ ]), the markup is clearly distinguished from the text itself. The characters used to indicate the markup are purely a matter of convention, one could also use other characters such as $ or *.

For example, if a specific string of characters which represents the title of a section should be printed in a large bold font, you could have the following HTML markup:

```
<font size="6"><b> Introduction to metadata</b></font>
```

Your browser would then render the text as:

Introduction to metadata

The above example is a typical illustration of how *markup* is merely used as *makeup*. The markup simply indicates how one particular string of characters, in our example 'Introduction to metadata', should be presented. Imagine you have a document containing several hundreds of section titles. Instead of presenting them in size 20, you actually prefer to have them slightly bigger. Making this modification with the above approach obliges you to manually update the markup for every section title in your document.

Conceptually, a whole new world of opportunities for automated processing appears when the markup focuses on the *function* of a specific string of characters within the structure of a document. Instead of hardwiring how every individual element of a text should be presented, the markup can indicate the role it plays within a text. Let us re-use the same example and apply this time genuine markup and not makeup:

```
<h1>Introduction to metadata</h1>
```

We no longer indicate how the string of characters 'Introduction to metadata' should be printed. Instead, we specify the role this string plays within the text, by stipulating that 'Introduction to metadata' is the title of a section. You can re-use the markup element h1 for all the titles of sections within the document. You only specify once how this specific structural element of your text should be formatted. This specification can take place either in the header of the document file or in a separate file linked to your document, which could contain the following definition:

```
h1 {
  font-size: 20pt;
  font-weight: bold;
}
```

This gives you the tremendous advantage that you can define in one central place how a specific structural element within your document should be displayed, from where it will then be implemented in a coherent manner across the entire document. Once the definition of the layout of a document is contained within a separate file, one can imagine having multiple files linked to a document in order to automatically switch between different designs. This is the idea behind the 'write once, publish many' principle. In a web context, it lets you automatically switch between a website with bigger or smaller fonts, or a standard version of a web page packed with images and colours and a Spartan page optimized for printing in black and white. The content stays the same, you just use another style sheet which indicates how the different elements of the web page should be rendered.

4.2 Model

Now that you understand the purpose of markup, we need to conceptualize its use. In order to make markup machine-processable, you cannot just randomly put commands contained within delimiters inside a document. The markup needs to respect a logical and consistent structure to be processed automatically.

Conceptually, you can think of marked-up documents as trees. They have one *root* and consist of branches which themselves contain smaller branches, as depicted in Figure 2.1. A node and its directly descending nodes have a *parent–child* relationship; all directly descending nodes of a parent are *siblings*. The hierarchical nature of this data model is central: child elements inherit by default all of the characteristics which have been predefined on the level of the parent element. However, this default inheritance can be overridden if a specific characteristic is defined on the level of the child element.

4.3 Meta-markup

Why have we called this section 'meta-' markup languages? The model described above asks you to define a hierarchy of structural elements which you could consider as the building blocks of the documents you manage. Thinking about books, one could easily say that the element 'book' represents the root level of the document, which encloses all other elements. A child element of the root would be 'chapter', which itself consists of a title and multiple sections. We could imagine that this standardized vision of a book could be re-used by many people. But perhaps you like to use an epigraph at the beginning of every chapter, whereas other people would never make use of this element.

The early developers of meta-markup in the 1960s and 1970s foresaw that different application domains would have very different needs for the structural elements of their documents. For example, stanzas are an important structural building block of classical poetry. The documentation of production phases and testing of drugs might have specific elements which structure the quality procedures that need to be respected during the development of a drug.

It was therefore decided not to predefine all potentially interesting markup elements. Instead, a syntax and grammar was developed which allows everyone to develop their own specific markup language. Hence the use of *meta*, which refers to something at a higher, more abstract level. Out of the idea of a meta-markup language, the *Standard Generalized Markup Language* (SGML) was born. In hindsight, the heritage and impact of SGML, adopted as an ISO standard in 1986, has been enormous. SGML was used as a conceptual foundation for all the major standards which made the web a success: HTML, XML and CSS. Ironically, SGML has been considered by most as a failure, as the industry never largely adopted the standard due to its complexity. Bob Boiko's metaphor 'SGML became like those backwoods blues players of old to whom the pop stars give honor but no money' sums up the situation quite correctly (Boiko, 2005). The use of SGML required a thorough analysis of the domain and content to be represented, followed by an intensive modelling exercise in which all essential structural elements of a document had to be predefined in a schema. The implementation itself was terribly expensive, due to costly software and the need for highly specialized staff. The success of HTML can be linked to exactly the opposite conditions: anyone can write HTML and the tools are freely available.

4.4 The Hypertext Markup Language

Around 1990, Tim Berners-Lee developed and implemented HTML. SGML was a major source of inspiration, but for reasons of simplicity a fixed set of elements was defined, representing the basic building blocks of a web page (e.g. <head>, <title>, <body>, <link>). Notice how these elements indicate structural elements of a web document, and do not stipulate any layout. This markup is to be parsed by a web browser, which is responsible for interpreting the HTML tags and for displaying the web document on the computer screen. HTML is therefore a markup language (and not a meta-markup language). This implies that you can only make use of a pre-defined set of tags which can be interpreted by a web browser. Nothing holds you back from inventing your own HTML tags, but in order to use them you would need to build your own browser.

Needless to say, HTML was a success. However, after a decade Berners-Lee's brainchild was corrupted from a markup into a makeup language. The focus on the aesthetics (and not on the semantics or structure) of web pages was beginning to undermine the potential of the web as a global information system. What happened?

From the mid to the end of the 1990s, web publishers were building up the dot com bubble. During this period, one of the biggest business model underlying the web was born. Within this model, the value of a company does not lie in its net income acquired through the commercialization of a product or a service offered to its user base. The mission of a company is to rapidly build up a user base by offering a free commodity (email, social networking, photo sharing, etc.). This business model is based on the assumption that the company will be able to monetize its customer base at a latter stage through advertising and the aggregation of consumer profiles for example.

With this in mind, it is easy to understand why web developers focused in the first place on an attractive and distinctive layout. This tendency played an important role in the browser war between Netscape Navigator (precursor of Mozilla Firefox) and Microsoft Internet Explorer. In order to attract the biggest user base, both browsers developed, independently one from the other, HTML elements that would render web content attractive and original. To fully understand the impact of these practices, do the following small exercise. Launch Notepad or any other simple text editor and encode the following HTML:

```
<html>
<blink>This text only blinks in Firefox</blink>
</html>
```

Make sure to save the document with the .html extension. Now start up the Firefox web browser and open the HTML document you just created. Congratulations, you have just created your first makeup'ed web page: the text contained within the `<blink></blink>` tags should blink. Now open up the same document in any other web browser (Microsoft Internet Explorer, Google Chrome, Apple Safari...). Nothing happens. The browser understood that there are tags but does not understand them and therefore just displays the text contained within them.

The blink element is a non-standard presentational HTML element introduced in Netscape Navigator, but not supported by other browsers. Anyone who is old enough to have surfed the web in the late 1990s will think fondly of all the weird and utterly user-unfriendly websites which held flashing and hovering content. On top of that: exactly the same page displayed differently across browsers.

4.5 The eXtensible Markup Language (XML)

The interoperability issues described above, coupled with the exploding volume of HTML documents containing no exploitable structure or semantics, resulted in a growing unease within the information retrieval and information science community. A standard was needed to ensure a more structured web, and XML saw the light. The standard is built as an application profile of SGML, but simplifies its use. An effort was made to keep 80% of SGML's functionality with only 20% of its complexity.

XML being a meta-markup language, realizes that user communities have the possibility of defining their own markup elements, hence the adjective 'extensible' in the name of XML. The big advantage of XML, especially at the time of major incompatibility issues on the web, is its platform and application independence. With its open and standardized format, XML allowed the web community to make a big step forward with the publication of structured content.

4.6 Designing XML documents

Similarly to relational database schemas, the design of XML documents also involves extensibility and simplicity trade-offs. The main discussion in XML is whether to model an entity as an element (serialized as *tags* surrounded by angle brackets) or as an *attribute* (key/value modifiers of a tag). Every XML document begins with an XML declaration, a *processing instruction* that identifies the document as a specific XML version. Processing instructions are special tags that start and end with questions marks inside the angle brackets. For instance, a minimal XML document for our collection would be:

```
<?xml version="1.0" encoding="UTF-8"?>
<Art title="Modern art"/>
```

So what we see here is the XML declaration, followed by an Art tag that has a title attribute with value Modern art. The Art element is the *root element* of our document, and every XML document should have exactly one root element. Since there are no other elements yet, we have made Art *self-closing* by including a slash before its ending angle bracket. Note how we were free to choose the names of the tag and the attribute, in contrast to more specified languages such as HTML. That does however not imply total freedom: the mandatory version attribute and its value are predetermined by the XML standard. The encoding attribute is not mandatory, but as we said before when explaining tabular data, plain text files always have a risk of being interpreted in a different encoding from that intended. Therefore, by specifying the encoding, we ensure that the interpretation will happen uniformly.

The root element is not difficult to get right, but modelling questions arise when we add data elements. For instance, let's add a work to the collection.

```
<?xml version="1.0" encoding="UTF-8"?>
<Art title="Modern art">
  <Work title="Guernica" year="1937" creator="Pablo Picasso"
        collection="Museo Reina Sofia" location="Madrid"/>
</Art>
```

The *hierarchical structure* of XML documents now becomes apparent: the Work element is a child of the Art element. Initially, we have chosen to model the work's elements as properties. However, this might not prove extensible enough. For instance, it is difficult to add more structure to the creator field, and there is currently no relation between the collection and location fields. The opposite approach would be to model everything as child elements:

```
<Art title="Modern art">
  <Work>
    <Title>Guernica</Title>
    <CreationDate>
      <Year>1937</Year>
    </CreationDate>
    <Creator>
      <FirstName>Pablo</FirstName>
```

```
        <LastName>Picasso</LastName>
      </Creator>
      <Collection>
        <Name>Museo Reina Sofia</Name>
        <Location>Madrid</Location>
      </Collection>
    </Work>
</Art>
```

This leaves us maximum flexibility to extend the document at any point. However, this also comes at a cost: the hierarchy is now relatively deep to express simple concepts, even for straightforward properties such as a year of creation. Even though the original design goals for XML state that 'terseness in XML markup is of minimal importance', it might be important for our application. Although software does not have any more difficulty parsing hierarchies as opposed to attributes, unnecessary complexity is never an asset. Understanding the XML document at a glance becomes more difficult for humans (and XML was designed to be read by both humans and machines), and the job of programming the format reader on top of the XML parser becomes more complex. In practice, a compromise often works best:

```
<Art title="Modern art">
  <Work title="Guernica" year="1937">
    <Creator firstName="Pablo" lastName="Picasso"/>
    <Collection name="Museo Reina Sofia" location="Madrid"/>
  </Work>
</Art>
```

Here, we have chosen to model all values that will not be decomposed or require further properties as attributes. For instance, a work's title does not require further description, but we would add additional information to a Creator, such as date and place of birth.

This might remind you of the discussion on relational model design, where we first determined *entity types*. Indeed, the decision is similar: things that would end up as entities in databases are likely represented as elements in an XML document as well. In contrast with databases, XML documents are more flexible and there is an even larger grey area for modelling choices. As always, this extended flexibility comes at a cost: databases are made for rapid data search and manipulation; searching XML documents is more than an order of magnitude slower.

Speaking of databases, you might wonder how to represent relations in XML. The answer is that you are free to choose that, but some choices are wiser than others.

For instance, we can simply continue the model as above and add another work:

```
<Art title="Modern art">
  <Work title="Guernica" year="1937">
    <Creator firstName="Pablo" lastName="Picasso"/>
    <Collection name="Museo Reina Sofia" location="Madrid"/>
  </Work>
  <Work title="First Communion" year="1895">
    <Creator firstName="Pablo" lastName="Picaso"/>
    <Collection name="Museo Picasso" location="Barcelona"/>
  </Work>
<Art>
```

However, this duplication of information is harder to maintain and it might lead to errors. In fact, the last name of the creator of the second work is incorrectly spelled 'Picaso', even though it appears correctly in the first. Therefore, it makes sense to model the information only once and refer to it using identifiers:

```
<Art title="Modern art">
  <Work title="Guernica" year="1937" collectionId="Co20">
    <CreatorRef creatorId="Cr43"/>
  </Work>
  <Work title="First Communion" year="1895" collectionId="Co22">
    <CreatorRef creatorId="Cr43"/>
  </Work>
  <Creator id="Cr43" firstName="Pablo" lastName="Picasso"/>
  <Collection id="Co20" name="Museo Reina Sofia" location="Madrid"/>
  <Collection id="Co22" name="Museo Picasso" location="Barcelona"/>
</Art>
```

In contrast to database systems, you are responsible yourself for the correct assignment and use of identifiers. Note how we modelled collectionId as an attribute of work, but Creator as a child element. The rationale behind that is that a work only resides in one collection, whereas there might be many creators of a single work, and a separate element allows us to specify a role for each of them (as with the many-to-many relationship of a database schema). This design choice allows the specification of multiple creators, since attribute names on an element must be unique.

4.7 XML Schema
The flexibility of XML documents might seem a drawback if you want to

consume XML. After all, your application will expect to see specific elements and attributes, but if anybody has the freedom to create their own, how can you be sure that the things you need will be there? We briefly mentioned before that this is possible with an XML schema, a document that explains what kind of XML markup is allowed.

Different languages exist to express schemas, the oldest being Document Type Definition (DTD), part of the original XML specification. The DTD specification of our Work element might look like this:

```
<!ELEMENT Work(CreatorRef)+>
<!ATTLIST Work title CDATA #REQUIRED>
<!ATTLIST Work year CDATA #REQUIRED>
<!ATTLIST Work collectionId IDREF #REQUIRED>
```

We again note a special kind of tag, which starts with an exclamation mark. The above fragment states that Work is an element that can contain many CreatorRef elements. It can have title and year attributes of type CDATA (character data) and a collectionId attribute that is an IDREF (a reference to an identifier), all of which are REQUIRED. This allows a parser to check whether the Work element is specified in the right way. Additionally, it can verify whether the identifiers are used correctly, as it will check for each IDREF attribute whether an element with this ID exists.

However, DTD has a quite peculiar syntax and it does not have a strong expressive power. For instance, we could not specify that year is a numeric value. Also, more complicated hierarchical rules cannot be efficiently described. Therefore, XML Schema (note the capital 'S') has been created by W3C (the World Wide Web Consortium). It features an XML syntax to describe schema documents, which themselves can also be validated by XML Schema. A description of the Work element would be:

```
<xsd:element name="Work">
  <xsd:complexType>
    <xsd:sequence>
      <xsd:element name="CreatorRef" maxOccurs="unbounded" />
    </xsd:sequence>
    <xsd:attribute name="title" type="xsd:string"/>
    <xsd:attribute name="year" type="xsd:gYear"/>
    <xsd:attribute name="collectionId" type="xsd:IDREF"/>
  </xsd:complexType>
</xsd:element>
```

This says that Work is an element that can have several CreatorRef elements. It can have a `title` string as attribute, a `year` that has a *year* data type, and `collectionId` which is an `IDREF`. We see that the XML Schema syntax is more verbose, but it is also more expressive. For instance, the `year` field is now specified more precisely thanks to XML Schema built-in data types.

For documents with an associated DTD or XML Schema, various automated *validators* exist that either guarantee the validity of a document or show what type of errors occur. Many software libraries for XML parsing support this functionality. Checking the validity of an XML document upfront means the rest of your software chain can read and manipulate the document as expected, without causing errors because of missing or incorrect structure.

4.8 Namespaces

As anyone can make their own elements and attributes in an XML document, we need a mechanism to universally identify which ones are the same. For instance, two documents might use a `title` element, but one uses it to designate book titles, and the other for personal titles such as `Mr` or `Mrs`. While enforcing a specific document structure, schema documents alone do not provide a means for consistent re-use across *different* types of documents that need to re-use the *same* elements in another context.

This is the issue that *XML namespaces* address – they are a method of qualifying element and attribute names (Bray et al., 2006). Namespaces allow you to re-use what has already been developed by someone else, and by doing so you can explicitly state that you agree with outside parties on how your data should be interpreted. The link with metadata schemes is self-evident here, as they share the same goal: making explicit statements about how a specific value should be interpreted. For example, if I want to use an element in my XML document which represents the name of a creator, it would make a lot of sense not to issue an identifier on my own for that element, but to re-use the namespace issued for the Dublin Core element "Creator": `http://purl.org/dc/terms`. When used on a `creator` element, it indicates that this element is to be interpreted as defined by the Dublin Core schema, which defines it as "an entity primarily responsible for making the resource".

Namespaces can be indicated using the reserved XML attribute `xmlns` on an element, which then holds for this element and all of its descendants. Namespace declarations are mostly seen in the `schema` element, forming the root of the schema, and are applied to the entire document. For instance, an XML document could start with the following tag:

```
<Agent xmlns="http://purl.org/dc/terms/">
```

This indicates that all elements in the document, including the root element, are to be interpreted according to the Dublin Core specification, which defines this namespace. Multiple namespaces can be used in a single document by using prefixes. For instance, we could re-use elements from a generic schema such as Dublin Core in combination with more specific elements from VRA Core, as follows:

```
<Art title="Modern art"
     xmlns:dc="http://purl.org/dc/terms/"
     xmlns:vra="http://vraweb.org/vracore4.htm">
  <Work>
    <dc:creator>Pablo Picasso</dc:creator>
    <dc:title>Guernica</dc:title>
    <vra:technique>Oil painting</vra:technique>
  </Work>
</Art>
```

4.9 Search and retrieval

While relational databases are especially designed for maximal performance, XML documents are designed for maximal flexibility. As we have seen, information can be modelled in different ways. As such, we cannot expect XML to achieve the same level of speed for search and retrieval, even if the entire model is loaded into memory (which is not always possible, due to size constraints). Nonetheless, like databases that are accessible through SQL, XML has its own query language: XPath. Since XML is a tree, XPath allows us to traverse that tree and collect elements and attribute values along the way. The result of an XPath query is thus not an XML document, but a set of elements or values.

Given the structure of XML, it does not come as a surprise that XPath has a hierarchical division as well. For instance, the following XPath query selects all Creator elements that are children of any Work elements in an Art document:

```
/Art/Work/Creator
```

So we first select Art, the root element (note the leading slash /), then all possible Work children, and finally all Creator elements that are direct descendants thereof. To select LastName elements that are children of any Creator element, we can use:

```
Creator/LastName
```

Note how the XPath expression does not start with a slash this time, as we do not start from the root but rather from any possible Creator element. However, this will only select children, i.e., direct descendants, of `Creator`. To select *all* descendants of a node, we can specify an *axis* called `descendant`:

```
Work/descendant::LastName
```

This will find all `LastName` elements that are somewhere inside a `Work`, even if nested within other elements.

Finally, this expression selects all `year` attributes from `Work` elements:

```
Work/@year
```

Many more constructs are possible. We can filter elements based on attribute values or the elements they contain, much as you would expect from SQL queries. Bear in mind that XPath queries are executed by traversing the whole XML tree, in contrast with relational databases, which use indexes of the data.

4.10 Data- versus narrative-centric XML

One of the reasons why there are so many misconceptions about XML is the fact that it can be used for a wide range of purposes. Even if there are a lot of concrete projects and applications which do not fall exclusively in one of the two categories, it is important to distinguish the data- and narrative-centric approach to XML. These two categories largely coincide with how the two different communities we talked about in the beginning of the section understand XML. The IT community has a data-centric view, in the sense that XML is used to define a structure, which is then filled up with data. The example of a Simple Object Access Protocol (SOAP) message below illustrates this approach. The XML file allows to facilitate, in an automated manner, the communication of a specific value between two computers, here the insurance value of Guernica at the Reina Sofia Museum, in a structured format.

```
<?xml version="1.0"?>
<soap:Envelope xmlns:soap="http://www.w3.org/2003/05/soap-envelope">
  <soap:Header/>
  <soap:Body>
    <m:GetInsuranceValue xmlns:
       m="http://www.example.org/insurance_value">
      <m:Insurance_value>DE00050</m:Insurance_value>
    </m:GetInsuranceValue>
  </soap:Body>
</soap:Envelope>
```

The digital humanities and computational linguists tend to have a narrative-centric vision of XML, in the sense that XML is used to insert some level of structure in documents. The Text Encoding Initiative (TEI) is a classic example of the narrative-centric approach. Below you can find an excerpt from a TEI example file from Wikipedia. The choice tag can be used to represent variants of the same section of text. In the example below, choice is used to indicate an original and a corrected value and to differentiate an original and regularized spelling:

```
<p xml:id="p23">
   Lastly, That, upon his solemn oath
   to observe all the above articles,
   the said man-mountain shall have a daily allowance of
   meat and drink sufficient for the support of
   <choice>
     <sic>1724</sic>
     <corr>1728</corr>
   </choice> of our subjects,
   with free access to our royal person, and other marks of our
   <choice>
     <orig>favour</orig>
     <reg>favor</reg>
   </choice>.
</p>
```

The fact that XML can accommodate both approaches is due to the fact that XML was conceived to be both human- and machine-readable. This feature of XML is one of both its biggest advantages and its biggest pain points. Any XML file can be opened and modified in a text editor. In theory, you could describe your entire collection in all of its detail by just using Notepad. This platform and application independence makes it particularly easy to exchange XML documents between heterogeneous environments. XML files are in this sense one of the best serialization formats that make the case for non-binary files.

4.11 Change

Most changes in XML are difficult and should be carefully considered, as they need to propagate to different documents. In the case of relational databases, changing the structure was cumbersome, but nonetheless always limited to a single system. With XML, if a document format evolves, there are two main options:

- The change is completely *backwards-compatible*; for example, adding an optional element. Existing documents can then remain as-is, and parsers can be extended. However, this needs careful planning in advance, and is not always possible.
- The change is not backwards-compatible; for example, renaming a tag or changing an attribute into a child element. We distinguish two sub-options:
  - Through schema *versioning*, different document structures can be supported. Existing documents do not have to change, but parsers must support the different versions (for example, one with the old element name and one with the new name).
  - The change is *breaking* and existing documents and parsers have to be updated to conform to the new schema. This leads to maximal consistency, but many modifications must be carried out (for example, all documents and parsers have to switch to the new name).

The first option is clearly optimal, but only applies to certain cases. In general, change is difficult and thus progresses slowly. Between changes, data cannot be stored optimally.

4.12 Why do IT people prefer JSON?

According to the followers of the XML hype around the year 2000, XML was soon going to take over the web (and then the world). There are several reasons why this did not happen – even though XML is still very popular in many application domains. First, there is XML's verbosity. By design, XML tries to be as explicit as possible, but this sacrifices clarity in the end. For many XML documents, it is difficult to understand what it going on with a single look. There is also a lot of repetition in the markup.

More importantly, the web has witnessed an enormous growth of JavaScript applications. At first regarded as inferior to compiled languages such as Java (which has many XML-driven parts itself), it soon became clear that JavaScript's dynamic nature made it a perfect fit for the web. While JavaScript can parse XML, it also has a native format to express data: the JavaScript Object Notation or JSON, with a more terse syntax that focuses on 'just getting things done'. As a result, we should not expect much portability between different contexts. However, data exchange over the web between clients and servers, and between different applications, happens mostly in JSON. Severance (2012) neatly describes this oddity of the winning underdog. An example JSON fragment of a work could look like this:

```
{
  "title": "Guernica",
  "year": 1937,
  "creator": {
    "firstName": "Pablo",
    "lastName:" "Picasso"
  },
  "collection": {
    "name": "Museo Reina Sofia",
    "location": "Madrid"
  }
}
```

Note that JSON has also a hierarchical structure; in fact, the above document translates directly into XML (with the exception that JSON does not offer distinct structures for child element and simple attributes).

4.13 Does XML make your data smart?

In the introduction of this section we mentioned the high expectations collection holders have of XML, due to the common belief that XML makes your data *smart*. We hope to have demonstrated throughout the section that XML is nothing more, but also nothing less, than a standardized syntax to encode data in a structured manner. The semantics of data can be made explicit through the use of XML elements, but it is important to realize that outside the community which defined the elements, the meaning of the elements is not explicit. The use of namespaces does offer the opportunity to share amongst different communities the same element, but this practice mostly applies to a limited set of the elements. So at the end of the day, even with our metadata in a more portable format we are still confronted with the same problem: if we want other people to re-use our metadata, they are forced to study the schema and documentation describing their semantics.

5 Linked data

We have travelled all the way from previous data models to come to this specific point. Relational databases and XML both offer wonderful possibilities to manage structured metadata, but they also have the big drawback that you need to understand the schema describing the structure and interaction between the data. This is exactly where our last data model comes in.

5.1 The semantic web vision

Before we get into details regarding the data model, let us first fully understand why exactly we need to bypass the problems associated to the re-use of locally defined semantics. The vision behind the semantic web was born out of the frustration of having only human-readable information on the web, which restricts the ways in which software can help us find information. For instance, keyword-based search works well for terms such as 'Picasso'. Queries such as 'paintings by Picasso' are already more difficult, since pages can use different wording. But without an interpretation of a page's content, queries such as 'paintings by artists who have met Picasso' are impossible. In the semantic web vision, the web also becomes accessible for software agents instead of containing only human-readable information (Berners-Lee, Hendler and Lassila, 2001). It enables a vast array of novel applications by making information machine-interpretable.

5.2 RDF

By adopting an extremely simple data model consisting of *triples*, data represented in Resource Description Framework (RDF) become *schema-neutral*. An RDF triple consists of a *subject*, *predicate* and an *object*, as seen in Figure 2.1. This allows for maximum flexibility. Any resource in the world (the subject) can have a specific relationship (the predicate) to any resource in the world (the object). There is no limit on what can be connected to what. This model allows us to express statements in a straightforward way, such as for example the statement that Jeff Koons is the artist who created the work 'Puppy':

```
:Jeff_Koons :created :Puppy.
```

Figure 2.4 represents some of the metadata of the example we have been using throughout this chapter. By simplifying to a maximum the data model, all of the semantics are made explicit by the triple itself. By doing so, there is no longer a need for a schema to interpret the data. Within the world of databases and XML, only the data conforming to the rules defined in the schema may exist and be encoded in the database or XML file. With RDF, you just make statements about facts you know, but these statements might interact with statements made outside your information system. This data model allows heterogeneous data to connect and interact. For instance, in Figure 2.4 you can see two pieces of metadata which were previously not mentioned.

Note, however, that schema-neutral does not mean that no schema-related issues remain. Any piece of data still needs to be expressed in a certain vocabulary, and each vocabulary has its own way of expressing things. The main difference between RDF and XML and other technologies is that in RDF everything is self-describing: each vocabulary is expressed in terms of other

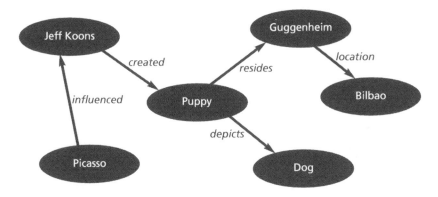

Figure 2.4 Illustration of how to use triples to express metadata

vocabularies. In order to extract meaning from a given RDF fragment, the unique identifiers of each used resource allow its definition to be looked up. This look-up mechanism is enabled by the principles of linked data, which is the topic of the next section.

5.3 The linked data principles

The implementation of the RDF model in the open and distributed context of the web is based upon their capability to issue identifiers for subjects, predicates and objects, which can be freely re-used. Software is then able to interpret this information, because the identifiers create unique meaning, as opposed to the names of columns in databases or elements in XML, which only have local significance and change from application to application.

However, the semantic web was mainly developed from the artificial intelligence (AI) standpoint. Ever since the 1960s, the AI community worked on automated reasoning, expert systems and intelligent agents. Underlying all of these fields and applications is a core belief in the power of logic to formalize all aspects contained within an information system. Chapter 4, in section 4, will come back to the reasons why this vision is currently deemed unworkable on the scale of the web.

In order to move forward with a machine-readable web, Berners-Lee (2006) drastically reduced the ambitions of the full-blown semantic web and came up with the *linked data principles*. These four rules specify a simple way to format data so it can be interpreted by software:

1 Use URIs as names for things.
2 Use HTTP URIs so that people can look up those names.
3 When someone looks up a URI, provide useful information, using the

standards (RDF, SPARQL).
4 Include links to other URIs so that they can discover more things.

As you can see, these principles require a clear understanding of URLs and URIs. A URL is a *uniform resource locator*, which, as the name says, enables to locate resources in a unique way. The most widely known URLs are those used on the web; they start with http: or https:. Given any such URL, your browser is able to locate the underlying resource, no matter where it is physically stored. A URI, *uniform resource identifier*, is a generalization of the concept that permits resources anywhere in the universe to be given a unique identification. However, not all URIs are URLs; for instance, the URI urn:lex:eu:council: directive:2004-12-07;31 uniquely identifies a European Union directive, but does not directly give its location.

Let's now look at the role of URIs and URLs in the linked data principles. The first principle demands unique identification for each concept, and URIs are the most appropriate mechanism to provide this. Additionally, the second principle states that these identifiers must be HTTP URIs, in other words URLs on the web. The third principle asks for the representation of the resources identified by those URLs by using standards, such as the machine-readable format RDF. Finally, the fourth principle makes sure that data contains links to other data, allowing software agents to look up related information.

5.4 The central role of URLs

Remember how XML namespaces uniquely identified elements and attributes. With linked data, URLs are used to uniquely identify concepts. For example, a more meaningful way to express the fact that Jeff Koons created 'Puppy' is the following triple:

```
<http://guggenheim.org/new-york/collections/collection-
online/artwork/48>
    <http://purl.org/dc/terms/creator>
      <http://viaf.org/viaf/5035739>.
```

In this example you see that the artist Jeff Koons is identified with the URL of his authority file available on the Virtual International Authority File (VIAF) website. What is the added value of using the URL instead of the string of characters 'Koons, Jeff, 1955–'? Rules have been developed for decades to formalize the spelling of names in authority records, and in order to disambiguate with other people with exactly the same name, his date of birth has been added. Therefore, one could think that the text string serves well as an identifier. Imagine, however, what needs to happen if Jeff Koons dies in 2025? All of the metadata which used the text string to designate the name of the creator will need to update the creator field to 'Koons, Jeff, 1955–2025'. Instead, if the VIAF URL is used, the information only needs to be updated centrally in the VIAF authority file, but the URL as such does not change. From the moment the date of death has been added, this new information will become automatically available to everyone who uses the VIAF URL as an identifier for Jeff Koons. The fact of looking up more information about a subject through its URL is called *dereferencing*. Chapter 5 will explain the use of URLs for both virtual and real-world resources.

The basic condition for this approach is a stability of the identifier, and URLs tend to have a very bad reputation on that level. The URL used to identify the work 'Puppy' is simply the URL of the record displaying the metadata of the object. But what would happen if this work is transferred from the Bilbao to the Venice Guggenheim museum? This would imply that the URL loses its validity. To avoid such trouble, Chapter 6 discusses sustainable URLs.

5.5 Serialization

As the initial semantic web vision was launched in 2001, it comes as no surprise that the first standardized syntax was based on XML, and consequently named RDF/XML. Unfortunately, RDF/XML inherits the verbosity of XML as well, resulting in a serialization format that admittedly can be parsed by an XML parser, but is hard to follow and understand. Therefore, the Turtle syntax was developed, in which triples are native elements. Turtle is currently in the final stage of standardization, and is bound to take the place of RDF/XML.

The triples above were expressed in Turtle, but here we will review its syntax in more detail. In Turtle, triples are serialized by separating each of the components (subject, predicate, object) by white space and ending it with a dot. URLs are surrounded by angle brackets.

Since URLs can be rather long, it includes an abbreviation mechanism through the @prefix directive:

```
@prefix gh: <http://guggenheim.org/new-york/collections/collection-
    online/artwork/>.
@prefix dc: <http://purl.org/dc/terms/>.
@prefix viaf: <http://viaf.org/viaf/>.

gh:48 dc:creator viaf:5035739.
```

We first define three *prefixes*, consisting of certain characters ended by a colon, which can subsequently be re-used. This makes the actual triples shorter and easier to understand, and can also eliminate possible mistakes in the URL by avoiding duplication.

Multiple statements about the same object can be written tersely by using a semicolon if the subject is repeated, and a comma if the subject and predicate are repeated:

```
gh:48 dc:creator viaf:5035739;
      dc:title "Puppy".
viaf:5035739 :influencedBy viaf:15873,
                           viaf:95794725.
```

The above fragment states that the creator of the artwork is Jeff Koons (viaf:5035739) that its title is 'Puppy', and that Jeff Koons is influenced by Pablo Picasso (viaf:15873) and Ed Paschke (viaf:95794725). In addition to the use of semicolons and commas, we note two other things. First, the word 'Puppy' is surrounded by double quotes, as it is not a URL but a *literal value*. RDF includes literal values in its model as well, as some properties eventually do not point at another object but rather at a non-decomposable value. Literal values can have an associated *type* (such as string, number, or date), and in case of a string, a *language code* (such as en-us). Second, the predicate :influencedBy has an empty namespace prefix, which indicates that it is local to the current document. This is a convenient way of introducing new concepts in a document, which are then defined in terms of other properties later on.

5.6 Search and retrieval

Like relational databases and XML before, RDF also comes with its own query language, *SPARQL*. Queries in SPARQL are based on *graph patterns*: the form of the desired data is described in a WHERE clause. A simple SPARQL query is the following one:

```
SELECT ?predicate ?object WHERE {
  <http://dbpedia.org/resource/Pablo_Picasso> ?predicate ?object.
}
```

This searches for triples that have Picasso as subject and *any* predicate and *any* object. The question mark before a word means that it is a *variable*. Out of those triples, the query will return the predicate and the object.

We can be more specific as well. For instance, if we want to find works by Picasso, we can use the following query. Note the use of prefixes to abbreviate common terms.

```
PREFIX dbpedia: <http://dbpedia.org/resource/>
PREFIX dbpprop: <http://dbpedia.org/property/>

SELECT ?work WHERE {
  ?work dbpprop:artist dbpedia:Pablo_Picasso.
}
```

This illustrates the simplicity of the linked data model, while at the same time showing its immense power and flexibility.

5.7 Change

We hope you understand an essential feature of the RDF data model by now: that all of the semantics of the data are made explicit through the model itself. In a sense, we have come full circle with a return to the idea of a flat file, if we think of a collection of triples contained in a single file, composed of three columns with the headers *subject*, *predicate* and *object*. Confronted with a new reality which needs to be handled, new triples are simply added. However, this comparison does not do justice to the RDF model, as the strength of triples is that every value points to other triples that have this value as subject or object. The context of every row is thereby augmented by other rows.

Change in RDF is therefore supported easily: adding new data comes down to adding new triples, without needing to alter the existing data or structure. This gives the data maximum flexibility, at the cost of dealing with an open world. Whereas databases are guaranteed to give you all the data they have, finding all facts about a concept is more complicated with RDF, as different identifiers might be used for the same thing. Nonetheless, when such issues are managed properly, for instance by creating sufficient links between datasets, schema-neutrality can be a very powerful concept.

6 Conclusion

This chapter provided an answer to the question of *why* we need linked data. The answer might seem self-evident and straightforward: in order to *link* data across the web. To achieve this goal, we need to be able to interconnect data across independent islands. We use the word 'islands', as each information system is modelled for its particular needs and application domain, resulting in systems that cannot hold hands with one another in an automated manner. For sure, it is easy to embed a link in your collection database which points to the record of a similar object from another institution. But this requires you to know how to access the database of the other institution, to know what fields are used to describe the object. Once you have found the record to which you want to link, you need to embed its URL manually within the record of your database. We cannot reasonably perform these actions manually for all of our collection items. We therefore need to think about how we can automate the linking process.

6.1 Understanding trade-offs

In order to understand the obstacles to the automation of linking, this chapter gave a comprehensive overview of the most recurrent data models used to build the current islands of metadata. Hopefully the red thread between the four data models has appeared clearly. A *trade-off* has to be made between the complexity of the data model and the ease with which the outside world can re-use and connect to your data. The collection management databases which are currently forming the backbone of our cultural heritage institutions allow complex data to be stored in a way which minimizes redundancy and dependency. You only need to encode once all the information you have in relation to an artist or some very rare and complex technique which requires a lot of documentation to be understood. The day the artist dies, you only need to update the attribute 'Date of death' of the entity 'Artist', and this update will be shared across all the records pointing to this entity.

However, we have seen that this advantage comes at a cost. A collection management database can easily contain several hundreds of tables, inter-connected with relations. Modifications and extra tables are often added in an ad hoc manner in order to fulfil an urgent need, and are often left un-documented. It should therefore come as no surprise that migration operations from one software to the other (or even just to another version of the same software) can be very time-consuming for IT staff, as they need to interpret the database schema to understand how the tables are interconnected.

The development of XML made it easier to share metadata across applications, due to its platform and application independence. In contrast to databases, you do not need any specific software to read and create XML documents. The advantage of being readable both for humans and machines also resulted in XML's major drawback, namely its verbosity. More importantly, complex data described in XML rely on a schema documenting and prescribing how elements and attributes interact within an XML file. Establishing a consensus inside and outside an institution on how to interpret and update the schema often causes problems.

The last section of this chapter introduced RDF, which we referred to as schema-neutral. The simplicity of the data model (subject-predicate-object) brings back the idea of a flat file, consisting of three columns representing subjects, objects and predicates. No extra documentation or schema is needed to interpret these data, and any new type of information can be added without a need to modify the structure of the data model.

6.2 The law of instruments

'Give a small boy a hammer, and he will find that everything he encounters needs pounding'.[2] This expression, also referred to as the 'law of the instrument', describes how people have a tendency to attribute too much importance to the tool they are using, at the expense of their objectives. One would think that engineers evaluate what data model most suits the needs of an application, and then choose a technology allowing them to implement the model. In practice, the opposite often happens. People build up experience with a specific technology and are not very eager to switch to another tool, as this sometimes requires a substantial effort. Academics and consultants, on the other hand, occasionally tend to get overly enthusiastic about a new technology, regardless of whether the underlying data model is best for the purpose at hand.

6.3 When to use what

This chapter hopefully made it clear that every model has been developed for a specific use. If the only tool you have is a hammer, you treat everything as if it were a nail. This was the case with the use of XML in the context of SOAP, for example. The verbosity of XML is now considered inadequate for data exchange over the web between clients and servers, and its role is taken over by JSON. The current hype on linked data reminds us of the unbounded enthusiasm for XML, in the sense that a lot of applications which are currently built based on linked data technologies could be better and more cheaply realized with a classic relational database. At the end of this chapter, the reader hopefully has acquired a sufficient historical, conceptual and technical understanding of which data

Table 2.3 Summary of the (dis)advantages of different data models

data model	(dis-)advantages	use
tabular data	+ intuitive approach + very portable + technology agnostic – prone to redundancy and leading to inconsistencies – inefficient search and retrieval	import and export of data with a simple structure
relational model	+ handling of complex data + optimized queries + mature software market – binary format – schema-dependent	management of complex data which require normalization
meta-markup	+ platform-independent + both human- and machine-readable – complicated implementation for complex data – verbosity	import and export of complex data
RDF	+ schema-neutral approach + discovery of new knowledge – loss of normalization – immature software market	making data available for linking

model to use in which context.

To conclude this chapter, Table 2.3 summarizes the essential characteristics of every data model we discussed.

The case study at the end of this chapter will now demonstrate how the linked data approach results in a dynamic view of data, allowing heterogeneous information sources to interconnect in a standardized manner. Through the example queries, issues regarding data inconsistency and incompleteness, which is the drawback of this *open world* approach, will also be underlined. While practising with concrete examples with SPARQL queries, try to reflect specifically on one of the characteristics of the RDF data model that we identified: it is schema-neutral from a conceptual point of view. However, what happens in practice when you want to query a dataset you are not familiar with in SPARQL? We will come back to this issue in the concluding chapter.

7 CASE STUDY: linked data at your fingertips

This case study is slightly different from the others in this book, in that it doesn't focus on a particular dataset. Instead, we will explore linked data from various sources to get a feeling of the possibilities and limitations in practice. Earlier on in this chapter, we referred to the schema-neutral character of the conceptual RDF data model. The exercises of this case study will help you understand how this theoretical model has been implemented in practice. As you will see, the open-world assumption definitively offers opportunities but can be challenging to implement. To demonstrate this, we will retrieve in this case study metadata on Pablo Picasso in various ways, to understand the capabilities of each data source. First, we will examine DBpedia, which is a version of Wikipedia automatically converted into RDF. Next, we will try queries on Freebase, which is a collaborative linked data source with partly automated input (from Wikipedia and other sources) and partly human input. The difference between DBpedia and Freebase is that Freebase can be edited publicly, whereas DBpedia only has a single automated process. Finally, we will zoom in on Sindice, an index that brings together many large datasets of the linked data cloud and is easily accessible through its front-end Sig.ma.

7.1 DBpedia, the Wikipedia of data

DBpedia is a publicly accessible RDF store with content that is automatically extracted from Wikipedia, the free online encyclopedia. A substantial proportion of articles on Wikipedia have semi-structured data in the form of infoboxes (usually displayed to the right of an article) listing key/value data such as names, birth dates, etc., which are available on DBpedia. Two versions of DBpedia are available: a periodically updated version at http://dbpedia.org/ and a *live* version at http://live.dbpedia.org/, which follows the rapid change on Wikipedia. DBpedia currently contains more than 250 million triples. In this case study, we will look at DBpedia and investigate how we can browse and query data.

7.1.1 Browsing DBpedia

Finding a topic page is as easy as going to http://dbpedia.org/page/Topic_Name. For instance, the DBpedia page of Pablo Picasso can be found at http://dbpedia.org/page/Pablo_Picasso. At the top of this page, we see its title Pablo Picasso, followed by a short English description. The remainder of the page consists of a long two-column table with properties and values that contain the information we are interested in. Take your time to look around and discover what DBpedia has to say about Picasso. In addition to human-readable abstracts in many different languages, we see many key-value pairs that contain machine-interpretable information. Using the DBpedia ontology, knowledge about Picasso is expressed, such as birth date and place, multi-language labels, influences, spouse, and nationality.

If you wonder where the triples are, well, you can reconstruct them by taking the page's subject, a predicate from the Property column and an object from the Value column. For instance, one of the triples is:

```
dbpedia:Pablo_Picasso dbpedia-owl:birthPlace dbpedia:Málaga.
```

There are also several properties in the reverse direction as well, indicated by the key 'is *property* of'. For instance 'is dbpedia-owl:parent of' translates to:

```
dbpedia:Paloma_Picasso dbpedia-owl:parent dbpedia:Pablo_Picasso.
```

As we expect from *linked* data, we can click through on any value to learn more. If we click on dbpedia:Málaga, we see a page with detailed information on the city. As we explained earlier, even the properties can be examined. Clicking dbpedia-owl:birthPlace reveals that this is a relation between a person and a place. Interestingly, some links go outside DBpedia, thus connecting this dataset to others, something that is not possible with relational databases. For instance, http://data.nytimes.com/N855344257183137093 is indicated as the same resource, with the owl:sameAs relation, and this link leads to Picasso's data sheet on the *New York Times* website. This reveals the true potential of linked data.

At the bottom of the page, there are links to view the data in different formats. The 'N3/Turtle' link leads to an RDF serialization that can be interpreted by software. You might notice a lot of strange-looking sequences in the file which take up a large amount of space. They are escape sequences for non-ASCII characters, such as å, ä, or ö for example, from the full-text abstraction fields.

However, towards the bottom of the file, you will notice more familiar triples such as:

```
dbpedia:Noel_Rockmore dbpedia-owl:influencedBy
  dbpedia:Pablo_Picasso.
dbpedia:Ben_Shahn dbpedia-owl:influencedBydbpedia:Pablo_Picasso.
dbpedia:Piet_Mondrian dbpedia-owl:influencedBy
  dbpedia:Pablo_Picasso.
```

If possible, we recommend that you switch off line wrapping in your editor, so the long lines with escape sequences will simply flow off the screen.

7.1.2 Querying DBpedia

Once we get to know some basic properties of the data, we have sufficient information to start querying it in a more complex way. We have seen some predicates and some objects, which can help us construct queries. We advise you to keep the Picasso page open in one tab while you bring up the SPARQL query interface at http://dbpedia.org/sparql. You are greeted by the following default query:

```
SELECT DISTINCT ?Concept WHERE { [] a ?Concept. } LIMIT 100
```

We are already familiar with the WHERE and SELECT clauses, and as their names suggest, DISTINCT asks for unique items and LIMIT 100 for only the first 100 results. The [] syntax is a way to say 'any node', like a variable without a name. If we execute this query, we will receive a (quite random) list of 100 Concepts in DBpedia. These are not only DBpedia topics, but also concepts such as owl:Thing and http://schema.org/CreativeWork.

Let's now try a query of our own, to verify if we can get the same information on Picasso as we did when browsing DBpedia. To see all triples on Picasso, enter the following SPARQL query:[3]

```
PREFIX dbpedia: <http://dbpedia.org/resource/>
PREFIX dbpedia-owl: <http://dbpedia.org/ontology/>
SELECT ?p ?o WHERE { dbpedia:Pablo_Picasso ?p ?o. }
```

This will show us all triples we saw earlier on the Picasso page. Well, at least those triples that have Picasso in the subject. To find all triples where Picasso is the object, issue the query:

```
SELECT ?s ?p WHERE { ?s ?p dbpedia:Pablo_Picasso. }
```

This yields results like the following:

s	p
dbpedia:The_Three_Dancers	dbpedia-owl:artist
dbpedia:The_Accordionist	dbpedia-owl:artist
dbpedia:Desire_Caught_by_the_Tail	dbpedia-owl:author
dbpedia:Olga_Khokhlova	dbpedia-owl:spouse
dbpedia:Stanley_William_Hayter	dbpedia-owl:influenced
...	...

The values in the s column correspond to bindings of the ?s variable, the p column to bindings of the ?p variable. To understand where the found information comes from, we substitute s and p in the original WHERE clause. The first row thus belongs to a match of:

```
dbpedia:The_Three_Dancers dbpedia-owl:artist dbpedia:Pablo_Picasso.
```

To receive just 30 triples, add the LIMIT clause:

```
SELECT ?p ?o WHERE { dbpedia:Pablo_Picasso ?p ?o. } LIMIT 30
```

If you want to see all predicates used with Picasso as the subject:

```
SELECT ?p WHERE { dbpedia:Pablo_Picasso ?p ?o. }
```

Note the omission of the ?o variable in the SELECT clause, as we only want to see the predicates. This yields the following list:

p
http://www.w3.org/1999/02/22-rdf-syntax-ns#type
http://www.w3.org/1999/02/22-rdf-syntax-ns#type
...
http://www.w3.org/2002/07/owl#sameAs
http://www.w3.org/2002/07/owl#sameAs
http://www.w3.org/2002/07/owl#sameAs
...
http://purl.org/dc/terms/subject
http://purl.org/dc/terms/subject
http://purl.org/dc/terms/subject
...

You might be surprised to see that there are duplicates in the result list. How come we have duplicates here when we did not have them in the previous query? The answer is that triples are unique in the triple store, i.e., a triple can only occur once.[4] However, many triples can use the same predicates, and indeed, several Picasso triples use the rdf:type and owl:sameAs predicates. To have the unique predicates, we need to add the DISTINCT modifier:

```
SELECT DISTINCT ?p WHERE { dbpedia:Pablo_Picasso ?p ?o. }
```

So far, we have received tables of variable values as a result, but what if we want triples? Besides SELECT, SPARQL also has a CONSTRUCT clause that creates triples instead of variable bindings. For example, this shows all Picasso triples:

```
CONSTRUCT { dbpedia:Pablo_Picasso ?p ?o. }
WHERE     { dbpedia:Pablo_Picasso ?p ?o. }
```

These include the following:

```
dbpedia:Pablo_Picasso rdf:typefoaf:Person,
    yago:SpanishPotters,
    yago:PeopleFromParis,
    yago:BalletDesigners.
dbpedia:Pablo_Picasso dcterms:subject category:Cubism
    category:Spanish_expatriates_in_France,
    category:Spanish_sculptors,
    category:Modern_painters.
```

It might seem strange to duplicate the graph from the WHERE clause into the CONSTRUCT clause, but they actually signify two different things. The WHERE clause tells the SPARQL engine to look for all triples that have Picasso as the subject and to store their predicates and objects in the variables ?p and ?o respectively. The CONSTRUCT clause instructs the engine to collect all ?p and ?o values – regardless of how they were retrieved – and to create triples from them using the specified pattern.

This means that we can choose to generate a different pattern. For instance, suppose that we just want to express that Picasso is somehow connected to the object of the triple, instead of exactly specifying this relationship. Then we can simply do:

```
CONSTRUCT { dbpedia:Pablo_Picasso <isConnectedTo> ?o. }
WHERE     { dbpedia:Pablo_Picasso ?p ?o. }
```

This will yield triples such as:

```
dbpedia:Pablo_Picasso <isConnectedTo> category:Modern_painters.
```

This allows you to convert the queried data into the form that you prefer. Finally, to receive 100 random triples from DBpedia, try the following:

```
CONSTRUCT { ?s ?p ?o. } WHERE { ?s ?p ?o. } LIMIT 100
```

7.2 More complex SPARQL queries

WHERE patterns can be as complex as you like. The most simple case is a single triple. For instance, the birth place of Picasso can be retrieved by:

```
SELECT ?place WHERE {
   dbpedia:Pablo_Picasso dbpedia-owl:birthPlace ?place.
}
```

This turns out to be http://dbpedia.org/resource/M%C3%A1laga. Note the use of escape sequences in the URL to encode the accented character in 'Málaga'. We can now find all people born in Málaga:

```
SELECT ?person WHERE {
   ?person dbpedia-owl:birthPlace
<http://dbpedia.org/resource/M%C3%A1laga>.
}
```

Unsurprisingly, this list includes Picasso himself:

person
...
dbpedia:Pepe_Romero
dbpedia:Pablo_Picasso
dbpedia:Edu_Ramos
dbpedia:Carlos_Aranda
...

We could simplify the same question by describing the pattern in one query with a WHERE clause consisting of two triples:

```
SELECT ?person WHERE {
   dbpedia:Pablo_Picasso dbpedia-owl:birthPlace ?place.
   ?person dbpedia-owl:birthPlace ?place.
}
```

This will select all people whose birthplace is the same as Picasso's, without having to specify that exact place. We just instruct the SPARQL engine to find the birthplace for Picasso and look for people with this birthplace at the same time. Were you surprised to see Picasso in the result list? It might seem strange, but this is actually logical: Picasso has the same birthplace as Picasso, hence he is included in the list. Always remember that computers execute what you ask for, not what you intended to ask: Picasso satisfies the query pattern, so his name is returned, even though you already knew this.

We could place further restrictions on this list. For instance, we see many different kinds of people. If we are only interested in *artists* born in Málaga, we can say:

```
SELECT ?person WHERE {
    dbpedia:Pablo_Picasso dbpedia-owl:birthPlace ?place.
    ?person dbpedia-owl:birthPlace ?place.
    ?person a dbpedia-owl:Artist.
}
```

The list has fewer members, and Picasso is still in there (since he's an artist):

person
...
dbpedia:Javier_Conde
dbpedia:Pepe_Romero
dbpedia:Pablo_Picasso
dbpedia:Juan_Antonio_Arguelles_Rius
...

Let's ask for people who were influenced by Picasso:

```
SELECT ?artist WHERE {
    ?artist dbpedia-owl:influencedBy dbpedia:Pablo_Picasso.
    ?artist a dbpedia-owl:Artist.
}
```

And let's see where those people were born, to have an idea of how Picasso's legacy spread geographically:

```
SELECT ?artist, ?place WHERE {
    ?artist dbpedia-owl:influencedBy dbpedia:Pablo_Picasso.
    ?artist a dbpedia-owl:Artist.
    ?artist dbpedia-owl:birthPlace ?place.
}
```

This reveals the following data:

artist	place
dbpedia:Sarah_Stein	dbpedia:San_Francisco
dbpedia:Helmut_Kolle	dbpedia:Charlottenburg
dbpedia:Karel_Appel	dbpedia:Amsterdam
dbpedia:Karel_Appel	dbpedia:Netherlands
...	...

Note how some artists occur twice in the list, but with a different place. For instance, Karel Appel has a birthPlace of Amsterdam but also The Netherlands, both of which are correct. It might be confusing that they appear twice, but this is because the values are coming from different triples and both answers conform to the query pattern we gave. When we ask for the data as triples, this connection becomes more obvious.

```
CONSTRUCT { ?artist dbpedia-owl:birthPlace ?place. }
WHERE {
   ?artist dbpedia-owl:influencedBy dbpedia:Pablo_Picasso.
   ?artist a dbpedia-owl:Artist.
   ?artist dbpedia-owl:birthPlace ?place.
}
```

Triples indeed better illustrate the connection between the pieces of data:

```
dbpedia:Dick_Bruna dbpedia-owl:birthPlace  dbpedia:Utrecht,
                                           dbpedia:Netherlands.
dbpedia:Wifredo_Lam dbpedia-owl:birthPlace dbpedia:Sagua_La_Grande,
                                           dbpedia:Cuba.
dbpedia:Karel_Appel dbpedia-owl:birthPlace dbpedia:Netherlands,
                                           dbpedia:Amsterdam.
```

Another perspective is time: when were the people who were influenced by Picasso born?

```
SELECT ?artist, ?date WHERE {
   ?artist dbpedia-owl:influencedBy dbpedia:Pablo_Picasso.
   ?artist a dbpedia-owl:Artist.
   ?artist dbpedia-owl:birthDate ?date.
}
```

   This gives the following people:

artist	date
dbpedia:Wifredo_Lam	1902-12-08
dbpedia:Karel_Appel	1921-04-25
dbpedia:Piet_Mondrian	1872-03-07
...	...

We have a considerably shorter list then when we asked for all people influenced by Picasso. This appears strange, because the amount of people should be the same, no matter when they were born. The issue here is that DBpedia does not contain birth data information for all people. As a result, only people with a birth date are included. In contrast, a relational database would include all people but leave unknown birth dates empty. We can obtain the same behaviour from DBpedia by marking the triple with the birth date OPTIONAL:

```
SELECT ?artist, ?date WHERE {
   ?artist dbpedia-owl:influencedBy dbpedia:Pablo_Picasso.
   ?artist a dbpedia-owl:Artist.
   OPTIONAL {
      ?artist dbpedia-owl:birthDate ?date.
   }
}
```

This will give us all influenced people, some of which have an unknown birth date:

artist	date
dbpedia:Wifredo_Lam	1902-12-08
dbpedia:Karel_Appel	1921-04-25
dbpedia:Dick_Bruna	
dbpedia:Piet_Mondrian	1872-03-07
dbpedia:Joan_Glass	
...	...

To obtain a chronological overview, we can ask DBpedia to ORDER the results:

```
SELECT ?artist, ?date WHERE {
   ?artist dbpedia-owl:influencedBy dbpedia:Pablo_Picasso.
   ?artist a dbpedia-owl:Artist.
   OPTIONAL {
      ?artist dbpedia-owl:birthDate ?date.
   }
}
ORDER BY ?date
```

This will list artists without a known birth date first, followed by an ordered list of those with a known birth date.

Finally, we might be interested to dig even deeper. All artists in the current list were influenced by Picasso, but who did those artists influence?

```
SELECT ?artist, ?influencedArtist WHERE {
    ?artist dbpedia-owl:influencedBy dbpedia:Pablo_Picasso.
    ?influencedArtist dbpedia-owl:influencedBy ?artist.
}
```

The SPARQL engine first looks for all ?artist matches who were influenced by Picasso. For each ?artist value, it looks for ?influencedArtist matches who were influenced by ?artist:

artist	influencedArtist
dbpedia:Karel_Appel	dbpedia:Jan-Hein_Arens
dbpedia:Piet_Mondrian	dbpedia:Charmion_Von_Wiegand
dbpedia:Piet_Mondrian	dbpedia:Robert_Cottingham
dbpedia:Georges_Braque	dbpedia:Piet_Mondrian
dbpedia:Georges_Braque	dbpedia:Byron_Galvez
...	...

Now is the time to reflect on what we have achieved. The above query selects people influenced by people who were influenced by Picasso. We sincerely challenge you to try finding this information on Google (do let us know how many searches and clicks you needed).

One important remark though: the returned information by DBpedia is *incomplete* and likely *incorrect*. There are two reasons for incompletion. First, not all data might be there. Some artists might not be in DBpedia, others might not have their influences listed. If DBpedia does not know an artist's influences, that result will simply not be included. Second, SPARQL endpoints are not obliged to return all results. RDF has an *open-world assumption*: just as on the web, we are never sure that all information is there. Hence, the SPARQL engine gives its best effort to find your query results, but without the guarantee that they will be complete. You can try to formulate a query that gives you all the data from DBpedia (it's really easy in fact), but you will notice that you only get a few thousand results. It is not that the other triples are not there; it is just that the SPARQL engine decided it has worked hard enough already. The reason for incorrectness, apart from missing information, is that the information in DBpedia stems from the online encyclopedia Wikipedia, which is edited by volunteers. That information might contain errors, or might be outdated. The SPARQL endpoint of

DBpedia Live (http://live.dbpedia.org/sparql) might give you more up-to-date results, but unfortunately, no correctness guarantee either. However, results from a search engine such as Google can also be incomplete and incorrect.

7.3 Freebase, the community-curated database

7.3.1 Browsing Freebase

While DBpedia data stems from Wikipedia, an encyclopedia that can be edited by anyone, DBpedia data itself is not publicly editable. Freebase (http:// freebase.com/) is a database of linked data where users can add and edit information directly. That does not mean that Freebase contains only human-added data: many entries are loaded automatically from external sources (such as Wikipedia and Netflix) by specialized software tools. However, human curation is an important aspect of the Freebase philosophy.

Freebase is not based on RDF, but its contents are still considered linked data because a triple-like model is followed. Data is organized by topic, and typed relations to other topics can be added; topics and triples are identified by URLs. In contrast to DBpedia, each piece of data also contains fields detailing by whom and when it was created. Furthermore, facts are grouped by *types*. For instance, people have the type *People*, which contains properties such as *Date of birth*, *Gender*, and *Children*. These properties are not always filled in for all members of the *People* type; they just provide an easy template for editors to encourage them to use the correct properties.

Let's have a look at the page for Pablo Picasso on Freebase. You can visit it directly at https://www.freebase.com/m/060_7 or search through the homepage https://www.freebase.com/ for the artist's name. This page starts with an image and an abstract of the topic, as well as various links to pages on the web about the same topic. In the 'Properties' tab below, we see all data on Picasso, grouped by type that belong to categories. The first type is **Topic** and lists general information such as name, description, website and notability. These properties apply to all topics on Freebase. Scrolling down the page, we note other types such as **Person** and **Visual Artist**, as well as **Literature Subject** and **Film Actor**. It might seem strange to label Picasso as a *film actor*, but this is actually merely a grouping of properties per topic. As we expect from linked data, clicking values leads to the information pages about the subjects. Hovering over types and relationships also reveals their properties.

On the top of the page, we can see different tabs. The default view is the **Properties** view. The **I18n** tab (an abbreviation of 'Internationalization') shows attributes with multi-language fields, such as transliterations of Picasso's name in different languages. The **Keys** tab lists different identifiers of the subject, together with their namespace and who created them. Finally, the **Links** tab shows a tabular overview of all properties of the subject, together with the

person who added or last edited them and the modification date. This can also
serve as a history of all data about the topic.

Freebase is more human-targeted than DBpedia, as the pages are designed to
be browsed and edited easily, whereas DBpedia offers primarily data tables. This
is already apparent from Freebase's homepage, which allows you to navigate data
in an interest-driven way. Similarly to DBpedia, data about topics is also offered
in RDF, although this might not be obvious at first sight. Starting from the regular
URL for a topic such as https://www.freebase.com/m/060_7, you can obtain the
RDF version by changing the URL to http://rdf.freebase.com/rdf/m.060_7.

7.3.2 Querying Freebase

Freebase does not support SPARQL queries; rather, it uses its own query
language, MQL, which is based on JSON. The reason for this is historical;
SPARQL was not yet standardized when Freebase came into existence. The
query form of Freebase is located at https://www.freebase.com/query.

The following query retrieves all personal data about Pablo Picasso:

```
{
   "name": "Pablo Picasso",
   "type": "/people/person",
   "*": null
}
```

The idea is to pass a *template* to the query engine, and all empty fields will be
filled out in reply. The fields name and type narrow the query down to a single
topic. The field * ('all') with value null ('a single unknown value') instructs
Freebase to select all values that belong to this topic. The result is a JSON
document similar to the following:

```
{
"result": {
   "place_of_birth": "Málaga",
   "id": "/en/pablo_picasso",
   "parents": [
     "José Ruiz y Blasco",
     "María Picasso y López"
   ],
   "gender": "Male",
...
```

The results you receive depend on the type you specify. If we want to retrieve properties about Picasso's work as an artist, we set the type accordingly:

```
{
  "name": "Pablo Picasso",
  "type": "/visual_art/visual_artist",
  "*": null
}
```

This then results in the following data:

```
{
  "result": {
    "type": "/visual_art/visual_artist",
    "id": "/en/pablo_picasso",
    "name": "Pablo Picasso",
    "art_forms": [
      "Painting",
      "Sculpture",
      "Ceramic art",
...
```

If we are interested in specific properties, we can specify them in the template. For instance, to only show the artworks by Picasso:

```
{
  "id": "/en/pablo_picasso",
  "type": "/visual_art/visual_artist",
  "artworks": []
}
```

The two square brackets [] denote an empty list ('multiple unknown values'), which will be filled out by the query engine:

```
{
  "result": {
    "id": "/en/pablo_picasso",
    "type": "/visual_art/visual_artist",
    "artworks": [
      "Guernica",
      "Garçon à la pipe",
      "Les Demoiselles d'Avignon",
...
```

Note that a null value would not have worked here, because there is more than one artwork.

If we want more details on the artworks, we have to extend the template. For instance, to retrieve all artwork properties:

```
{
  "id": "/en/pablo_picasso",
  "type": "/visual_art/visual_artist",
  "artworks": [{ "*": null }]
}
```

Inside the list, we place a single template object whose properties will be filled in. This returns an extensive list of all works and their properties. If we are only interested in specific properties, we can name them as we did before:

```
{
  "id": "/en/pablo_picasso",
  "type": "/visual_art/visual_artist",
  "artworks": [{ "name": null, "date_completed": null }]
}
```

The templating mechanism thus works on every label of the data. The following query lists all of Picasso's artworks with title and date:

```
{
"result": {
  "artworks": [
    {
      "name": "Guernica",
      "date_completed": "1937-06"
    },
    {
      "name": "Garçon à la pipe",
      "date_completed": "1905"
    },
    {
      "name": "Les Demoiselles d'Avignon",
      "date_completed": "1907"
    },
...
```

The main difference between MQL and SPARQL is that SPARQL still employs the triple model (with variables for unknowns), whereas MQL has proprietary templating mechanisms.

7.4 Sindice, the semantic web index

7.4.1 Querying the entire web

So far, we have only been querying single datasets. However, the central idea of linked data is of course to be able to cross dataset boundaries. On the web, we mostly discover information through search engines, so analogously, a search engine for linked data could help us find datasets and navigate to other datasets from there.

Sindice (http://sindice.com) is an index of the semantic web. It collects linked data in RDF and other formats, and helps you discover more resources. For instance, we can inspect the data Sindice has about Picasso by putting Picasso's URL, http://dbpedia.org/resource/Pablo_Picasso, into the text box and clicking 'Search'. Even though Sindice finds hundreds of matching documents, you might initially be disappointed by the results. While the ranking of results on traditional search engines has considerably improved over the past decades, raking of semantic data is still in its infancy. However, going through the result pages, we discover various datasets that indeed mention Pablo Picasso.

More targeted searches are possible through Sindice's SPARQL endpoint at http://sparql.sindice.com/. For instance, we can see what data Sindice has available on Picasso:

```
SELECT ?s, ?p WHERE { ?s ?p dbpedia:Pablo_Picasso. }
```

In addition to a lot of data from DBpedia, we also see triples from other datasets such as the *New York Times*. The Sindice SPARQL endpoint is also still under development, so not all triples that are available through the search function can be found in the SPARQL endpoint. Another reason we do not see more data is the issue of identity. Indeed, triples in DBpedia are mostly of this form:

```
dbpedia:Pablo_Picasso dbpedia-owl:birthPlace dbpedia:Málaga.
dbpedia:Pablo_Picasso rdf:type dbpedia-owl:Artist.
```

However, in the *New York Times* dataset, triples use another URL to represent Picasso:

```
nytd:N855344257183137093 skos:prefLabel "Picasso, Pablo".
```

This is a common practice in linked data, since there is no central identity authority. Fortunately, both identifiers are connected together by an owl:sameAs predicate:

```
nytd:N855344257183137093 owl:sameAs dbpedia:Pablo_Picasso.
```

Therefore, we can find more triples about Picasso by adapting our query. Instead of demanding that the triple contain the DBpedia identifier dbpedia:Pablo_Picasso, we say that they can use any identifier, as long as it corresponds to the same concept as dbpedia:Pablo_Picasso. In SPARQL, we can express this as:

```
SELECT ?picasso, ?p, ?o
WHERE {
   ?picasso owl:sameAs dbpedia:Pablo_Picasso.
   ?picasso ?p ?o.
}
```

This instructs Sindice to find all ?picasso identifiers that have a owl:sameAs relation to DBpedia's Picasso entry, and for each of them, find all matching triples. We now retrieve results from the *New York Times*, Yago, and several other datasets. This provides an interesting opportunity to harmonize the triples using one single identifier. Therefore, we can construct the triples while explicitly using the DBpedia identifiers as the subject:

```
CONSTRUCT { dbpedia:Pablo_Picasso ?p ?o. }
WHERE {
   ?picasso owl:sameAs dbpedia:Pablo_Picasso.
   ?picasso ?p ?o.
}
```

Note the explicit mention of dbpedia:Pablo_Picasso in the CONSTRUCT clause, which ensures that all found triples use this identifier, no matter what dataset they originate from.

7.4.2 Browsing Sindice through Sig.ma

While Sindice gives you a more raw view on the web's data, Sig.ma (http://sig.ma/) is an interface built on top of Sindice that lets you collect information about a topic easily. Sig.ma looks through different data sources using Sindice, but groups the information visually together, turning it into a *mash-up*.

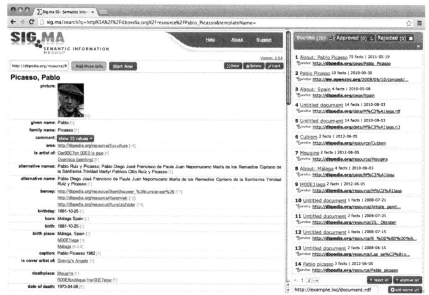

Figure 2.5 A search for http://dbpedia.org/resource/Pablo_Picasso on Sig.ma

Figure 2.5 shows the result of searching for http://dbpedia.org/resource/ Pablo_Picasso. On the left are the different pieces of information, grouped together by category, starting with images at the top. On the right, we see the sources that contributed to the information on the page. They consist of the original URL we entered, but also all URLs that are mentioned on that page. Scrolling down, we see many information sources, and if we hover above them, the corresponding data sources are highlighted on the right. Similarly, we can hover in the sources sidebar on the left to see which pieces of information they contributed.

However, as you would expect, this mostly shows information associated with the single identifier http://dbpedia.org/resource/Pablo_Picasso and so a lot of potential sources are not included. Therefore, we can also search for the artist by typing 'Pablo Picasso' in the search box, which will lead to much more data. However, Sig.ma text search is a little liberal, so some data might only be marginally relevant to Picasso. Even worse, some data is simply incorrect because the topic was not matched precisely. Here are some examples we found:

- Picasso is created by 'darj33ling'. Upon closer inspection of the data source containing this fact, it turns out that this actually refers to a *slide deck* titled 'Pablo Picasso', created by a user account 'darj33ling'.
- Picasso is 425 pixels wide, because a photograph of him is.
- Picasso is a product or service. This seems to come from an online shop that sells puzzles with Picasso's artworks on them.

This indicates the kind of problem that can occur when automatically combining data from different sources. It also shows the importance of having URLs as identifiers on the semantic web instead of plain text. Fortunately, Sig.ma allows you to discard sources you do not trust by removing them from the right sidebar. Additionally, you can add new data sources there. Sig.ma will extract data from them on the fly and categorize it on the left.

All in all, Sig.ma is an exciting visualization of the possibilities of linked data, because it connects so many sources together. If we understand its limitations and are careful with selecting sources, very meaningful results can be generated. Do try to put your own name in the search box, as there might even be linked data sources about you that you weren't aware of. And if you have your own data, you can submit it to Sindice so it will be included in Sig.ma results.

Notes

1 We based our overview of data modelling on chapters from Ramsay (2004) and Segaran, Evans and Taylor (2009).
2 See https://en.wikipedia.org/wiki/Law_of_the_instrument.
3 You are not strictly required to add the PREFIX declarations here, as DBpedia inserts them automatically for its common prefixes. However, not all SPARQL endpoints support this and so, in general, always include all declarations (even though we will not repeat them in this book due to space constraints).
4 At least, a triple can only occur once in the same graph. Triple stores might contain different graphs, but this is a different story altogether.

References

Berners-Lee, T. (2006) *Linked Data*, http://www.w3.org/DesignIssues/LinkedData.html.

Berners-Lee, T., Hendler, J. and Lassila, O. (2001) The Semantic Web, *Scientific American*, **284** (5), 34–43.

Boiko, B. (2005) *Content Management Bible*, Wiley.

Bray, T., Hollander, D., Layman, A. and Tobin, R. (2006) *Namespaces in XML 1.1*, 2nd edn, W3C Recommendation, http://www.w3.org/TR/xml-names11/.

Lynden, A. and Fenn, J. (2003) *Understanding Gartner's Hype Cycles*, Technical Report, Gartner.

Manovich, L. (2001) *The Language of New Media*, MIT Press.

Ramsay, S. (2004) *A Companion to Digital Humanities*, Blackwell, chapter on Databases.

Segaran, T., Evans, C. and Taylor, J. (2009) *Programming the Semantic Web*, O'Reilly.

Severance, C. (2012) Discovering JavaScript Object Notation, *Computer*, **45** (4), 6–8.

Shafranovich, Y. (2005) *Common Format and MIME Type for Comma-separated Values (CSV) Files: request for comments 4180*, Internet Engineering Task Force, http://www.ietf.org/rfc/rfc4180.txt.

3

Cleaning

Learning outcomes of this chapter

- Adopting a broader view of metadata quality
- Why you need to clean your metadata in the context of linked data
- Identification of most common metadata quality issues
- Understanding the possibilities and limits of automated metadata cleaning
- Case study: cleaning metadata of the Schoenberg Database of Manuscripts

1 Introduction

'It is not a bug, it is a feature' is one of the more interesting lines one of us learnt when working for a software company. When a customer noticed an inconsistency in one of the products, the challenge was to convince the client the issue was not a shortcoming but actually a quality of the software. This line comes to mind when we think about the relation between linked data and metadata quality. The lack of consistent, formalized and well structured data on the web is often presented as the biggest Achilles' heel for the realization of the semantic web and linked data vision. However, we prefer to see the same reality from another viewpoint. Even the most ardent critic of linked data must admit at least one positive outcome: linked data have put metadata quality in the spotlight, finally giving this topic the attention it deserves.

If you only remember one thing from this chapter, it should be this: all metadata is dirty, but you can do something about it. Recurrent metadata quality issues such as duplicate records or inconsistent encoding of dates or names all have a negative impact on the use of your metadata but also on the implementation of linked data methodologies. As Chapters 4 and 5 will demonstrate, the success rate of methods such as reconciliation and enrichment depends to a large extent on how consistent and well structured your metadata are. Data profiling and cleaning techniques will teach you how to spot these issues and where possible mitigate them.

1.1 The difficulty of combining theory and practice

Data quality has attracted a lot of attention recently within academic circles. A large number of papers and books describe data quality with the help of theoretical concepts, models and frameworks which often refer to and build upon one another. Academia's self-referentiality is not always what practitioners need when they want to learn how to handle, for example, duplicate records and spelling inconsistencies within their day-to-day work practices. When taking a defective car to a repair shop, one does not expect the mechanic to develop an abstract model of how exactly your car stopped functioning and why it broke down. You just want your car repaired.

The same thinking can come to mind when consulting some of the metadata quality typologies and frameworks which will be briefly presented in this chapter. Many publications develop theoretical models and typologies (or present critiques and extensions of existing ones), without making it explicit how they can be put into practice to actually help you enhance your metadata.

You know that a better conceptual understanding of your car, for example through a model explaining the relations and dependencies between its different parts, can help you avoid unnecessary damage to your car in the future or to calculate when you should take it in for maintenance. The same applies to abstract frameworks which allow a better understanding of metadata quality. Models certainly can be useful but it should be clear what their practical benefits are. Unfortunately, research concerning data quality has notoriously 'failed to combine and cross-fertilize theory and practice' (Floridi, 2013). This chapter hopes to avoid this pitfall.

1.2 Overview of the chapter

From the very beginning of this chapter, we want to emphasize that there is no such thing as perfect metadata, making the discussion on how to obtain total quality data irrelevant. The theoretical considerations presented at the beginning of this chapter will give us a frame to better interpret and understand the practical outcomes of data profiling. This method brings to the surface inconsistencies within metadata in a (semi-)automated manner. Once inconsistencies are detected, techniques can be used to clean metadata where possible. In order to ensure a good practical understanding of these methods and tools, an extensive use case based upon metadata from the Schoenberg Database of Manuscripts (SDBM) from UPenn Libraries is presented at the end of the chapter. The SDBM has evolved over the years from a personal tool of a manuscript collector to a research database used by an international community of scholars. Technically it has evolved from a spreadsheet to a standalone database into a web-based application, with a current intention to embrace linked data principles in order to connect with outside data sources. The constant evolution of its purpose and technological framework resulted in a database containing multiple inconsistencies. All these factors make it an ideal case study for this chapter.

2 A new field of data quality

It is difficult to overstate the importance of data quality in our current information-driven society. The implementation of Freedom of Information acts throughout Europe, the Sarbanes Oxley Act in the USA and the political support for the Open Data movement received by the UK and US governments are all illustrations of how governments are trying to promote transparency and accountability through access to information. In parallel with these top-down regulations, activists and journalists are engaging in bottom-up initiatives. Projects such as http://opented.eu and http://govtrack.us aggregate data provided on the web by public bodies but also provide tools to interpret and re-use large volumes of data regarding political or economical decision-making processes (Robinson, Yu and Felten, 2010).

In parallel with this movement, concerns about the quality of the data have also arisen. At its best, publishing bad data is useless. At its worst, it can have disastrous consequences. More importantly, it is sometimes extremely complex to find a consensus on whether data are of good or bad quality. The complexity of the debate regarding Al Gore's use of data in his documentary *An Inconvenient Truth* and the problem of the assessment of data in relation to climate change as a whole illustrates why data quality has become such a hot but also troublesome topic (Meshkin, 2010).

Unfortunately, the increasing attention has not yet resulted in a better understanding of what exactly data quality is. Enacted in 2000 in the USA, the Information Quality Act, also known as the Data Quality Act, remains notoriously vague on how the notion can be understood and should be implemented on the ground.

2.1 Fitness for purpose

Why is data quality such a difficult topic to handle? Quality has been (and remains) a very intangible notion. Boydens (1999) refers to three different interpretations of the concept of 'quality':

1 **Common understanding:** the distinctive attribute or characteristic possessed by someone or something.
2 **Philosophical context:** refers to the sensible aspect of someone or something, as opposed to quantity.
3 **Specialized meaning:** the degree of excellence of someone or something.

It is the third interpretation to which we refer here, which immediately brings up the question of how the degree of excellence can be evaluated. This leads us to the ISO 9000 definition for quality, which states the following: 'The totality of features and characteristics of a product, process or service that bears on its ability to satisfy stated or implicit needs' (ISO, 2005). This definition is heavily referred to in the literature, and commonly abridged as 'fitness for use' (Boydens, 1999; Bruce and Hillmann, 2004).

2.2 As data are re-used, purposes change

In the paper 'Increasing Returns and the Two Worlds of Business', Arthur (1996) describes how the information economy confronts the traditional economic law of diminishing returns. This law describes how traditional businesses run at some specific point into limitations (e.g. distribution costs, access to raw materials, maintenance of stocks) which mean that augmenting the production results in lower per-unit profits. At some specific point, the costs associated, for example, with the transport of more raw materials or storing bigger stocks implies that, relatively speaking, less profit is made per unit. These *decreasing returns to scale* imply that companies cannot expand their production continuously as they reach an equilibrium regarding per-unit profit. This leaves space for other players in the market.

The specific affordances of data as an economic product, such as important up-front investments but marginal storage and transportation costs, give rise to the contrary (Arthur, 1996). Businesses within the information economy benefit from *increasing returns to scale*, which explains the presence of monopolies such as Microsoft and Google.

What does this have to do with data quality? As Arthur mentions, 'adaptation is what drives increasing-returns businesses, not optimization'. How does this relate to data quality? Returning to our 'fitness for purpose' definition of quality, we need to be aware that data offers the opportunity to be used in multiple contexts. This results in a tension between *purpose-depth* and *purpose-scope*. In the best of worlds, high-quality information is 'optimally fit for the specific purpose/s for which it is elaborated (purpose-depth) and is also easily re-usable for new purpose/s (purpose-scope)' (Floridi, 2013). It is therefore dangerous to speak of purpose-fitness from one specific point of view, which can be analysed (or measured as some pretend) according to a variety of parameters (completeness, accuracy, timeliness, etc.).

Floridi gives a good example with postcodes. Originally developed to speed up the automated processing of mail, postcodes are currently used for a wide range of purposes such as calculating insurance premiums, designating destinations in route planning software and making decisions in relation to the type of public services (health care, education, social housing) a citizen receives.

As the national post offices in the UK commercially exploit the use of their postcode database, the project http://www.freethepostcode.org/ promotes a crowdsourced encoding of how postcodes map to a specific latitude and longitude and vice versa. The initiative promotes users to make use of postcodes in unexpected ways.

On the level of the purpose-depth, the quality of postcodes is high: they function well to help the attribution of mail. However, when it comes to the allocation of public services such as health care or social housing, their quality is a lot more debatable, leading to the use of terms such as 'postcode lottery' (Floridi, 2013).

Not only the purpose but also who is consuming the data can radically change how we assess data quality. Let us think, for example, about the CAPTCHA application. This challenge-response test is used on the web to check whether or not it is a human user who is submitting information in a form, in order to avoid bots automatically submitting content containing spam. The small images used for these online tests represent tiny portions of scanned textual documents which cannot be converted to text with a sufficient degree of certainty. In the OCR context, these parts of the scan are considered of poor quality, as they can not be converted automatically into text. The *bug* is in this context converted into a *feature*, in the sense that the impossibility of automatically converting the image into text constitutes exactly the quality in the context of the CAPTCHA. Confronted with partly incomplete or incorrect data, humans have an amazing capacity to deal with errors. By putting specific values or representations of data in a larger context, we manage to complete this test. Computers cannot.

This distinction between purpose-scope and purpose-depth is very relevant for cultural heritage metadata, as different and sometimes conflicting visions and expectations exist about the use of metadata.

2.3 What do users expect from metadata?

How can we relate the 'fitness for purpose' view on data quality to the cultural heritage sector? Is there actually a shared view on what users expect from metadata? Despite efforts amongst the cultural heritage community to analyse the needs of their patrons, no clear understanding about users and their expectations has been gained over the last few years. As Darren Peacock notes:

> This confusion results in research and analysis in the form of inconsistently modelled snapshots of what is happening online. Despite the large amount of effort going into user research over more than a decade, we still have a very fragmented understanding of users and the user experience on museum Web sites.
>
> Peacock and Brownbill, 2007

In his article, Peacock identifies four different terms that have been used to refer to patrons in the context of the online use of cultural heritage. Each term reflects a specific view on the user and his needs:

1 **The audience:** this term refers to a subject, passive population, as identified within the context of traditional broadcast media such as the radio and television. This model has its roots in 19th-century paternalistic ideas about how cultural institutions could attract and educate the masses. This understanding of the user was in line with the vision of the 'virtual museums' created in the early days of the web.
2 **The visitor:** the public is considered as visitors who make an active choice to visit a museum. The visitor studies paradigm prefers an ethnographic methodology to study visitor 'behaviour', which can also be applied in an online environment.
3 **The user:** usability analysis focuses on the way agents can achieve their tasks within an interface. User-centred design tests rely on experts or representatives of users to test the fitness for use of search and display interfaces.
4 **The consumer:** this approach is driven by market research that focuses on how needs can be satisfied and relies on 'behaviorist models of stimulus and response'. As Peacock adequately notes, this 'market conception completely alters the relationship of supply and demand for museums, inverting the dependency of consumer on producer to its reverse.'

The last view especially, that of the user as *consumer*, has had a big impact over the last decade. Cultural heritage institutions increasingly feel they are put in competition with private companies in the quest for attention from the user. When interpreted literally, the 'fitness for purpose' metadata quality definition refers strongly to the idea of self-regulating markets, where the demand has a direct impact on the offer.

To what extent may we consider the cultural heritage as a self-regulating market? Matarasso warns us of the difficulties and dangers of applying the 'fitness for purpose' definition in a too narrow or literal manner within the cultural heritage domain. He explains that free market regulation cannot be the only quality criterion:

> The market is never as free as we might wish it to be. There is a strong commercial interest in a standardization of taste, whether in music, films or coffee, since it enlarges markets and reduces overheads. These forces are dangerous enough when it comes to ordinary commodities: they are all the more when it comes to the space where we shape, question and transit our values. The views of audiences and participants in the arts are a component of evaluation.

> Only in the commercial sector do they act as a determinant measure of worth: and the point of having a public sector is precisely to introduce other values and safeguards to our cultural life.
>
> Matarasso, 2002, 3

These considerations underline the importance of not only attributing importance to what we have called the purpose-depth, or the adequacy of something for its immediate use, but also the purpose-scope, which designates the fitness for potential re-use.

The introduction mentioned that we do not expect our mechanic to elaborate a theoretical model on how exactly your car broke down. We will now demonstrate with concrete examples how to handle metadata quality in practice. The next section will focus on how data profiling can be used to analyse to what extent the values contained in a database correspond to the restrictions laid down in the definition of each field. The results of this analysis can be used to assess their purpose-scope and -depth.

3 Data profiling

Metadata practitioners who worked on aggregation projects, harvesting metadata from different partners, must acknowledge that the quality of existing metadata is hardly questioned and only becomes visible once they are put to work and queried by a large number of users. After all, what collection holder wants to stand up in the middle of his or her peers and warn them about the low quality of his or her metadata? This misplaced trust causes delays and failures when metadata do not live up to expectations (van Hooland, Kaufman and Bontemps, 2008). To put it bluntly in the words of Diane Hillmann: 'There are no metadata police' (Bruce and Hillmann, 2004).

In the absence of concrete methodologies and tools, metadata practitioners usually believe that producing information describing the quality of their metadata is too big a step to be taken. This section will therefore present the notion of data profiling, defined by Olson as 'the use of analytical techniques to discover the true structure, content, and quality of a collection of data' (Olson, 2003). Data profiling is the first and the essential step towards data quality, in the sense that it consists of gathering factual information on the data quality, that can be used, first, to decide which actions to take in order to enhance the quality and, second, to inform the users on the quality of the data they are consulting.

3.1 Flattening out your metadata

Before we dive into the details of data profiling, we need to prepare our metadata for analysis. The methods and tools we will be using assume you are working with metadata represented as tabular data, which is the data model we described in Section 2 of Chapter 2. In other words, we need to work on metadata stored as a flat file, consisting of rows and columns. However, we saw in Chapter 2 that most institutions use relational databases to manage their metadata, which store metadata across different tables. Your metadata might also be stored in an information system which uses XML as a native data model.

It might take substantial effort, but in most contexts metadata records contained within a database can be flattened out in one large table. We will not focus on the extraction process, as this involves in-depth knowledge of database management. It is the task of the database manager to aggregate all relevant values related to a resource (be it a collection object, bibliographic item or an archival fonds) which are spread out over multiple tables into one flat file. Your help will probably be required to indicate what exactly are the values you want to include in what is commonly called a database dump. If your metadata are stored as an XML file, there might be a need to flatten out hierarchical data. This might involve the duplication of certain values of the parent element, which need to be repeated on the level of every child. If you are unaware of this step when looking at the flat file, it might drastically disturb your interpretation of the data. For example, the metadata from the general description of the archival fonds, e.g. who is the owner of the fonds, will be incorporated on the level of each individual archival item contained within that file. If this inheritance of a specific value from a more general level is not documented and taken into account, the values might be interpreted incorrectly.

3.2 Guide to metadata diagnosis

In this section we will point out the most important features of metadata and databases that you should take into account when performing data profiling. This section should be read in combination with the hands-on exercises of the case study at the end of the chapter. The importance of, for example, storage and value properties will be illustrated within this section with some short examples. Through the use of filters and facets within OpenRefine you can experiment on your own in order to assess the impact of inadequate definitions of these properties. Most of the rules and procedures presented below are described in more detail by Olson (2003). Consult his work for more details and how to link data profiling with database management.

3.2.1 Columns as the point of departure

Throughout the different analyses, the focus will reside on the level of the metadata fields. These fields are represented as columns when stored as tabular data. All of the cleaning tasks performed in the case study with OpenRefine will also use the column as the point of departure.

Data contained in a column share a common meaning. The more detailed the common features and constraints of these data are, the easier it will be to verify whether the values contained in the column conform to the expectations and constraints defined. When you create a new field within your metadata schema, the collection management software you use will probably offer all sorts of features to delimit the type of values that the field can accommodate. For example, you could oblige the user to encode only values for the style of an artwork from a controlled list, or to encode dates within the ISO 8601 standard.

For the moment, let us get rid of all the whistles and bells your software might be able to implement and let's get back to basics. A minimal SQL query to add a column with the name 'title' to the table 'artwork' would look like this:

```
ALTER TABLE artwork ADD title VARCHAR(60);
```

It is surprising how many things can go wrong with just these three variables: the name of the column, its data type and the maximum length.

The very first indication of what values to expect in a column should be reasonably given by the name of a column. When creating a table in a database, the database management software will ask for a name. The name of a column therefore represents the most minimal level of documentation. It can also be considered as the most valuable, as it is often the only documentation available.

You might wonder why we discuss something as trivial as the name of a column. Its presence seems self-evident, but column names are surprisingly often dubious and difficult to interpret. Sometimes names of columns are given in a rush and giving a proper title is forgotten. Instead of a new column being created, an existing but unused column might be re-appropriated without a modification of the title.

The metadata export used in the case study offers some classic examples of what can go wrong with column names. Who would intuitively know for example what content to expect under column titles such as 'MIN_FL' or 'MIN_LG' mean? We might have a rough understanding of what a column name 'Sold' might refer to, but are we expected to find the date of a sale, or a Boolean value (yes/no) telling us whether something has been sold or not? The content of the column called 'Seller' seems clear, but what is exactly the difference with its neighbour column called 'Seller2'? Is it the person or the organization involved in a second sell, or is it column which allows to store the name of a second party which is involved in the same sale? These concrete examples demonstrate that column names are no trivial matter. Most collection management systems, such as OpenAccess for example, force users to add an explicit descriptive name to document the title of the metadata field, which is often short and might contain abbreviations.

When diagnosing your metadata with OpenRefine, the use of a facet will allow you very rapidly to check whether the name of the column actually matches the values the column contains by giving you an overview of the distribution of the values. If, based on the name of a column, you expected person names and half of the most popular entries represent dates, you know there is a problem.

Unused columns

This might come as a surprise to those of you who never had a look into the back-end of a collection management database, but almost every database we have come across contains a high number of unused columns. This phenomenon occurs for different reasons.

Off-the-shelf collection management software contains a large number of preconfigured columns, out of which often only a small portion is effectively used. Even if a proper analysis is made at the time of the configuration of a database to match the needs of an institution with the columns that are actually needed, people include too many rather than too few columns.

Used columns can also lose their purpose at some point, but continue to persist within the system. The strange thing is that very often these unused columns are migrated from one system to another. The fear of losing information tends to win over a desire to keep a database tidy. However, the presence of many unused columns distorts reporting and analytics.

3.2.2 Storage properties

After having defined a name for a column, two other basic properties are defined in our minimal SQL query:

```
ALTER TABLE artwork ADD title VARCHAR(60);
```

Apart from naming the column, we need to indicate how the database should store the values within that column. The variables VARCHAR(60) refer to the data type and the maximum field length.

The most common data types include (but are not limited to):

- text: textual data
- number: integer or decimal numbers
- Boolean: true or false
- date: standardized format (e.g. ISO 8601) to represent dates.

In theory, these different data types seem to offer a wealth of opportunities to keep a tight grip on how metadata are encoded. However, note that all types of data can be stored by using the data type *Text* (often referred to as *Character*). The practice of storing all different data types as text could seem like a good and practical idea at first, just like organizing an open-invitation house party. At first, the idea that everyone, regardless of whether you know them or not, can just show up and join in might seem the most sociable thing to do. However, you might soon regret the idea when strangers are emptying your fridge. The same thing happens when all fields are of the *Text* data type: you lose control. It becomes increasingly difficult to automatically check the coherence of what is encoded.

Why does this happen on such a large scale? Often, you might want to encode values which do not belong to the global data type respected by the majority of the values. For example, if you choose to use the *Date* data type, you cannot encode values such as 'unknown' or 'End of the 19th century'. Especially when importing legacy data, you could be obliged to store everything into the *Text* data type, as you might not have the time to streamline values which do not conform. Also, flat files frequently do not support any other data type than *Text*.

During data profiling, try not to settle too easily with this common denominator data type. Through simple operations with the help of facets, you will learn in the case study how to get a quick overview of what the most used data type is in a column. If the number of entries which do not conform to the overall data type is not too high, you might decide to invest some time in manually cleaning them up or to use regular expression to automate the conversion process.

With the decrease of storage costs, it may appear that the length of a database field has lost a lot of its pertinence. However, the length of a value can give very valuable indications. First of all, the average length of the encoded values gives a very good indication whether the content of a field is being used for its original intent or what you think is stored in the column. If you think you are handling a field which should contain the name of a donor and the average length is three characters, something is wrong. The distribution of the length of the values encoded throughout an entire collection also gives precious insights. If 95% of the values of a field have in between 10 and 20 characters, the outliers on both sides, values representing less than 10 or more than 20, should probably be looked at manually.

3.2.3 Value properties

Once these basic aspects of a metadata field have been analysed, we can go a step further and have a closer look at the content of the values. Fields can restrict the content to a fixed set or a range of values. Controlled vocabularies are a good example of a fixed set of values, as the cataloguer has to use a value offered by a controlled list.

Data profiling can in this context provide an opportunity to get a deeper understanding of how a controlled vocabulary is being used to index a collection. The analysis of the distribution of the values used for indexing can result in strategic information. When the distribution of the use of indexing terms is visualized, typically it takes on the form of a power law: a small number of indexing terms is used very often, whereas the majority of the terms are almost hardly used. Figure 3.1 shows you, for example, the distribution of the indexing terms used at the Powerhouse Museum in Sydney, Australia.

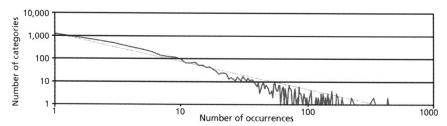

Figure 3.1 Distribution of values from a controlled vocabulary across a collection

This type of information can give you valuable insights in how to assess your indexation process. The presence of both over- and underused values gives you indications as to how to modify controlled lists. An overused value might be split up into more specific values, and under- or unused values might be taken out.

The content of metadata fields can also be limited through a range. Here we typically think of fields such as, for example, insurance value or dates. A common issue with ranges is that the unit of the range is taken for granted and not, or not systematically, mentioned. When describing the dimensions, the weight or the cost of an object, it is important to know whether you are expressing the values in inches or centimetres, in pounds or kilograms and dollars or euros.

3.2.4 Dates

One specific type of field on which we can focus a bit more in depth are dates, beyond any doubt one of the most problematic fields. Everyone who has hands-on experience of the management of metadata knows how difficult it is to streamline the encoding of dates. During the evaluation of one collection management database, we identified for example *52 different ways* to encode a date. Table 3.1 represents the ten most frequent patterns to represent a date of acquisition in the database we assessed.

Dates are problematic fields throughout all application domains, but the cultural heritage sector has a particularly hard time encoding dates in a coherent manner and making them machine-processable for search. Not only is a lot of uncertainty involved about when exactly something took place, but the granularity (day, month, year, decade, century, millennium) of expressing a date or a period may vary widely inside and outside an institution. For example, 2007, June 2007, June 7 to June 10 2007 and June 7 2007 are all valid dates to be used. In our experience, forcing the encoding of dates in a strictly preformatted

Table 3.1 Overview of the ten most recurring formats to encode a date, based on an export of legacy metadata from the Royal Museum of Central Africa, Belgium

Pattern	Examples
(empty)	
9999-9999	1891-1912
9999	1909
99-99/9999	09-10/1992
99/9999	01/1994
99-9999	08-1950
99/99/9999	04/08/1963
AAA 9999	May 1938
AAAAAAA-AAAAA 9999	January-march 1999
99-99 9999	01-02 1993

manner is not workable. In most cultural heritage contexts, a certain flexibility is needed to express temporality. Then the question is: how do you allow structured queries through all these different formats?

Fortunately, you can make use of tools which will convert any date to a standardized date range consisting of a beginning and an end date. This information can be stored internally, invisible to the end-user. For example, the collection management system CollectiveAccess would store the dates 2007, June 2007, June 7 to June 10 2007 and June 7 2007 respectively as:

```
January 1 2007 @ 00:00:00am - December 31 2007 @ 12:59:59pm
June 1 2007 @ 00:00:00am - June 30 2007 @ 12:59:59pm
June 7 2007 @ 00:00:00am - June 10 2007 @ 12:59:59pm
June 7 2007 @ 00:00:00am - June 7 2007 @ 12:59:59pm
```

This approach allows the database to search and sort dates independently of the format and the language used to encode them, but also to transform on the fly the display format of dates independently of how they were originally encoded.

One needs to leave the freedom to both refer to exact dates but also to periods, such as the end of the Bronze Age or the Interbellum period, for example. In a configuration file, CollectiveAccess allows users to set up a list of periods which are frequently textually expressed in a collection. These might be highly specific to a given domain, such as archaeology or anthropology. These text expressions are then again converted to a beginning and an end date stored internally:[1]

```
expressions = {
  us civil war = 1861 to 1865,
  world war 2  = 1939 to 1945,
  qin dynasty = 221 to 206 bc
}
```

3.2.5 Empty fields

Behind the apparent simple and very recurrent phenomenon of not having a value in a field lies a surprisingly complex set of problems (Olson, 2003). The first problem lies in the variety of options which exist to express the absence of a value. The most obvious option is to leave the field empty. However, when configuring a metadata schema, the decision could be made not to allow empty fields. If no standardized expression is foreseen, users will improvise all sorts of different solutions: 'null', 'unknown', 'no value', etc. The diversity of these expressions can lead to the false conclusion that the field does contain a value. There are also different reasons why there is no value to encode for one or more records:

- lack of resources to adequately fill in the field
- the value is not known
- the value is not applicable
- the value is not known yet.

Applications very rarely offer the opportunity to document why no value is given.

The spaces in between

A particularly interesting and important case of empty values is *trailing white spaces*. You could consider these as null values in disguise. To the human user, a field might seem empty. However, a white space was for some reason encoded. We tend to forget that whitespace characters are encoded as any other character. Software therefore legitimately interprets whitespace as a value. Interestingly, Unicode offers codes to define 26 variants of the whitespace character.[2] Trailing whitespace can distort your analytics and therefore need to be removed as much as possible.

3.2.6 Field overloading

Field overloading is the opposite phenomenon of empty fields: too much information is packed into one field. This phenomenon refers to the bad practice of encoding in one field values which should be split out over multiple fields. Field overloading can have negative consequences for searching and sorting, but also severely limits the type of analysis and cleaning of the metadata.

Two different reasons can be the source of field overloading. There might be a need to encode multiple values of the same type in one field. If the field does not offer the facility to be repeated, the multiple values are repeated after one another in the same field. This typically happens in, for example, the subject field, in which multiple keywords are contained in one and the same field. The keywords are divided by a comma, white space or any other separator character (e.g. 'Madonna with child, medieval mural painting'). The other type of field overloading occurs when different realities are described within the same field. This often is due to the fact that the content of a field is too generic and should be subdivided in more specific subfields. Classic examples are the encoding of addresses, which pack in one field the street name, house number, postcode and city name.

As long as the separator character which divides the different values has been used in a consistent manner, and the order in which different types of values appear is respected, the content can be split out very easily. However, the separator signs are rarely used in a consistent manner, especially in large metadata sets built up over many years. The use of regular expressions, as will be explained in the case study, can come in very handy to write short scripts to address these issues. Regular expressions also make it possible to check whether values respect a predefined pattern. URLs, e-mail addresses, phone numbers, postcodes, etc., are all examples of values for which a pattern can be defined and used for validity checks.

3.2.7 Duplicate records and accession numbers

Another recurring problem is the identification of duplicate records. Duplicates can arise for different sorts of reasons in a database, but these mainly occur when metadata are migrated from one application to the other and some consolidation has to take place between different sources of the metadata. Here we want to specifically focus on the issue of unique identifiers. Once you have a solid method of issuing unique identifiers for records in your database, preventing or finding duplicates seems a straightforward operation. Reality, however, is more complex.

A lot of the problems we are currently facing with duplicate or missing records is immediately related to how traditional accession numbers have crept into the digital world. Accession numbers are usually assigned in a sequential manner as new collection holdings are acquired and catalogued. They are composed of multiple sections, out of which at least a couple have *meaning*. Typically, an accession number might start out with the year it was acquired, the department to which it belongs and potentially also the type of object (manuscript, sculpture, etc.). Only at the very end comes a sequential number. By interpreting the structure of the accession number you already learn a lot about the object.

However, having semantics in a unique identifier is currently considered to be bad practice. Why? First of all, because semantics change over time. Institutions and their departments are constantly being restructured, which requires a modification of the identifiers. It is not uncommon to find three or four generations of accession numbers in a database, which all need to be maintained. Second, due to the combination of character and numeric elements, a great many human errors are made when creating accession numbers but they are also difficult to sort and query in an automated way. A new context could also imply that the semantics of the identifier are inappropriate. Third, making the access-ion number available to the general audience could, for example, give away too much detail on where exactly a precious object would be stored in an institution. For all these reasons, the semantics of accession numbers are more of a burden than an advantage within an electronic environment.

As a practical workaround, most collection management systems will allow you to create accession numbers but will create internal identifiers consisting of automatically generated numbers. In order to ensure consistency in the format and to allow the database to use the accession number for sorting, CollectiveAccess allows users to customize configuration files. The file illustrated below allows users to set up a rigorous encoding of the structure of the accession number and to indicate how the values should be sorted:

```
sort_order = [item_num, lot_num, acc_year],
             elements = {
                  acc_year = {
                          type = YEAR,
                          width = 4,
                          description = Year,
                  },
                  lot_num = {
                          type = NUMERIC,
                          width = 6,
                          description = Lot number,
                  },
                  item_num = {
                          type = SERIAL,
                          width = 6,
                          description = Item number,
                          table = ca_objects,
                          field = idno,
                          sort_field = idno_sort,
                  } }
```

A last practical recommendation in relation to accession numbers: hands-on experience with digitization and retro-cataloguing projects has shown that things go terribly wrong with unique identifiers. Time and time again, projects across all types of institutions are delayed due to the incapability to create and maintain links between a physical object, its existing metadata residing in a collection management database and the digital representation of the object. Issuing unique identifiers for files created in a digitization workflow is a straightforward operation, but ensuring that these identifiers are linked to the pre-existing metadata record which describes the digitized object is a tremendous challenge. In a production setting, where hundreds or thousands of objects are scanned and photographed on a daily basis, mistakes are quickly made. Often the physical objects only have a label with a legacy accession number. Manually looking up the corresponding metadata record of the object in the database takes up valuable time. It is therefore absolutely not a luxury to have a feature within your collection management system for printing out barcodes, according to a standard such as COD128, or 2-dimensional QR codes, on labels. This allows you to print out barcodes on stickers, which might also include legacy accession numbers, to be attached to the container of the objects to be digitized. This involves some preparation effort but it ensures to have a fluent digitization workflow and limits errors as the identifier of the object is scanned in and not encoded manually.

Keep in mind that assigning unique identifiers becomes even more complex when digitizing composite objects, such as historical photo albums. There is a need to assign identifiers on three levels: the album, the pages and the individual photographs, which could exist on both the front and the back if interesting information is recorded on the back. Within the pre-existing database, there is probably only one global metadata record, and therefore one accession number, for the album as a whole. The digitization process therefore introduces the need to create a whole new array of unique numbers. Conventions for assigning identifiers for these peculiar types of objects tend to be developed in an ad hoc manner, resulting over the years in a cacophony of identifier patterns. Cleaning these up necessarily involves a lot of manual intervention, but data profiling can at least give you a quick overview of how bad the situation actually is.

3.3 Tools for data profiling

In the past, end-users had to rely on IT people in order to diagnose the quality of their data and to run cleaning tasks, as custom-written scripts were needed to act upon sizeable data sets. Luckily, the advent of interactive data transformation tools (IDTs) now allows for rapid and inexpensive operations on large amounts of data, even by professionals lacking in-depth technical skills.

IDTs resemble the desktop spreadsheet software we are all familiar with. While spreadsheets are designed to work on individual rows and cells, IDTs operate on large ranges of data at once. These tools offer an integrated and user-friendly interface through which domain experts can perform both the data profiling and the cleaning operations.

Several general-purpose tools for interactive data transformation have been developed over the last years, such as Potter's Wheel ABC and Wrangler. This handbook specifically focuses on OpenRefine (formerly Freebase Gridworks and Google Refine), as it has recently gained a lot of popularity and is rapidly becoming the tool of choice to process and clean large amounts of data efficiently in a browser-based interface. OpenRefine will be introduced and presented in the case study of this chapter.

4 Conclusion

Don't take your metadata at face value. That is the key message of this chapter, which focused on how researchers and practitioners can diagnose and act upon the quality of metadata. Methods such as the reconciliation and enrichment of metadata, which will be presented in the following chapters, depend to a large extent on string-matching algorithms. From the point of view of these algorithms, 'Post impressionism', 'post impressionist' and 'post-impressionism' are three different realities, as there is no complete match on the string level. Natural language processing can overcome to a good extent the issues raised in this specific example, but they nevertheless point out the importance of streamlining metadata as much as possible.

Even if more and more people are talking about the importance of data quality throughout different application domains, the topic remains difficult to handle. First of all, quality is an intangible notion. It is often defined as the extent to which a product or service satisfies a need. But needs change, making the quality of data to a large extent dependent on the context of use. It is therefore not only important to assess the purpose-depth (to what extent do the data fit their initial purpose?) but also the purpose-scope: how easy is it to re-use the data for other purposes? Making metadata available as linked data fundamentally is based on the premise that you allow others to re-use your metadata, regardless of the context of use.

After a global introduction to the notion of data quality, the specific context of the quality of metadata in the cultural heritage sector was discussed. First of all, to what extent may we consider our libraries, archives and museums as players within a self-regulating market? Over the years, we have witnessed how cultural heritage institutions have become increasingly dependent on how their products and services are consumed. This is not a place to have an ideological debate on the funding of the arts and culture, but probably everyone agrees that cultural heritage institutions also have a preservation role to play: therefore they should not take into account only the needs of their current users.

This aspect brings us to the most crucial characteristic of cultural heritage metadata: they have a longevity which is atypical for other application domains. As the majority of large national institutions have been created since the 19th or the beginning of the 20th century, all institutions are managing to a large extent what we commonly call legacy metadata. Over the course of the average lifecycle of an institution, several disruptive technologies (preformatted indexing cards, databases, the web) made their entrance. Confronted with limited resources and often little experience with the logistical and technical aspects of moving data back and forth, the conversion process is usually a painful experience for all of those involved. One museum we know has been working on the migration from a closed to an open-source system for over three years. The proprietary collection management system it has been using over the last decade stores the metadata in a very peculiar manner, scattered over a very large number of database tables. The future system also has its own internal data model, which clashes to a significant extent with the way the data were managed previously. Moreover, during the preparation for the migration of the metadata, it became clear that a lot of the fields should be normalized before moving them over to the new application. As a result, the museum and its metadata have been in limbo for the last couple of years. In the meantime, ad hoc solutions such as spreadsheets and web-based forms are being developed individually across departments in order to manage specific projects and exhibitions.

Normalizing and cleaning data is one thing, but it is also necessary to understand the underlying problems. Inconsistencies which are introduced in the database might simply be the result of occasional human errors. However, if violations appear to a large extent and are made visible through data profiling, it could also mean that the metadata schema and the integrity constraints are no longer adequate and need to be reassessed. The emergence of a new category of activity or a change in the interpretation of a concept might be at the root.

The need to modify the metadata schema might also rise very gradually over time. For example, the preformatted indexing cards which were made around the 1950s to document the collection of the Belgian Royal Museum for Central Africa contained a field 'ethnic group'. This field reflects the views of the early ethnologists, which are now considered as overly simplistic and the result of a colonial-coloured vision. These common denominator terms for ethnic groups might have worked well with the administrative ways of dividing the Congolese territory and its inhabitants during the colonial Belgian rule. However, they did not do any justice to the big differences which might exist between groups classified together under one label. This inadequacy becomes apparent in the different spellings and subdivisions made for the tribes. For example, the specific tribe Chokwe was encoded over the years in 47 different manners ('Djok', 'Badjoko', 'Tshokwe Kasai', etc.). Normalizing all these different forms to 'Chokwe' is an easy technical operation, but by doing so, one is making an abstraction of the complexity of the reality (van Hooland and Vanhee, 2009). This example illustrates once more that through the prism of metadata a wide diversity of technological and social changes can be observed.

In the last section of the chapter, we turned to the practical analysis of formal metadata quality issues. Through the method of data profiling, it is possible to obtain a quick overview of the consistency of what is stored in metadata fields. Through the analysis of apparently simple features such as the storage properties (column title, data type and length) and value properties (distribution of values, null values, dates and identifiers), an overview was given of classic metadata quality issues.

In order to take the practical understanding of metadata quality to another level, this chapter will now put forward a case study based on the Schoenberg Database of Manuscripts, managed by UPenn Libraries.

5 CASE STUDY: Schoenberg Database of Manuscripts

Through the use of a concrete metadata set, this case study aims to explore some functionalities of OpenRefine which are relevant to anyone wishing to clean up their own metadata. First of all, the context of the metadata used in the case study is described. It is important to understand how certain inconsistencies have found their way into the Schoenberg Database of Manuscripts (SDBM). A database documenting manuscript transactions might appear as a unique project, but the issues with its metadata are universal and can be found in most collections. Once the context and the structure of the metadata are explained, OpenRefine is introduced. Three out of the five case studies within our handbook are based around this software. We will therefore take some time out to explain some general aspects of the tool which you will also need for the other two case studies (Chapters 4 and 5). After the introduction of general features, we dive into specific data profiling and cleaning operations. As we are limited in space, we will focus on the most essential operations, which are bound to be interesting for all metadata managers. We will not be able to solve all of the issues with the dataset, nor address all features of OpenRefine. If you want to discover more advanced features of the software, please consult the specific literature (Verborgh and De Wilde, 2013).

5.1 The context of the SDBM

Lawrence J. (Larry) Schoenberg, an American manuscript collector, created in 1997 the Schoenberg Database of Manuscripts.[3] The database, maintained since 2005 by the University of Pennsylvania Libraries, contains over 200,000 records, representing approximately 90,000 medieval and early modern manuscripts, drawn from over 12,000 auction, sales and library catalogues from institutional and private collections, with new records being added daily. The SDBM has two primary, interrelated aims:

- to be an interactive research tool for the history of manuscript transmission
- to create a universal finding aid for the current locations of the world's manuscript books.

Purpose: documenting manuscript transactions

It should be understood that the primary purpose of the database is not to document manuscripts as such, but transactions. Each record in the database hence represents a catalogue (auction, sale, or institutional) or inventory entry, and not a unique manuscript.

The SDBM in its current form assists researchers in locating and identifying manuscripts from Europe, Asia, and Africa produced before 1600, establishing provenance and aggregating descriptive information about specific classes or types of manuscripts. Available online at no charge, the SDBM is used internationally by scholars, students, librarians, dealers and others interested in provenance research. Figure 3.2 gives a good example of the value of the SDBM. Thanks to the intervention of William Stoneman, curator of early books and manuscripts at the Houghton Library of Harvard University, the SDBM was able to receive Harvard's MARC records for its manuscript collection and crosswalk them into the database. The values in the field **Duplicate Ms** allow one to link manuscript transactions across time. Many of these records also have current location data, making it possible, for example, to find a manuscript listed in a catalogue from the 17th century.

Despite its value, the SDBM provides data on only a selection of the world's manuscript books and is limited by a number of factors, including its operational infrastructure and technological platform. Currently the team from the Schoenberg Institute for Manuscript Studies at the University of Pennsylvania (UPenn) Libraries is undertaking a global action plan to enhance the use of the database and the unique metadata it holds. UPenn has given us the unique opportunity to make use of their metadata for pedagogical

	Manuscript ID 58152	
	Transaction Details	
Duplicate Ms	46576,58152,182376,201624	Possible Dups:
Catalog Date	19470000	
Sellers	Seller 1: Robinson, W.H. Ltd	Seller 2:
Buyer / Recipient	Harvard University	
Institution / Collection		
Price		Currency:
Cat ID		
Cat / Lot No.		Sold:
Source		
	Manuscript Details	
Current Location	Cambridge, MA, Harvard University, Houghton Library, MS Typ 8	
Author	Ovid	Author (variant): Publius Ovidius Naso
Title	Heroides Epistolae	
Year	1500	Circa: C
Artist		
Scribe		
Language	Latin	
	Material: V	Use:
Place	Italy, Naples	
Description	Folios: 104 Columns: Lines: 0 Height: 170 Width: 100 Alt Size:	
Miniatures	Full Page: 19 Large: 0 Small: 0 Unspecified:	
Initials	Historiated: Decorated:	
Provenance	Hebert/Phillipps, Thomas, Sir/Harvard University	
Binding		
Link		
Comments	Bond P251;18the Italian red binding; Phillipps8416	

Figure 3.2 Example record from the SDBM

purposes. A global export from the database was made in August 2013. It is therefore important to understand that we are working on a temporal snapshot of the SDBM, which was taken just before a major restructuring and cleaning operation.

The SDBM offers a terrific opportunity to illustrate in a hands-on manner the impact of the phenomena described in the theoretical part of this chapter. The following elements make the analysis of the SDBM particularly interesting:

- The initial purpose of the database evolved from documenting manuscripts to documenting transactions of manuscripts.
- The user base expanded from an individual manuscript collector to an international community of scholars from potentially different domains.
- The technological context underwent multiple changes.
- The metadata are based on the aggregation of pre-existing metadata created by a very wide diversity of institutions.

5.2 The evolution of the database

In 1997 Larry Schoenberg purchased a dataset describing transaction details of Books of Hours, medieval manuscripts containing religious texts such as prayers and psalms, which are often decorated. On the basis of this dataset contained in a spreadsheet, the first initial version of the SDBM was created in Microsoft Access in 1997. Early on, the initial scope of Books of Hours was extended to all manuscripts passing through auction houses and booksellers. Researchers were hired to encode new entries, based on library catalogues. In 2005, Larry Schoenberg handed over the management of the database to UPenn Libraries. A first public interface was developed and 12,000 records from the Jordanus database of scientific manuscripts were imported.

Over the course of the following years, modifications were made to the metadata fields. Due to the heterogeneous ways of the encoding of records and various massive importation procedures, a lot of inconsistencies crept into the database. In order to mitigate these issues, new fields were created and a data dictionary was added to have reference data from Library of Congress Name Authorities (LCNA) and Getty's Union List of Artist Names (ULAN), in order to streamline data entry for author and artist names. In order to enhance the metadata encoding and management workflow in a more distributed manner, the database transitioned from Access to Oracle in order to create a web-based back-end for data encoding.

With current trends and developments in crowdsourcing and metadata aggregation, these limitations caused by inconsistencies in the metadata can and should be overcome. A New Schoenberg Database of Manuscripts is currently under development, which will be an online, collaboratively built, universal finding aid. Building upon existing data, the SDBM will be transformed into a global open-access tool, allowing anyone to contribute information as a by-product of their own research into both the current and the historic locations of the world's manuscript books.

5.3 Metadata

Table 3.2 gives an overview of the metadata fields available for end-users on the public front-end of the database. This description is also available on the database website.[4]

Again, it is crucial to realize that the records contain a mix of information not only about transactions of manuscripts but also about the manuscripts themselves.

5.4 OpenRefine, an interactive data transformation tool

OpenRefine (http://openrefine.org/) is a free, open-source software package that allows you to analyse and enhance your dataset in an automated way. It has been designed for large datasets, while still giving you control over every operation as if you were dealing with only a handful of records. OpenRefine started its life under the name Freebase Gridworks as a support tool for people

Metadata field	Definition
Table 3.2 Overview of the metadata elements used in the SDBM	
ID	Unique identification number assigned to each record
Duplicates	Linkable ID numbers to related records in the database
Catalogue or transaction date	Records date (yyyy/mm/dd) of sale catalogue, publication date of institutional catalogue, date of private and/or unpublished transaction if known
Primary seller	Name of auction house, dealer, or private seller. Used if the transaction represents a sale or attempt at a sale or represents an exchange between one individual or institution and another
Secondary seller	Name of private collector or institution selling manuscripts through an auction house or dealer (included in facet list under Seller)
Institution or Collection	Name of institution or private collector holding or receiving a manuscript in a given transaction. Used if data comes from an institutional catalogue; if there is a cited recipient in a published or non-published transaction; or if an institution is identified in a secondary source
Buyer	Name of buyer or recipient of a donation, if known, in a transaction
Catalogue ID	Title or identifying statement of a catalogue
Lot or cat.#	Lot or catalogue number
Price	Amount paid for manuscript. Numerical values only
Currency	Composed of a 3-digit standard currency abbreviation, e.g. USD for American dollars, GBP for British pounds, EUR for euros, and prices in outdated currencies *Continued overleaf*

Table 3.2 Overview of the metadata elements used in the SDBM *(continued)*

Metadata field	Definition
Sold	Indicates if a sale took place, with 'yes' or 'no'
Source	Secondary source of transaction data. This field is used when identifying source of data imported from an electronic source or data taken from printed source that records data from a primary transaction source. Examples are 'Jordanus', for an electronic source, or 'De Ricci, vol. X, p. XXXX, no. XXX'.
Current location	Current location of manuscript, if known, including shelf mark, if known
Author	Authorized name of author and other associated authorial names with applicable code, e.g. Translators (Tr), Glossators (Gl), Commentators (Com). Names follow Library of Congress guidelines, though exceptions are sometimes made if the author is better known by another name
Author (variant)	Name given in the data source if different from name given in the Author field
Title	Title of text(s)
Language	Language(s) identified in a manuscript
Material	Physical material on which the text is written (e.g. paper (P) or vellum (V))
Place	Geographical location where the manuscript was produced
Liturgical use	Liturgical use for a liturgical text (e.g. missal, breviary, antiphonary, etc.) or a book of hours
Date	Year that the manuscript was created. Dates given in century form are entered as follows: formula: 15th century = 1450, 14th century = 1350; 13th century = 1250, etc. Qualified in Circa field
Circa	Descriptive code to qualify approximate date given in Date. The following codes are used: C (circa); Ccent (circa a century); C?(very uncertain circa); C1H (circa first half of century); C2H (circa second half of century); C1Q (circa first quarter of century), C2Q (circa second quarter of century); C3Q (circa third quarter of century); C4Q (circa fourth quarter of century); Cearly (circa early part of century); Clate (circa late part of century); Cmid (circa middle of century).
Artist	Name of artist(s), using the Getty Union List of Artist Names as the name authority
Scribe	Name of scribe(s) as given in data source
Folios	Number of folios in codex
Columns	Number of columns in text block
Height	The height of a manuscript in millimetres
Width	The width of a manuscript in millimetres
Binding	Description of binding
Provenance	Names of previous and current owners as known
Comments	Comments or other distinguishing characteristics, such as the notes on provenance or the physical structure of a manuscript, including an explanation of the physical relationships among various texts and/or parts of a miscellany, etc.
URL	URL to related website or digital image if one is known to exist

who wanted to clean up their dataset for upload into Freebase. Following Google's acquisition of Metaweb, owner of Freebase, Gridworks was renamed Google Refine and developed further. After two years, in 2012, Google transferred the control of Refine to the open-source community, who rebranded it as OpenRefine.

OpenRefine is designed for tabular data. Remembering the data model evolution from Chapter 2, this might sound like a severe limitation. However, the key driver behind this choice is simplicity: OpenRefine feels like familiar spreadsheet software, even though it operates on a totally different scale. Furthermore, it allows one to import data from various sources, including tabular formats (TSV, CSV, Excel), meta-markup languages (XML and JSON), and linked data (RDF). The tabular model is only a temporary view on the data to enable complex transformations in a straightforward way. After that, the data can be exported again in a multitude of formats. The best way to learn OpenRefine is to experiment with it yourself. Therefore, this case study will guide you through the cleaning of the SDBM data with OpenRefine with actions that you can repeat on your own.

OpenRefine runs locally: you remain in control of your metadata!

Some people initially have some reluctance about OpenRefine, as they think it is a software-as-a-service, like for example Google Docs, which runs in the cloud. Understandably, a lot of people would have issues in uploading their metadata to a server over which they do not have control.

In fact OpenRefine is a local application, and so the data never leaves your computer. The confusion arises from the fact that the interface is browser-based. You will notice this when you launch OpenRefine: it opens in your default browser. However, it is important to realize that the application is run locally: you do not need an internet connection to use OpenRefine, unless you want to reconcile your data with external sources through the use of extensions. You can also be reassured that your sensitive data will not be stored online or shared with anyone. In practice, OpenRefine uses the port 3333 of your local machine, which means that it will be available through the URL http://localhost:3333/ or http://127.0.0.1:3333/.

5.5 Installing OpenRefine

OpenRefine is available for different platforms (Windows, Mac, and Linux), so it should certainly run on your system. The software itself doesn't occupy a lot of hard disk space (but the projects you create can). The latest instructions are available at the OpenRefine website, http://openrefine.org/, where you can also download the version for your operating system. However, we will briefly summarize them here.

- **Windows** Download the ZIP archive file and extract its contents to a folder of your choice. The software can be started by double-clicking the `refine` file.
- **Mac** Download the DMG disk file and open it. You will see an OpenRefine icon, which you can drag into your Applications folder. Then double-click the icon to start it.
- **Linux** Download the archive file and extract it. OpenRefine can be started by the `./refine` command.

5.6 Creating an OpenRefine project: importing the SDBM metadata

Before we import the SDBM metadata, we first need to download them locally. An export of the SDBM metadata, made in August 2013, is available both in a zip file and as a .csv file from http://book.freeyourmetadata.org/chapters/2/. The SDBM project also gives you the facility to download the metadata from its own website, which will be constantly expanded and improved. We encourage you to do so and to experiment with different versions of the same dataset. However, if you want to follow the different steps of this case study, please use the download available on the above-mentioned website of our handbook. That way, you will be sure to have access to exactly the same operations and results mentioned in this case study.

When you first open OpenRefine, the start screen will present three tabs on the left which consist of the following options:

- **Create Project:** This option loads a dataset into OpenRefine. This is what we will do in this case study. There are various supported formats: TSV, CSV, Excel (.xls and .xlsx), JSON, XML, RDF as XML and Google Data documents. You can import data in different ways:
  — This Computer: select a file stored on your local machine
  — Web Addresses (URLs): import data directly from an online source
  — Clipboard: copy-paste your data into a text field
  — Google Data: enable access to a Google Spreadsheet or Fusion Table.
- **Open Project:** This option helps you go back to an existing project created during a former session. The next time you start OpenRefine, it will show a list of existing projects and allow you to continue working on a dataset that you have been using previously.
- **Import Project:** With this option, we can directly import an existing OpenRefine project archive. This allows you to open a project that someone else has exported, including the history of all transformations already performed on the data since the project was created.

Creating a project with OpenRefine is straightforward and consists of three simple steps: selecting your file, previewing the import, and validating to let OpenRefine create your project. Let's create a new project by clicking on the **Choose Files** button from the **This Computer** tab, selecting the SDBM metadata you downloaded (refer to the following information box) and then clicking on **Next**. On the next screen, you get an overview of your dataset as it will appear in OpenRefine. In the bottom-right corner, you can see the following parsing options as shown in Figure 3.3.

By default, the first line will be parsed as column headers, which is a common practice and relevant in the case of the SDBM metadata. OpenRefine will also attempt a guess for each cell type in order to differentiate text strings from integers, dates, and URLs among others. This will prove useful later when sorting your data. If you choose to keep the cells in plain text format, 10 will come before 2, for example.

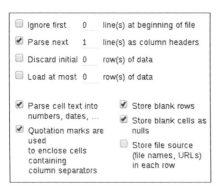

Figure 3.3 Parsing options when loading data

Another option demanding attention is the **Quotation marks are used to enclose cells containing column separators** checkbox. If you leave it selected, be sure to verify that the cell values are indeed enclosed in quotes in the original file. Otherwise, deselect this box to ensure that the quotation marks are not misinterpreted by OpenRefine. In the case of the SDBM metadata, quotes are used inside certain fields, **Title** for example. Quotation marks therefore do not carry a synthetic meaning: the checkbox needs to be deselected before going further. The other options may come in handy in some cases; try to select and deselect them in order to see how they affect your data. Also, be sure to select the right encoding to avoid special characters being mixed up. When everything seems right, click on **Create Project** to load your data into OpenRefine.

5.7 Finding your way in the OpenRefine interface

Once OpenRefine has loaded the dataset, it doesn't appear very different from how the same data might be shown in a spreadsheet (Figure 3.4). Nevertheless, there are important differences. Conceptually, four zones should be distinguished when interpreting Figure 3.4; let's go through them from top to bottom:

1 Total number of rows: If you did not forget to specify that quotation marks are to be ignored, you should see a total of 206,253 rows from the SDBM file. When data are filtered on a given criterion, this bar will

display something like, for
example, 123 matching rows
(206,253 total).

2 Display options: Try to alternate
between **rows** and **records** by
clicking on either word. Not
much will change, except that
you may now read 206,253
records in zone 1. The number of
rows is always equal to the
number of records in a new
project, but they will evolve

Figure 3.4 First overview of the
OpenRefine interface

independently from now on. This zone will also let you choose whether
to display 5, 10, 25, or 50 rows/records on a page, and it also provides
the right way to navigate from page to page.

3 Column headers and menus: You will find here the first row that was
parsed as column headers when the project was created. With the
SDBM metadata, the columns read ID, Duplicates, Cat./Trans.date,
and so on. If you deselected the **Parse next 1 line as column headers**
option box, you will see Column 1, Column 2, and so on instead. The
leftmost column is always called All and is divided in three subcolumns
containing stars (to mark good records, for example), flags (to mark
bad records, for example), and IDs. Every column also has a menu that
can be accessed by clicking on the small dropdown to the left of the
column header.

4 Cell contents: This option shows the main area displaying the actual
values of the cells.

5.8 Getting to know the metadata through filters

Our first task is trying to understand the metadata which we have loaded into
OpenRefine. Let's inspect the different columns of the dataset and their values
by scrolling slowly to the right. Let us try out the first functionality of
OpenRefine: filters. Go, for example, to the column **Seller** and click on the
triangle to the left of the field name and select **Text filter**. When typing a,
OpenRefine displays only records involving sellers whose name contains the
letter 'a' (anywhere in the word, not just the beginning). Changing this to ab
leaves even fewer rows. Note that the matching row count is displayed at the
top of the application.

We can now add a new filter on another column to narrow down the
selection. For instance, create a text filter on the **Title** column and type in bel.
This results in the dozen of records that have 'ab' in their seller name *and* 'bel'

in their title. To remove this filter, click the small cross displayed on its top right corner. Alternatively, you can also click the **Remove All** button to remove all filters, or **Reset All** to clear their text. Let's indeed remove them for now and try something else. Instead of trying to guess values ourselves, we can let OpenRefine make a list of all different sellers. This is done through facets.

5.9 Understanding the values of the fields through faceting

Although the most titles of the columns speak for themselves, some confusing fields also appear. For example, what exactly is the difference between **Seller** and **Seller2**? You could scroll manually through samples of the values, but the use of facets often allows you to understand the content of a column in a matter of seconds. Facets do not affect the values of your data, but they allow you to get useful insights into your dataset. You could think of facets as various ways to look at your metadata, just like the facets of a gemstone that still have to be refined. Facets also allow you to apply a transformation to a subset of metadata, as they allow you to display only rows corresponding to a given criterion.

We will explore the various ways of faceting data depending on their values and on your needs: text facets for strings, numeric facets for numbers and dates and a few predefined customized facets.

5.9.1 Text facets

Facets allow you to see at a glance what the different values are for that field and the number of occurrences for each one. Of course, faceting is only useful when a limited number of choices are at hand; it does not make sense to list all the object titles or descriptions, as it is very unlikely that they will appear twice (except in the case of duplicates, which will be dealt with later on).

So let's dig a little deeper in our metadata by understanding the difference between the two columns we mentioned above. Click the **SELLER** triangle and select **Facet – Text facet**. The result of this facet appears in the Facet/Filter tab on the left of the screen. Unfortunately, OpenRefine informs us that there are a total of 2275 choices, which is too much for your computer's memory to display. The default upper bound for facet choices is only 2000. We can get over this limitation by clicking on the **Set choice count limit** link and raising the upper limit to 10,000, for instance. However, be aware that this is likely to slow down the application.

Managing memory allocation

If you choose to raise the limit of facet choices, what OpenRefine really does is change the value of a Java variable called ui.browsing.listFacet.limit. OpenRefine will always offer to step up when the choice count oversteps the mark, but never the opposite. To do that, go to the system preferences at http://127.0.0.1:3333/preferences, edit the preference with key ui.browsing.listFacet.limit, and set its value to something smaller. To go back to the default 2000 value, you can also delete this preference altogether.

For large datasets, you might find that OpenRefine is performing slowly or shows you OutOfMemory errors. This is a sign that you should allocate more memory to the OpenRefine process. A word of caution: the maximum amount of memory you can assign depends on the amount of RAM in your machine and whether you are using the 32-bit or 64-bit version of Java. When in doubt, try to increase the amount of memory gradually (for example, in steps of 1024MB) and check the result first. The steps to change memory allocation are different for each platform:

- Windows: you will have to edit the openrefine.l4j.ini file in OpenRefine's main folder. Find the line that starts with -Xmx (which is Java-speak for 'maximum heap size'), which will show the default allocated memory: 1024M (meaning 1024 MB or 1 Gb). Increase this as you see fit, for instance to 2048M. The new settings will be in effect the next time you start OpenRefine.
- Mac: after closing OpenRefine, hold control and click on its icon, selecting Show package contents from the pop-up menu. Then, open the info. plist file from the Contents folder. You should now see a list of OpenRefine settings. Navigate to the Java settings and edit the value of VMOptions (these are the properties of the Java Virtual Machine). Look for the part that starts with -Xmx and change its default value of 1024M to the desired amount of memory, for example, -Xmx2048M.
- Linux: instead of starting OpenRefine with ./refine as you usually would do, just type in ./refine -m 2048M, where 2048 is the desired amount of memory in MB.

Once these modifications are made, a new window appears on the left-hand side of the interface. By default, the different values are presented alphabetically. Switch to the sorting by count, as this will give you a quick overview of the most popular values. If we now apply the same text facet on **Seller 2**, we have in two boxes on the left-hand side a quick overview of the most popular values, as illustrated by Figure 3.5.

For **Seller**, these are Sotheby's (26,975), Evans (4263) and Quaritch (4128), whereas **Seller 2** has Thomas Phillipps (3609), Guglielmo Libri (903) and Frederick North (877). Based on this information, you can deduce that the first field is used to refer to auction houses and the other field to individuals or libraries who have played a role in the manuscript transaction.

We invite you to apply textual facets on other fields, like for example **Institution, Artist** or **Author**. Facets, when sorted by count, allow you to get an immediate view of the most used values. By clicking on the number of choices available, a pop-up window appears representing the different values and their frequency within the data set. From this window, you can copy/ paste the data into a spreadsheet and create graphical representations of the distribution of the values in a collection. It's a simple way to create valuable information which can play a central role in annual management reports of collection management.

Please also get into the habit of completely scrolling down to the bottom of the list. Here you have access to the values which are only used once throughout a collection. Especially in fields where you expect a small number of variant values (e.g. country names or languages), you are bound to find surprises in a long tail of unique values.

Figure 3.5 Application of text facets on the fields **Seller** and **Seller 2**

There might be perfectly valid reasons for the presence of these outliers, but often spelling errors, typos or just simply improvisation on the behalf of the metadata creator are the reason behind the presence of these 'fake' outliers. They are fake, because they are merely outliers by form, and not by content. Two concrete examples to demonstrate the presence and impact of these false outliers:

1 Apply a text facet on **Material**, which is used to document the material from which a manuscript is made. A total of 69 different choices appears. Are there that many different types of material used to create manuscripts? Let's have a closer look. At the top of the list, we find the obvious values 'V' and 'P', which are codes used to indicate vellum or paper. Now take the navigation bar and scroll all the way down. Down here, you find a jungle of inconsistencies. For example, eight different ways to indicate that a manuscript is composed of both vellum and paper appear: 'VP', 'V P', 'V|P', 'V/P', 'Vellum|Paper', 'V,P', 'V, P' and 'V ,P'.

2 For the second example we can have a closer look at the field **Buyer**. Apply a text facet and scroll down the list to dive into the jungle of inconsistencies. For example, the values 'Ullman, B. L, Professor', 'Ullman, B.L.' and 'Ullman, Prof. Berthold Louis' all appear individually and represent different values. For us humans it is quite easy to see that these three values relate to the same person. Due to the different spellings, the three values are considered as different by a computer. Faceting has helped to put the finger on these inconsistencies. We will see later how we can solve this issue through clustering. Let us first discuss another related issue.

5.9.2 Managing field overloading

As you may already have noticed, certain columns are prone to the issue we described earlier on in this chapter: field overloading. Fields such as **Author**, **Author variant**, **Place** and **Provenance** contain multiple values in the same cell. Different values of the same type are repeated, illustrated by the practice of putting two authors (e.g. 'Guillaume de Lorris|Jean de Meung') next to one another in the same field. For a computer, the content is just one long string of textual data, making it hard to perform actions on individual names. If we want to apply data profiling techniques to discover the distribution of values across a collection or perform reconciliation with external vocabularies, we need to split out these different values. Fortunately, the pipe character (|) is used in a consistent manner to separate the different values. OpenRefine offers a handy functionality to manage this type of problem. Go to the **Author** dropdown and select **Edit Cells | Split multi-valued cells**. OpenRefine now asks what separator currently separates the values. As we have seen, the values are separated by a vertical bar or pipe character. Therefore, enter a vertical bar | in the dialog window.

This seems like a simple operation, but something important happened. OpenRefine has added extra rows for every unique value from the previously overloaded field. Please notice that you still have the same number of records, but records with, for example, two authors now consist of two rows. Visually, this is made explicit by displaying the rows which belong to the same record in the same colour (either white or grey).

More complex types of field overloading exist. The **Place** field is a classic example. In one and the same field, names of countries are combined with regions and cities. Typical entries are for instance 'Germany, western, Rhineland' or 'Netherlands, Delft'. These are more complex, as there is no clear order in which the different values appear. The first value consistently represents a country name followed by a comma, but the second value is sometimes a region or the name of a city, such as Delft. As the values represent different realities, there is no sense in splitting out the content over multiple rows of the same column. Instead, we can take out the first value which represents a country name and put the value in a new column. Next to the column name **Place**, select **Edit columns | Split into multiple columns**. In the pop-up window you are now able to indicate what separator should be used. This time we will not be using the pipe character but the comma, which is already indicated by default. Remember that it is unclear exactly what the second or third value represents: sometimes it is the name of a region but it can also refer to a city. For the time being, we just want to split out the country names. Therefore, indicate that you want to split the column into 2 columns at most, and indicate that you will keep the original column after splitting. On the right from the column **Place**, we now have a new column **Place 2**, which you can rename as

Country. Another new column has been created, in which the rest of the values have been stored. As there is no consistency in these values, this column can simply be deleted. We will see a more elegant solution later on, which will avoid the creation of this second column. By applying a text facet on our newly created column **Country**, we can quickly see that the large majority of the values effectively represent a country, but there are also some names of cities and continents when we scroll all the way down to the more unique values. These should be cleaned up manually.

5.9.3 Clustering

Now that we have split multi-valued cells and all values are uniquely represented in different rows, we are ready to deal with the different spelling of the same values through clustering. We already illustrated the problem of spelling inconsistencies with the help of the **Material** and **Buyer** fields. Let us this time focus on **Artist**: access the dropdown list next to the column name and navigate to **Edit cells | Cluster and edit**. OpenRefine presents you with a dialog box where you can choose between different clustering methods, each of which can use various similarity functions. When the dialog opens, **key collision** and **fingerprint** have been chosen as default settings. OpenRefine will execute the clustering algorithm and list the found clusters in rows along with the spelling variations in each cluster and the proposed value for the whole cluster, as shown in Figure 3.6.

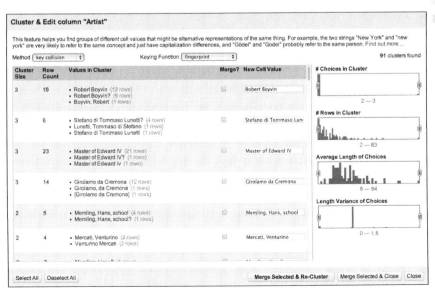

Figure 3.6 Overview of clustering features and configuration options

OpenRefine does not automatically merge the values of the cluster. Instead, it wants you to confirm whether the values indeed point to the same concept. The **Cluster Size** column indicates how many different spellings of a certain concept were thought to be found. The **Row Count** column indicates how many rows contain either of the found spellings. In **Values in Cluster**, you can see the different spellings and how many rows contain a particular spelling. Furthermore, these spellings are clickable, so you can indicate which one is correct. If you hover over the spellings, a **Browse this cluster** link appears, which you can use to inspect all items in the cluster in a separate browser tab. The **Merge?** column contains a checkbox. If you check it, all values in that cluster will be changed to the value in the **New Cell Value** column when clicking on one of the **Merge Selected** buttons. You can also manually choose a new cell value if the automatic value is not the best choice.

So, let's perform our first clustering operation. We strongly advise you to scroll carefully through the list to avoid clustering values that don't belong together. In this case, however, the algorithm hasn't acted too aggressively: in fact, all suggested clusters are correct. Instead of manually ticking the **Merge?** checkbox on every single one of them, we can just click on **Select All** at the bottom. Then, click on the **Merge Selected & Re-Cluster** button, which will merge all the selected clusters.

Let's see what happens when we try a different similarity function. Perform the clustering on, for example, the field **Seller 2** by picking the 'nearest neighbor' method, combined with the Levenshtein distance function. Leave the default settings of the radius and the block chars. We now work with a more aggressive clustering. It still delivers interesting results but you might want to check in detail whether the spelling differences in the personal names mentioned on Figure 3.7 are mistakes or actual valid differences.

How do clustering methods function?

OpenRefine offers two different clustering methods, 'key collision' and 'nearest neighbor', which differ fundamentally in the way they function. With key collision, the idea is that a keying function is used to map a field value to a certain key. Values that are mapped to the same key are placed inside the same cluster. For instance, suppose we have a keying function which removes all spaces; then, A B C, AB C, and ABC will be mapped to the same key: ABC. In practice, the keying functions are constructed in a more sophisticated and helpful way. Nearest neighbor, on the other hand, is a technique in which each unique value is compared to every other unique value using a distance function. For instance, if we count every modification as one unit, the distance between Boot and Bots is 2: one addition and one deletion. This corresponds to an actual distance function in OpenRefine, namely Levenshtein.

| 2 | 19 | • North, John (17 rows)
• Worth, John (2 rows) | ☐ | North, John |
| 2 | 8 | • de Berny, Gerard (7 rows)
• de Berney, Gerard (1 rows) | ☐ | de Berny, Gerard |

Figure 3.7 Results of a more aggressive clustering, applied on the field **Seller 2**

5.9.4 Customized text facets

Now that we have demonstrated how clustering can be used to resolve issues brought up by text faceting, let us have a look at more complex text facets. An interesting feature is the text length facet, which organizes values according to the number of characters contained in a field. Let us apply this facet on a field which traditionally becomes a melting pot of various types of values: Comments. By glancing through some records, we see that this column contains fairly logical content, such as for example 'Returned to England due to denied export license' but also more enigmatic values such as 'Phillipps129'. Text-length faceting can help us to get a very quick overview of the formal distribution of the values, again allowing us to gain a quick understanding of what the most common types of values are, and making outliers evident. Navigate to **Facet | Customized facets | Text length facet** in the column menu of **Comments**. The top box of Figure 3.8 represents the results you get. The content of the **Comments** field ranges from 0 to 4000 characters. By dragging the right bar handle of the graph all the way to the left, you can focus on comments shorter than 5 characters for example (no more than a word in most cases, and not very informative) or on comments longer than 250 characters (which often contain rich information that might best be stored in a more specific field). The distribution is so large (ranging from 0 to 4000 characters, although we see that the large majority is shorter than 100 characters) that it is quite difficult to make sense of it. This is where the log of text length facet (the next box on

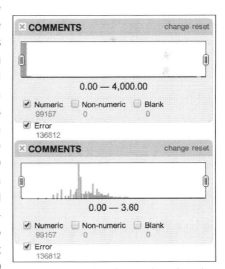

Figure 3.8 Results of a text length and the log of text length facet applied on **Comments**

Figure 3.8) comes into the picture, allowing for a much clearer overview of the distribution of the values: 2.8 are mistakes or actual valid differences.

5.9.5 Numeric facets

A specific type of facet can be applied on numerical values. Numbers are easily spotted, as they are coloured in green, assuming the **Parse cell text into numbers, dates** checkbox was selected at the time of the project creation.

Let us, for example, have a look at the column **Price**. A numeric facet will allow us to have an overview of the distribution of prices, and to check to what extent transactions are associated with a price. In the **Price** dropdown menu, navigate to **Facet | Numeric facet** and look at what appears in the **Facet/Filter** tab on the left. Whereas a text facet returned a list of different choices, numeric facets yield ranges of values, just like the one we had when faceting by choice counts. By inspecting the range, you quickly see there are outliers which will probably need your attention. First of all, you see that there are negative values, which does not make any sense for prices. By placing the right cursor of the distribution graph on zero and leaving the left one on the smallest value of the dataset, you can immediately inspect the concerned values.

Afraid to make mistakes? Don't be . . .

You might be hesitant to click on buttons which will execute massive changes over an entire metadata set, as deleting and moving columns, for example, are quite drastic changes. Rest assured – nothing can go wrong. First of all, OpenRefine works on a copy of your dataset, so the original data remains unharmed. Furthermore, it maintains a history of all actions you have performed so far. Not only does this mean you can go back at any time, you can also replay the steps on another dataset. To view your history, click the **Undo/Redo** tab at the top right of your screen. Click any step to restore your dataset to that stage. Exporting your history is possible with **Extract**, replaying it with **Apply**.

5.10 Exporting data for further analysis

OpenRefine is packed with functionalities, but you will sometimes need to rely on external tools for specific functionalities. For example, the field **URL** proposes a link to a related website or digital image if one is known to exist. As we know, broken or dead links are an important quality issue which regularly occurs. We therefore would like to check in an automated way how many of the links are still valid. We can easily automate this process with various freely available link checkers.

But how do we get the relevant data out of OpenRefine? First of all, we need to select only the records which contain a link. To do this easily, go to the field **URL** and apply **Facet | Customized facets | Facet by blank**. The left-hand box which pops up allows you to switch to records either with or without a URL. Only 14,308 records offer a link, so we only need to analyse those records. With **Facet by blank** still active, click on the **Export** button which you find in the top right corner of the interface. The dialog window offers different export options, such as tab- or comma-separated values or as an Excel file. Note that it is not possible to export only specific columns.

5.11 Learning more

5ith this case study we have barely scratched the surface of the functionalities of OpenRefine. You will see that the case studies of Chapters 4 and 5 explore exciting features such as reconciliation and NER in detail. Within this case study, we have only focused on metadata cleaning features which are bound to be relevant for all metadata managers. If you want to explore all functionalities in depth, please refer to the specific literature regarding the use of OpenRefine (Verborgh and De Wilde, 2013).

Notes

1 The description of the tool and the examples were taken from the CollectiveAccess documentation wiki. More information and examples can be found on http://docs.collectiveaccess.org/wiki/Date_and_Time_Formats.
2 http://en.wikipedia.org/wiki/Whitespace_character.
3 http://dla.library.upenn.edu/dla/schoenberg.
4 Please consult the list of metadata and their definitions on http://dla.library.upenn.edu/dla/schoenberg/ancillary.html?id=collections/schoenberg/fielddefinitions.

Bibliography

Arthur, W. (1996) Increasing Returns and the New World of Business, *Harvard Business Review*, **74** (4), 100–9.

Bovee, M., Srivastava, R. and Mak, B. (2003) A Conceptual Framework and Belief-function Approach to Assessing Overall Information Quality, *International Journal on Intelligent Systems*, **18** (1), 51–74.

Bowker, G. (2005) *Memory Practices in the Sciences*, MIT Press.

Bowker, G. and Star, S. L. (1999) *Sorting Things Out: classification and its consequences*, MIT Press.

Boydens, I. (1999) *Informatique, Normes et Temps*, Bruylant.

Boydens, I. and van Hooland, S. (2011) Hermeneutics Applied to the Quality of Empirical Databases, *Journal of Documentation*, **67** (2), 279–89.

Bruce, T. and Hillmann, D. (2004) The Continuum of Metadata Quality: defining, expressing, exploiting. Chapter in *Metadata in Practice*, American Library Association, 238–56.

Floridi, L. (2013) Information Quality, *Philosophy and Technology*, **26** (1), 1–6.

Hansen, M. (1991) *Zero Defect Data: tackling the corporate data quality problem*, PhD thesis, MIT Sloan School of Management.

ISO (2005) *Quality Management Systems – fundamentals and vocabulary*, ISO 9000:2005, Technical report.

Matarasso, F. (2002) The Weight of Poetry: the unique challenge of evaluating the arts. In *UK Evaluation Society*.

Meshkin, C. (2010) Unchecked Data: a tool for political corruption?, *Engage*, **11** (3), 44–50.

Olson, J. (2003) *Data Quality: the accuracy dimension*, Morgan Kaufmann.

Peacock, D. and Brownbill, J. (2007) Audiences, Visitors, Users: reconceptualising users of museum on-line content and services. In Bearman, D. and Trant, J. (eds), *Museums and the Web*, http://www.archimuse.com/mw2007/papers/peacock/peacock.html.

Redman, T. (1996) *Data Quality for the Information Age*, Artech House.

Robinson, D., Yu, H. and Felten, E. (2010) Enabling Innovation for Civic Engagement. Chapter in *Open Government: collaboration, transparency and participation in practice*, O'Reilly.

Tennis, J. (2012) The Strange Case of Eugenics: a subject's ontogeny in a long-lived classification scheme and the question of collocative integrity, *Journal of the American Society for Information Science and Technology*, **63** (7), 1350–9.

van Hooland, S., Kaufman, S. and Bontemps, Y. (2008) Answering the Call for More Accountability: applying data-profiling to museum metadata. In the proceedings of the *International Conference on Dublin Core and Metadata Applications*, 22–26 September 2008, 93–103.

van Hooland, S. and Vanhee, H. (2009),Van Steekkaart tot Webinterface: de evolutie van metadatabeheer in de culturele erfgoedsector. In Denil, B. and Walterus, J. (eds), *Erfgoed 2.0.*, Faro, 87–106.

Verborgh, R. and De Wilde, M. (2013) *Using OpenRefine*, Packt Publishing.

4

Reconciling

Learning outcomes of this chapter
- Why controlled vocabularies are important for linked data
- Being able to compare the lightweight linked data approach with the full-fledged semantic web
- Understanding the role of SKOS
- Learning to select the most suitable vocabularies to leverage your metadata
- Case study: reconciling the metadata of the Powerhouse Museum

1 Introduction

'Controlled vocabularies are like underwear. Everyone thinks they are a good idea but no one wants to use someone else's.' So goes a classic joke within library and information science circles. As this chapter will demonstrate, there are nonetheless important reasons why one would want to share and re-use vocabularies.

Thesauri, taxonomies, classification schemes or any other manifestation of controlled vocabularies constitute the very core of the LIS profession. The creation of library classifications such as the Dewey Decimal Classification (DDC) or the Universal Decimal Classification (UDC) represent in many ways the intellectual birth of the LIS discipline more than a century ago. The creation of a controlled vocabulary and its use to describe and give access to collections has been a central activity within the profession of librarians, archivists and curatorial staff.

1.1 Throwing money into a black hole?

The creation and use of a controlled vocabulary is expensive, as both the development of a vocabulary and its subsequent use for indexing has to be performed by domain experts. For decades, computer science has tried to automate both processes. On the whole, these attempts have not been terribly successful. Currently, data mining and natural language processing (NLP) techniques most certainly can be used to speed up the collection of potential terms for the construction of a thesaurus. The same techniques can at a second stage be used to analyse what terms from the thesaurus may be used to describe a document. In practice, both procedures need to be supervised by a domain expert, and are in that sense semi-automated methods.

The arrival of the web drastically affected views on the use of controlled vocabularies. Even their most ardent advocates from the LIS domain realize that maintaining and applying a controlled vocabulary on the scale of the web is a utopian idea. Moreover, the success of Google's indexing services based on a full-text search of unstructured HTML pages led to a questioning of the traditional indexing practices. Both the user community and the funding agencies, and also the cultural heritage institutions themselves, increasingly started to doubt over the last decade whether the investment in controlled vocabularies delivers a satisfying return.

One therefore often gets suspicious looks, rolling eyes or deep sighs when the development and use of a controlled vocabulary is suggested in the context of a digitization project. Creating and maintaining a thesaurus combines the drawbacks of both a short- and long-term investment: it is a risky enterprise which requires deep pockets. There are unfortunately no statistics to support this claim, but in our personal experience a lot of thesaurus projects are abandoned after a couple of years. More often than not, the complexity and required resources are underestimated. If the project manages to survive the first critical period, it can still takes many months or even years before the added value of more effective search and retrieval through a controlled vocabulary can be demonstrated. To managers or funding agencies that think in terms of a return on investment over the course of one to three years, subsidizing the development of a controlled vocabulary often is tantamount to throwing money into a black hole.

1.2 A little semantics goes a long way

Exactly the same type of criticism has been levelled at the semantic web. This reiteration of the artificial intelligence vision, in which automated agents perform complex tasks traditionally associated with human intelligence, acquired popularity in academic computer science circles around 2000. Within particularly well delineated domains, the use of ontologies can prove to be useful, but over the years a consensus grew regarding the failure of their application on a web scale. As a result, Berners-Lee developed a more pragmatic vision based upon the linked data principles, which have been presented in Chapter 2. Time will tell whether large-scale initiatives such as Facebook's Open Graph, Google's Knowledge Graph and projects such as http://schema.org manage to find the sweet spot between elegant but too ambitious semantics and the brutal force of full-text indexing.

The linked data movement clearly stirred a new interest in traditional controlled vocabularies. Let us come back to the third and fourth linked data principles, which stipulate:

- when someone looks up a URI, to provide useful information, using the standards
- the inclusion of links to other URIs, so that they can discover more things.

Controlled vocabularies can play a pivotal role in addressing these two principles. As will be demonstrated, a thesaurus expressed in Simple Knowledge Organisation System (SKOS) is available in an RDF-based data format and can contains links to other URIs, representing for example narrower, broader or related terms. This chapter will focus on how the work performed by cultural heritage institutions on the development of thesauri can be re-used in the context of linked data. It would be a waste not to re-use and value this work which has already been performed by others over decades.

1.3 Overview of the chapter

The chapter will start with an introduction to the basics of controlled vocabularies, and will focus on three different types: classification schemes, subject headings and thesauri. In order to interpret the results of the reconciliation process correctly, you need to understand in what context the Dewey Decimal Classification or DDC (example of a classification scheme), the Library of Congress Subject Headings or LCSH (example of subject headings) and the Arts and Architecture Thesaurus or AAT (example of a thesaurus) were constructed and how they evolved over the years. As in other chapters of this book, understanding the historical background will give you a better insight of the relevance of tools for current practices.

When making use of a controlled vocabulary, it is important to be aware of its disadvantages and limitations, especially with regard to full-text searching. Understanding these disadvantages will allow you to better frame the criticisms of the semantic web project, which was considered too ambitious to be successfully implemented on a large scale. A basic introduction to formal reasoning rules and the use of the Web Ontology Language (OWL) is given to explain the supplementary complexity of an ontology in comparison to a thesaurus.

We then come back to linked data by explaining how SKOS can be used to bring controlled vocabularies to the web. The added value of publishing, for example, thesauri on the web is not only to create links between objects and descriptors but also to facilitate interconnections between descriptors of multiple thesauri and to automatically map uncontrolled keywords as much as possible to a thesaurus published in the SKOS format.

The case study which concludes the chapter first of all demonstrates how to create a mini-thesaurus by making use of SKOS. The resulting file is then subsequently used as a reconciliation source with the help of the DERI RDF extension, which allows one to experiment with the reconciliation between the micro-thesaurus and a small sample set of metadata. Once the principles of reconciliation are understood, we move on to a real-life case study, based on a mapping of the keywords used by the Powerhouse Museum with the LCSH.

2 Controlled vocabularies

As the term suggests, a controlled vocabulary represents a restricted subset of language which has been explicitly created to avoid the problems which arise with the use of natural language during the indexing and retrieval of information. Humans have a talent for managing natural language, as we can (mostly) solve ambiguities based on the context in which a term is used. Machines cannot. Search engines simply look at whether there's a match between the string of characters encoded in a query and the text it has in its index. As the success of Google demonstrates, we can solve a lot of our information needs with a search engine, so why do we still need tools like thesauri?

There are domains where precise and timely information retrieval is of such importance that there is a need to express in a non-ambiguous way a concept in order to avoid problems related to synonymy, allusions, implicit language or the use of a different language. By providing synonymy control, controlled vocabularies improve *recall*, which is the proportion of the documents relevant to the search that were successfully retrieved. A query in a search engine with the term 'Outsider art', for example, would not allow you to find a document which only refers to the French term *Art brut*. Through the representation of the semantic relation between these two concepts, a thesaurus would allow you to retrieve the document and thereby augment recall.

Greater *precision*, which is the proportion of retrieved documents relevant to the search, can be achieved through the control of 'polysemy': when a term has multiple meanings and represents different concepts, the hierarchical position of the concept within the thesaurus can be used to disambiguate. For example, if you know that 'Jaguar' is a narrower concept of 'Feline', you know that the term 'Jaguar' should not be interpreted as the car brand. By doing so, the problem of polysemy is handled and the precision is enhanced.

Tremendous investments were made in the pre-search engine context to develop controlled vocabularies. As we will see later on in this chapter, these existing vocabularies represent decades and sometimes centuries of investment.

Despite the large amount of criticism every tool for knowledge organization has received, they somehow have always managed to survive. As long ago as 1959, the following claim was made about classification schemes:

> The curious fact remains that more and more libraries throughout the world continue to use it . . . somehow it works. We should fail . . . if we did not say that a scheme which has survived for eighty years in ever-growing currency in spite of merited criticism must have virtues which in practice outweigh our theoretical objections.
>
> Young, 1959, 73

A large variety of controlled vocabularies exist, which often gives rise to confusion. Every decade, new denominators are invented to rebrand existing approaches. The hype surrounding taxonomies to structure intranets around 2000 illustrated this. In this section, we will focus on three different controlled vocabularies:

- classification schemes
- subject headings
- thesauri.

All three share some characteristics, but also have important conceptual differences which need to be well understood before re-using these controlled vocabularies on the web.

2.1 Classification schemes

Classification schemes were the first controlled vocabularies to be developed within the newly established field of library and documentation sciences at the end of the 19th century. The gradual evolution at that time from a closed to an open access policy in libraries implied that users were increasingly allowed to browse through the bookshelves themselves, instead of having a librarian delivering the books upon request. Libraries therefore needed a method to physically organize their books by subject, allowing patrons to find their way to the book of their interest. Classification schemes therefore propose *systematically arranged classes*, offering placeholders to cluster documents on the same subject content (Broughton, 2004).

Classes are represented by *notations*, which are the short codes consisting of numeric and alphabetic codes you find on the spine of books on library shelves. These notations serve two purposes: they provide a systematic identifier enabling the location of classes within the scheme and documents classified with the use of the scheme; and they serve as an unambiguous label for the intended class

(ISO, 2013). The notations are independent from a specific natural language (e.g. English, French, etc.) That is why we refer to classification schemes as *artificial* controlled languages. Keep in mind this emphasis on a *systematic arrangement* through the use of notations. As we will see over the following sections, subject headings and thesauri are examples of *alphabetically* organized controlled languages, as they represent *concepts* through the use of *terms*.

Captions provide a short human-readable description of the scope of the class. Table 4.1 shows captions on the right of the notations for each class. Note that captions do not need to be unique across the entire classification scheme. The user is expected to interpret the caption by relating it to its superordinate class (ISO, 2013).

Table 4.1 Example of some DDC classes

5	art
591.1	Cubist sculptures
(084)	pictorial documents
(084.12)	photographs
591.1(084.12)	photographs of Cubist sculptures

Classes from a classification scheme can be *enumerated* in the scheme or *synthesized* by the user by following specific rules. Enumerative schemes explicitly contain all the potential classes which can be used. Synthetic schemes offer the possibility of combining existing classes in order to create new ones. In practice, most schemes are or have become synthetic. One of the very few enumerative classification schemes is the Library of Congress Classification (LCC, not to be confused with LCSH). The enumerative approach lowers drastically the skills needed for cataloguing, as the person merely has to put 'pre-existing stamps' on resources (Frické, 2012).

Table 4.1 gives some examples of notations and their captions. Note how the first four examples are enumerated in the scheme, the last class is synthesized. In the case of synthetic schemes, rules need to be laid down in order to indicate how exactly multiple classes should be combined. *Citation order* stipulates how synthetic components can be joined together. For example, it is indicated that periods should come before places.

Most well known classifications were created a century ago, such as Dewey's Decimal Classification (DDC), Cutter's Expansive Classification, LaFontaine and Otlet's Universal Decimal Classification (UDC), Hanson and Martel's Library of Congress Classification (LCC), and Brown's Subject Classification (SC). As we already mentioned, the original purpose of these classification schemes was to physically organize books on library shelves, and by doing so to facilitate retrieval. In an electronic environment, classifications can be used to facilitate browsing.

2.2 Example: the Dewey Decimal Classification

DDC is the oldest and probably most widely used classification scheme in libraries across the world. It is an enumerative scheme but which also possesses some synthetic elements. So-called Auxiliary Tables, covering form, period and place, allow the creation of new classes. Table 4.2 gives an overview of how DDC tries to span every possible domain of human knowledge.

Until the development of DDC, libraries used *fixed location* schemes, in the sense that the classes corresponded to a physical place where the book would be shelved. As libraries grew and books were moved from one shelf to another, this meant that the books also had to be given an updated class in order to reflect their modified position. DDC accommodates the notion of *relative location*, as the class is based on the subject of a book, and no longer where it is physically located (Broughton, 2004).

Table 4.2 Overview of the main classes in DDC	
0	Generalities
1	Philosophy, including psychology
2	Religion
3	Social sciences
4	Language
5	Mathematics and natural sciences
6	Applied sciences, technology
7	The arts
8	Literature
9	Geography, history, and auxiliary subjects

Another key feature is the hospitality of the decimal notation (Frické, 2012). As the world evolves, new topics arise and existing subjects might lose their relevance. The classification scheme therefore also has to accommodate change in subjects, but avoid at all cost that this implies modifying or updating existing notations. Through the use of decimals for the notation, new topics can always be inserted without affecting the pre-existing notations. For example, between the two existing notations 0.15 and 0.16, one can always insert 0.151. However, this approach has resulted in some extremely long notations. As Frické mentions, the subjects of Logic and Engineering each received one page within the first edition of DDC, each containing 10 three-figure notations to represent the main classes. Currently, all the notations for Logic are still contained on one page, but Engineering consists of 94 pages and some notations are ten digits long (Frické, 2012).

We mentioned that DDC is an enumerative scheme, but with some synthetic elements. Rules regarding the citation order are therefore needed to make it clear how classes should be combined. As compounding is only allowed in some specific contexts, there are no general rules, as is the case with other classification schemes (Broughton, 2004).

Maintenance and revision of DDC is carried out under the supervision of an Editorial Policy Committee, which includes representatives from Online Computer Library Centre (OCLC), Library of Congress, American Library Association and the Chartered Institute of Library and Information Science Professionals (CILIP). The first electronic version of DDC was published in 1993. The OCLC offers a (paying) access to DDC online called WebDewey, which is updated continuously. An experimental version of Dewey in RDF is available at dewey.info, which offers access to the top three levels of DDC in 14 languages.

2.3 Subject headings

Subject headings are a very different animal within the controlled vocabulary ecology. They consist of single words or phrases which describe the subject content of resources. Prominent examples include LCSH, Répertoire d'autorité-matière encyclopédique et alphabétique unifié (RAMEAU), Nuovo Soggetario and Schlagwortnormdatei (SWD), which have been incorporated into the Gemeinsame Normdatei (GND).

Remember the central role played by notations within classifications. These short codes play a crucial role in how a classification is systematically built up. That is also why we have called classifications *systematically* organized controlled languages. The human-readable captions allow one to interpret the notation, but they play no role in the actual organization of the scheme.

Subject headings, and also thesauri, are examples of *alphabetically* arranged controlled languages (Broughton, 2004). This represents a fundamental difference from classifications. Subject headings and thesauri do not use notations as classifications do, but words. Before we describe the implications of using words instead of notations, let us understand the different roles classification schemes and subject headings play.

The previous section described how classification schemes were developed to physically arrange and retrieve books. A classification scheme does this by clustering together books on the basis of their content, but the options to describe in detail a complex topic are limited. Complex subjects sometimes need to be attached under a class which has a much broader scope. More importantly, a resource can only be attached to one class. In practice, books often tackle multiple topics, which can make it very hard to decide under which class a book should be categorized.

As library collections grew, a need arose to describe the content of resources in a more adequate manner. Unlike the notations from a classification scheme, subject headings are not inscribed or attached to the documents themselves, but are represented on catalogue cards. This offers the possibility to libraries for creating subject catalogues, allowing users to alphabetically look for topics of their interest. Subject headings consist of either single or multiple words to represent the content of documents. Headings may also incorporate subdivisions, which allows the introduction of some structure. The following types of subdivisions are common:

- topical subdivisions, e.g. 'Economics' or 'History'
- geographical (place) subdivisions, e.g. 'Russia' or 'Europe'
- chronological (time) subdivisions, e.g. '500—1400' or '21st century'
- form subdivisions, e.g. 'Dictionaries' or 'Encyclopedias'.

Table 4.3 gives an example of both simple, compound and structured subject headings.

Table 4.3 Examples of simple, inverted, compound and complex subject headings
Animals
Architecture
Art, Modern
Atlas (Greek deity)
Cubism
Death in painting
Denmark
Ethiopia – Antiquities
Rococo – Great Britain
Spanish literature

Several things are to be noticed in this example. 'Architecture' and 'Animals' are examples of simple headings. 'Art, Modern' is an example of an inverted heading, where the natural word order has been turned around. This practice is again closely related to the technology of the time, the card-based catalogue. In order to make sure a user would find the appropriate heading, it was considered a good practice to focus on the most important word and to bring that to the front (Broughton, 2004). With the automation of search, this practice has lost its relevance, as words can be found automatically, regardless of the order in which they appear.

Compound headings, for example 'Death in painting' or 'Rococo – Great Britain', reflect the *pre-coordinative* character of subject headings, which was also the case with enumerative classification schemes. This aspect constitutes the main difference with thesauri, which are an example of *post-coordinated* vocabularies. We will come back to this point in the next section on the topic of thesauri.

A common characteristic between subject headings and thesauri is the use of *qualifiers*, which help to address the issue of synonymy. A term with multiple meanings, such as 'Atlas' in our example, can be disambiguated through the inclusion of one or more words enclosed within parentheses following the term. The inclusion of '(Greek deity)' in our example makes it clear to the user that the subject heading is not referring to a collection of maps or the first intercontinental ballistic missile.

More importantly, you will have noticed how the headings in Table 4.3 are organized alphabetically. This allows users to easily find specific terms, compared to the notations used to structure classification schemes. However, this alphabetic arrangement also has some important drawbacks. Headings which do not have any links are placed next to one another, which is the case with almost all the headings in Table 4.3. Headings which are related to one another, such as 'Art' and 'Cubism', are not put in a relation. For these reasons, subject headings make use of cross-references, which create meaningful links between headings. There are three basic types of cross-references:

- broader term (BT): indicates a term is more generic
- narrower term (NT): indicates a term is more specific
- related term (RT): indicates another type of relation between two terms.

The growth and professionalization of libraries in the second half of the 19th century resulted in a growing need to manage catalogues in a more rational and standardized approach. In order to avoid as much as possible in-house work on the development of indexing terms, a formal standard to assign subject headings for the indexing of bibliographic collections appeared at the beginning of the 20th century in the USA: the Library of Congress Subject Headings (LCSH).

2.4 Example: the Library of Congress Subject Headings

The LCSH are not only the most adopted subject indexing language worldwide, they are also the largest available controlled vocabulary in English. The LCSH has been developed for bibliographic descriptions covering a large variety of subject areas. As mentioned above, it is primarily a pre-coordinated system but, when confronted with a complex subject for which no single heading exists, a post-coordinated approach may be taken by cataloguers in order to reach a sufficient level of specificity (Chan, 2005). Subdivisions can be used to render a main heading more specific. This is a typical example of a structured heading in LCSH:

Cubism (May Subd Geog)
  BT Aesthetics
  BT Art
  BT Art, Modern – 20th Century
  BT Modernism (Art)
  BT Painting
  RT Post-impressionism (Art)
  NT Decoration and ornament – Cubism
  NT Drawing, Cubist
  NT Purism (Art)

LCSH is not only the most widely used but also by far the most criticized controlled vocabulary. Bashing the LCSH has become almost a subfield within Library and Information Science. Over several decades, the following characteristics have been criticized: complicated syntax, inadequate syndetic structure, outdated terminology, lack of specificity and complex, inconsistent application of subdivisions (Fischer, 2005). These criticisms are all justified but one should also bear in mind that LCSH was created long before the development of thesaurus construction standards. Confronted with the rising standardization of controlled vocabularies, the Library of Congress (LoC) decided in the 1980s to automatically replace the custom reference codes of LCSH with conventional thesaural codes. Visually, this created the illusion of having a thesaurus, without having a structure which respects the traditional thesaural relations. One of the most problematic aspects are the NTs, which should all be kinds of the broader term and reflect a hierarchical relation. In reality, NTs are often RTs. A typical example: 'Cat owners' is indicated as a NT of 'Cats', which semantically should be a RT.

2.5 Thesauri

Thesauri are probably the best known and most used type of controlled vocabulary within current information systems. The previous presentation of other types of controlled vocabularies makes it clear that thesauri in the strict information retrieval sense are a fairly recent concept. They emerged in the 1960–70s in the wake of automated information retrieval. The gradual introduction of electronic catalogues, metadata and full-text documents allowed a release from the limits of physical information storage and retrieval. In a digital environment, the limits of having a unique shelf number for a book and the strictly linear, alphabetical access of paper-based catalogue cards no longer apply.

Most importantly, the use of Boolean search techniques in early databases and indexes allowed patrons to perform searches regardless of word order. When combining two concepts with the Boolean operator AND, all documents which contain both those concepts will be retrieved, no matter the order of the concepts at the time of indexing. For example, the software performing a query on 'cubism AND photography' will simply look for documents indexed with both concepts, without taking into account the order in which they appear. This means that the combination and the co-ordination of concepts at the moment of indexing, two complex and time-consuming activities, lost a lot of their relevance. It is up to the user to combine concepts from a thesaurus at the time of search, the reason why thesauri are called post-coordinated controlled vocabularies. As we have seen in the previous section, pre-coordination refers to the practice of combining concepts at the time of the construction of the vocabulary, which results in the presence of compound terms in subject headings.

This difference between subject headings and thesauri also relates to how they are constructed. As we will see, the first step in creating a thesaurus consists of an analysis of the application domain, in order to identify the concepts and collect the potential terms. A lot of effort then goes into the modelling of the concepts as a logical and consistent whole. Subject headings are much more directly constructed in response to the need to describe specific documents, instead of focusing on the construction of a logical whole which represents an application domain in a coherent manner, as a thesaurus does.

An important distinct characteristic of thesauri is the fact that formal standards exist which give guidance on how they should be constructed. The ISO 25964-1:2011(E) (ISO, 2011) standard defines a thesaurus as a 'controlled and structured vocabulary in which concepts are represented by terms, organized so that relationships between concepts are made explicit, and preferred terms are accompanied by lead-in entries for synonyms or quasi-synonyms'. As with other controlled vocabularies, a thesaurus wants to ensure that both the indexing and searching process of a concept refer to the same term. We have already referred a couple of times to the notion of a *concept* and a *term*. This is a fundamental distinction. A concept can be defined as a 'unit of thought', whereas the term is a 'word or phrase used to label a concept'(ISO, 2013). A *preferred term* is the 'term used to represent a concept when indexing', whereas a non-preferred term is 'not assigned to documents but provided as an entry point'(ISO, 2013).

Below you can find a practical example of a mini-thesaurus, which models the world of cubist art:

Cubist
   — BT Modernism (Art)
   — BT Painting
   — NT Purist
   — RT Post-impressionism
   — UF Cubism

Cubist constitutes the preferred term, and cubism is provided as a non-preferred term, indicated by the UF (Use For). The concept has two broader terms (BT), which are 'Modernism (Art)' and 'Painting' and one narrower term (NT), 'Purism'.

This simple example allows us to illustrate and discuss some complexities of thesaurus construction. First of all, it is not an exact science. As mentioned with the modellization of a database or XML schema in Chapter 2, which are also exercises of making abstraction from reality, people can and do have different views of the same reality. For example, our small thesaurus mentions that 'Purist' is considered here as a narrower term of 'Cubist', which is in line with how the LCSH describes it. However, the French RAMEAU subject headings consider 'Purist' to be a related term to 'Cubist'. The question here is not to know which is right, but it is just a small illustration of the inconsistencies between controlled vocabularies, even inside the same application domain.

You might have noticed in the example that most terms consist of single words, not of multi-word phrases or expressions. Important exceptions exist, however, as compound terms such as 'Modernism (Art)' illustrate. This is an example of the use of a qualifier – here '(Art)' – a concept we already introduced with the use of subject headings. Their use can make the application of a thesaurus more cumbersome and may cause problems within automated systems. Therefore the ISO states that 'their use (especially in preferred terms) should be avoided. Multi-word terms should be preferred to a single-word term with a qualifier, as long as the compound form occurs in natural language' (ISO, 2011). However, the ISO also acknowledges that it is 'often difficult and subjective' to decide whether to include a compound term or not, so not opting for a qualifier often results in equally complex discussions (ISO, 2011).

2.6 Example: the Arts and Architecture Thesaurus

The AAT is the 'most widely known specialist thesaurus' (Broughton, 2004) developed for the cultural heritage domain, with a specific focus on art, architecture and material culture. Constructed and maintained by the Getty Foundation, the AAT is used for the description of works about art and works of art. AAT terms can therefore act both as cataloguing terms for books but also, more importantly, as descriptors of physical characteristics of objects, resulting in the presence of terms such as 'cracks' and 'colour shift'.

The history of the development of the AAT is very much intertwined with that of the LCSH. Dissatisfaction with the use of the LCSH by art librarians was an important factor in the development of the AAT in the 1980s, as the coverage of the arts and architecture by the LSCH was deemed insufficient. Archives and museums at the time either developed in-house specific vocabularies or did not have any controlled subject access. The need for a thesaurus for the cultural heritage domain increasingly arose in the 1970s, and work on the AAT took place throughout the 1980s (Petersen, 1990). Within the context of rising computerized cataloguing and indexing, specific importance was given to a rigorous and consistent hierarchical approach, allowing users to browse through nested terms and giving indexers the freedom to combine single concepts. Despite the criticism of the pre-coordinated approach of the LCSH and the inconsistencies within its syndetic structure, the AAT drew on the LCSH during the phase of terminology-gathering 'because of LCSH's long-term pre-eminence as an indexing vocabulary' (Petersen, 1990). The website of the Getty Foundation provides a clear overview of all other sources used for terminology-gathering.[1] As a thesaurus, the AAT is generally used for post-coordinate indexing. However, pre-coordinated compound concepts can be included within the AAT when a compound concept semantically refers to the union of two or more sets of documents rather than their intersection (Will, 2012). Furthermore, the AAT has its own specific rules for the encoding of compound concepts (Soergel, 1995).

2.7 Difficulties associated with controlled vocabularies

Despite the presented advantages, there are also serious drawbacks attached to the use of controlled vocabularies. The following sections will describe their disadvantages, when compared with the use of search engines handling natural language. These disadvantages are crucial to take into account, as they also help to explain the failure of the full-blown semantic web vision we will discuss later in this chapter. To resume, the disadvantages of using controlled vocabularies are:

- the cost: they are very expensive to create and maintain
- their complexity: end-users have problems using them
- their slow evolution: it takes time to update them
- the subjectivity: they tend to express a specific world view.

The following sections will discuss these disadvantages in more detail. Every disadvantage of controlled vocabularies is put into context by comparing how the issue is dealt with when using natural language queries with a search engine.

2.8 Money

There are no exact formulas to calculate how long it takes to build a thesaurus, as this is very much dependent on the context. As a general rule, it takes six man/months to create a thesaurus consisting of 2000 concepts and more than a year to create a thesaurus consisting of 10,000 terms (Boydens, 2013). A central question is how many terms a thesaurus should consist of. The growth of the volume of documents to be indexed can be used as a general indicator. Boydens proposes the following guidelines to indicate the relation between the yearly increase in the volume of documents (V) and the number of terms (T) to be added to the thesaurus:

- $V = 10,000/year \rightarrow T = 500$ to 1000
- $V = 100,000/year \rightarrow T = 3000$ to 6000
- $V = 1,000,000/year \rightarrow T = 8000$ to $16,000$

As the world evolves and new concepts arise and old ones get outdated, a thesaurus remains very much a work in progress. Resources need to be allocated to maintain a thesaurus relevant over time.

2.9 Complex to use and evaluate

As Stella Dextre Clarke mentions, 'to this day our profession divides into two faiths: the believers and the unbelievers in systems of vocabulary control' (Clarke, 2008). The unbelievers frequently refer to the complexity of the use of tools such as subject headings and thesauri to prove their inefficiency. The fact that the average end-user is not at ease with, for example, thesaurus-based search has been often illustrated with the help of web statistics, which demonstrate how little end-users make use of a thesaurus on the front-end of catalogues. And when a thesaurus is used for retrieval, some studies have claimed that precision and recall is actually negatively impacted, as a thesaurus is frequently used inadequately. Despite decades of user studies, it is difficult to find some consensus across the studies, leading Svenonius (1986) to state that 'an experiment sophisticated and large enough to control all of the necessary variables has never been conducted and probably never will'.

Unfortunately, search and retrieval through the use of either natural language or controlled vocabularies are still all too often presented as two exclusive methods, whereas in practice they can be, and are, combined. Where possible, one should avoid confronting an end-user with the complexity of a thesaurus search, but they can be used in the background to automatically enhance queries through machine inferencing. Software like PoolParty invests in the development of intuitive search interfaces built on top of controlled vocabularies.[2]

2.10 Slow updates

One of the biggest drawbacks of controlled vocabularies is the time-lag between the appearance of a new concept and the moment it becomes available as a term of a controlled vocabulary to be used for indexing and searching. For example, a concept such as 'War on terror' immediately played a big role in the USA and international community after the events of 11 September 2001. It was adopted quite quickly in the LCSH, as it was included as a heading in late December 2001. However, in March 2009 the Obama administration explicitly declared that it had ceased to use the expression. It took until March 2012 to revise the newly created heading and to make it explicit that the heading referred to an expression coined and used by the Bush administration. This is, unfortunately, not an exception. It took, for example, 13 years for the Library of Congress to eliminate 'Jewish Question', and 18 for 'Yellow Peril', from its vocabularies (Fischer, 2005).

The cultural heritage sector is not particularly a fast-evolving domain, but often neologisms appear to describe newly emerging art styles. Performing a quick search engine search will immediately return web pages which contain the newly coined term. Even if an artwork of this style is purchased and described by an institution, it will take a couple of months for this new style to be incorporated within their controlled vocabulary. The Getty Institute, which is responsible for the management and the publication of the AAT, allows registered contributors to submit candidate terms through an online contribution form, which are considered by an editorial team for inclusion. Thousands of records are added or edited in each vocabulary annually. In the traditional publishing model this means that the updated data files for licensing are released in June of each year. Making the AAT available as linked data will avoid this time lag. Despite faster communication of the updated terms, the editorial process necessarily will continue to take time.

Search engines clearly outperform controlled vocabularies on this aspect. The search engines we use do not give clear answers in regards to the time-lag between the publication of content on the web and its indexation. Commercial competition and a rapidly moving technological environment make it almost impossible to give clear answers about the time-lag between the publication of content on a web server and the moment a crawler indexes it. Services such as Google's Webmaster Tools give the opportunity to proactively submit URLs with new or updated content to Google, which should speed up the indexation process.

The crawling process of web content happens at varying depths and according to different schedules, but we can still safely say that changes on the web are almost immediately reflected in the indexes of a search engine when compared to the update process of controlled vocabularies. Evolution of content on the web can actually be used to identify important events as they are happening in the real world. The Wikipedia Live Monitor application, for example, monitors article edits on different language versions of Wikipedia, as they happen in real time. This analysis of concurrent Wikipedia edit spikes, coupled with social network plausibility, checks for breaking news detection (Steiner, van Hooland and Summers, 2013).

2.11 Subjectivity

Scholars such as Geoffrey Bowker have worked extensively on how classifications and other forms of controlled vocabularies cannot be considered as neutral tools for search and retrieval. They tend to express a specific world view. A classical example is Dewey's over-representation of Christianity under the heading Religion, leaving hardly any space for other religions.

Intuitively, search engines also score better on this aspect of information retrieval. However, the increasing importance given to the customization and personalization of search results from search engines may lead to questions about the objectivity of search engines. In his book *The Filter Bubble*, Pariser (2011) demonstrated how search engines, based on previous search queries and other parameters, such as the location and time of day, deliver customized search results. If users get different search results for exactly the same query, can we still speak about an objective search tool?

Now that we have addressed the opportunities but also the drawbacks of controlled vocabularies, we will discuss how the computer science domain has handled the use of semantics, and the development of the semantic web vision in particular.

3 Semantics and machines

Soon after the invention of the computer, scientists started wondering exactly how intelligent those machines could become. The initial optimism was quite high. After all, computers were able to quickly solve mathematical challenges that would take humans several days. Even complex computational problems, such as accurately forecasting the weather, were thought to be solved quite rapidly. So researchers assumed that computers would soon tackle 'simple' problems like our day-to-day thought and decision-making activities. It was Moravec (1988) who encapsulated this fallacy in what would become called Moravec's paradox: 'It is comparatively easy to make computers exhibit adult level performance on intelligence tests or playing checkers, and difficult or impossible to give them the skills of a one-year-old when it comes to perception and mobility.' This was considered the most significant discovery in the artificial intelligence field by Pinker (1994), who paraphrased it as 'the hard problems are easy and the easy problems are hard'.

In the 1950s, artificial intelligence gradually became a scientific research field. Initially, the focus was on problems from game theory, such as chess, as mastery of those games seemed to correlate somehow with intelligence in humans. However, it would notoriously take several decades before world champions could be beaten by algorithms. More than anything, an important part of the road towards artificial intelligence seemed to be to grasp the concept itself; 'artificial' was easily defined through the use of electronic devices, but 'intelligence' remained a tough nut to crack. Turing (1950) acknowledged that intelligence is difficult to define, and favoured an operational definition instead. He proposed the Turing Test, in which a human judge converses through a textual interface with both a computer and another human. If the judge cannot determine which of the two parties is human, the machine can be considered intelligent. Whether or not this also implies the machine *understands* the conversation is highly debatable, but actually irrelevant if we regard the system as a black box: only the effects are important, not the underlying process.

Very broadly speaking, artificial intelligence systems consist of a method of representing knowledge, and algorithms to devise other knowledge from it (such as conclusions or decisions). In the 1980s, expert systems came into existence. They are programs that assist with decision-making in specific domains, based on a large knowledge base of allowed facts and deductions. However, those systems were always limited to the specific domain for which their knowledge had been explicitly created. As such, they were only 'intelligent' within their own world, while *adaptability* seems to be a key characteristic of human intelligence.

3.1 Modelling the world: the semantic web vision

With the world wide web, information could be shared on a scale that had never been possible before. In the web's first decade, this information was expressed in natural language and therefore mostly consumed by humans. One important exception to this was search engines, which crawl the web for pages so they can be searched quickly later on. However, such crawlers made no attempt to interpret the contents of a page; they simply matched keywords typed by a user to words they had extracted from pages.

Since the web quickly became the world's largest source of information, some people wondered whether this huge knowledge base could also be employed by machines, thereby turning it into a world-scale expert system qualified in *any* domain. The main obstacle is of course that computers are currently not able to interpret natural language – even though several clever approximations exist – so none of the information is directly usable by machines. The vision of the *semantic web* (Berners-Lee, Hendler and Lassila, 2001) is to also provide information in a machine-interpretable way in order to enable *intelligent agents* to autonomously perform tasks for us. Rather than a disruptive change, the semantic web is a layer on top of the existing web infrastructure.

One building block of the semantic web is the Resource Description Framework (RDF) we discussed in Chapter 2. RDF introduces a simple language based on triples with subject/predicate/object entities, each of which is given meaning by the use of a unique identifier. Entities can be grouped together in *ontologies*, which define the relation between different concepts. These ontologies themselves are also expressed in RDF, so they are fully machine-interpretable as well. For this task, RDF Schema (RDFS) was introduced, offering a vocabulary with concepts such as classes, data types, labels, and relations such as 'has type' and 'is subclass of'. The Web Ontology Language (OWL) extends RDFS with more fine-grained concepts, allowing to precisely define ontological concepts.

RDFS and OWL provide ways to 'associate those classes and properties with formal reasoning rules that enforce constraints or produce new knowledge by inference' (Baker et al., 2013, 2). For instance, suppose we define a predicate that represents the 'has written' relationship. This could be expressed in our ontology as follows:

```
@prefix ex: <http://example.org/ontology#>.
@prefix rdf: <http://www.w3.org/1999/02/22-rdf-syntax-ns#>.
@prefix rdfs: <http://www.w3.org/2000/01/rdf-schema#>.


ex:hasWritten rdf:type rdf:Property;
              rdfs:domain ex:Person;
              rdfs:range ex:LiteraryWork;
              rdfs:subPropertyOf ex:hasAuthored.
```

Here, the hasWritten property has domain Person (meaning that people can be the subject of this property) and the range LiteraryWork (meaning that any literary work can be the object). Also, it is a specialization of the more general property hasAuthored. Note the use of prefixes to distinguish our own namespace ex from the standard rdf and rdfs namespaces.

To see the power of reasoning, suppose a computer finds the following fact somewhere:

```
:HermanMelville ex:hasWritten :MobyDick.
```

Then it can look up the hasWritten property through its URL, where it will find our little ontology with more machine-readable information on this property. This allows this computer to infer the following triples automatically:

```
:HermanMelville a ex:Person.
:MobyDick a ex:LiteraryWork.
:HermanMelville ex:hasAuthored :MobyDick.
```

Indeed, given the domain of ex:hasWritten, Herman Melville must be a person, and the range implies that *Moby Dick* must be a literary work. Also, since ex:hasWritten is a specialization of ex:hasAuthored, the latter relationship also holds between these two entities. Again, whether or not this implies an 'understanding' of the data is beside the point. The computer does not 'understand' that *Moby Dick* is a book in the way that humans do, but this doesn't matter. The crucial aspect is that a machine is able to apply the interpretation of the 'has written' relationship to infer new knowledge, without being constrained to a specific knowledge domain. This illustrates the power of ontologies, and the idea of reasoning that underlies the semantic web.

3.2 Less is more: lowering the ambitions for linked data

After a few years, the semantic web became synonymous with complexity, and adoption was slow. This sharply contrasted with the ease by which the web itself had been adopted only a decade earlier. The semantic web was perceived more or less as a playground of artificial intelligence researchers, while people actually wanted something that 'just worked'. Publishing data and writing applications was too complex for non-experts, so only few datasets were available.

This was exactly the inspiration behind Tim Berners-Lee's linked data principles, which we listed in Chapter 2. Rather than worrying too much about the underlying concepts, linked data prioritizes getting data out in a machine-readable format, emphasizing the importance of links to other concepts in order to create meaning. More specifically, RDF allows URIs for subjects, predicates, and objects, but not all URIs can be looked up directly through a web browser (for instance, a social security number is a URI, but not a web address). Linked data encourages the use of HTTP URLs, which allow the discovery of more information automatically if the link is followed.

Then the question of course is: which party will provide the URLs that identify well known entities? For predicates, which identify relationships, the answer is still ontologies. Well known metadata schemas such as Dublin Core provide properties that can be re-used across datasets, such as dc:creator, which makes it explicit to everyone that you are talking about an entity responsible for the creation of a resource. The same is possible with RDFS and OWL, the concepts of which are all identified by HTTP URLs. It is possible to issue your own URLs, but to enable automated interpretation, they should link to well known concepts. Therefore, it is better to use controlled vocabularies, which are more likely to be re-used than your own, and hence the resulting dataset is more portable.

The same reasoning techniques as on the semantic web are still possible. On more than one occasion, Tim Berners-Lee has called linked data 'the semantic web done right'. However, linked data and the semantic web are not competing visions; rather, linked data can be considered the building blocks of the semantic web.

4 Bringing controlled vocabularies to the web

The two previous sections allowed us to confront two different approaches regarding knowledge representation. The work on controlled vocabularies from the library and information science community was initiated with classification schemes at the end of the 19th century and lead up to the development of thesauri in the 1960s. We also saw that a different tradition from the artificial intelligence community worked on a far more ambitious agenda to formalize the use of natural language.

As with other chapters in the book, the elaborate historical overview given in the two previous sections brings a necessary sense of realism to the current debate about knowledge representation on the web. The difficulties of implementing the full-blown semantic web, based on the AI approach towards the formalization of natural language, led to a renewed appraisal of traditional controlled vocabularies. They clearly do not offer the same logical rigour and precision of RDFS and OWL. The standard hierarchical relations (broader and narrower term) do not have inferencing capacities as do, for example, relationships of class instantiation, class subsumption and part–whole (Baker et al., 2013). The inferencing capacities are therefore very limited.

However, the capabilities to improve precision and recall within an information retrieval context remain relevant. From a purely pragmatic point of view, people realized that existing vocabularies should be re-used, instead of developing new ones. The growing need to re-use and exchange controlled vocabularies on the web context has given rise to standardization efforts, of which SKOS has been by far the most successful.

4.1 SKOS: a lightweight approach

Simple Knowledge Organizing System (SKOS) proposes a data model to represent controlled vocabularies on the web (Alistair et al., 2005). The data model allows the expression of common characteristics shared between thesauri, classification schemes, subject headings and other forms of controlled vocabularies. It is compatible with thesaurus standards such as ANSI/NISO Z39.19 (2005). Because of its flexibility and standardization by the W3C, SKOS has been preferred over other formats such as Topic Maps[3] or zThes[4] (Pastor-Sanchez, Mendez and Rodríguez-Muñoz, 2009).

4.2 The difference between SKOS and formal ontologies

SKOS data are expressed in RDF triples, for which any of the mentioned serialization formats (RDF-XML, Turtle or N-Triples) may be chosen. RDFS and OWL can be used as building blocks alongside data expressed in SKOS. This interaction results in quite a lot of confusion about whether SKOS can be considered as a formal language to represent ontologies (Miles and Bechhofer, 2009). Let us therefore come back to the different functions played by formal ontologies (expressed in RDFS/OWL) and controlled vocabularies (expressed in SKOS). Ontologies make knowledge about a certain aspect of the world explicit by creating sets of axioms and facts. Controlled vocabularies on the other hand 'have typically been designed not as formally precise representations of domain knowledge but as informal structures reflective of the intuitive knowledge of human users in a form useful for resource discovery' (Baker et al., 2013). Concepts from a controlled vocabulary are hierarchically and associatively structured, but they do not have the same rigour as formal axioms or facts about the world. Remember that controlled vocabularies have been developed to describe the content of books and other resources, not to meaningfully represent the world as such. As Svenonius mentions:

> Subject language terms differ referentially from words used in ordinary language. The former do not refer to objects in the real world or concepts in a mentalistic world but to subjects. As a name of a subject, the term Butterflies refers not to actual butterflies but rather to the set of all indexed documents about butterflies. In a natural language the extension, or extensional meaning, of a word is the class of entities denoted by that word, such as the class consisting of all butterflies. In a subject language the extension of a term is the class of all documents about what the term denotes, such as all documents about butterflies.
>
> Svenonius, 2000a, 130

Let us take an example. Intuitively, one might assume that skos:narrower has the same expressivity of rdfs:subClassOf. However, if concept X is indicated as a narrower concept of Y in SKOS, one cannot automatically assume that X is the subclass of Y in the RDFS sense. In other words, one cannot automatically infer that 'every X is a Y' based on `skos:narrower`.

Apart from the fact that controlled vocabularies never had the intention to represent domain knowledge the way ontologies do, one should also take into account the context in which they have been created and are managed. Vocabularies, such as the LCSH, have been developed by so many different generations of librarians. We cannot reasonably expect these types of large-scale projects to have the same type of formal rigour of ontologies. Humans unavoidably make errors, resulting over time in a significant amount of error, where for example hierarchical and associated links are not managed in a consistent manner. Here we can recall the LCSH example where 'Cat owners' are indicated as a narrower term of 'Cats', which semantically should be a related term.

4.3 Distinguishing concepts and terms

The SKOS reference guide defines a concept as 'an idea or a notion; a unit of thought. However, what constitutes a unit of thought is subjective, and this definition is meant to be suggestive, rather than restrictive' (Miles and Bechhofer, 2009).

It is important to realize that concepts are the basis of SKOS, not terms. This distinction is also incorporated within the new thesaurus ISO guidelines. Concepts can be abstract and may be expressed in a different manner through concrete terms. SKOS therefore introduces the element `skosConcept`. Isaac et al. (2008) propose three properties of concepts:

- Labelling properties: link a concept to a concrete term which represents the concept. The two most common properties are `skos:prefLabel` and `skos:altLabel`. As the name indicates, `skos:prefLabel` is used to designate preferred terms. `skos:altLabel` can be used to indicate variant forms. Concepts can be linked to `skos:prefLabel` and `skos:altLabel` across multiple languages, facilitating by doing so multilingual search and retrieval.
- Semantic properties: used to represent typical hierarchical relations between general and more specific concepts, which are at the heart of thesauri and classification schemes. `skos:narrower`, `skos:broader` and `skos:related` describe *hierarchical* and *associative* relationships between two concepts within one thesaurus. Additionally, SKOS is designed to match descriptors of different vocabularies by assigning `skos:closeMatch`, `skos:exactMatch` or `skos:narrowMatch` as properties between two concepts.
- Documentation properties: these properties give the opportunity to provide

additional information regarding the concept, which can help with the disambiguation, such as skos:scopeNote, skos:definition, skos:example and to register evolution of the concept through skos:changeNote and skos:historyNote.

Let us look at a concrete example. Point your browser to http://id.loc.gov/authorities/subjects/sh85034652.html and see how the authority file for 'Cubism' is structured and displayed for human consumption on the HTML page. Scroll all the way down to the bottom of the page, click on the button to download the SKOS - N-Triples representation, and open up the file. Here you find all of the same information as on the HTML representation, but in a more structured and therefore machine-processable format.

In order to make the SKOS data more readable, we have slightly reworked the example by adding prefixes, appearing at the beginning, which allow us to reduce the length of the file:

```
@prefix : <http://id.loc.gov/authorities/subjects/>.
@prefix ch: <http://purl.org/vocab/changeset/schema#>.
@prefix org: <http://id.loc.gov/vocabulary/organizations/>.
@prefix skos: <http://www.w3.org/2004/02/skos/core#>.
@prefix xsd: <http://www.w3.org/2001/XMLSchema#>.


:sh85034652 a skos:Concept;
   skos:inScheme <http://id.loc.gov/authorities/subjects>;
   skos:prefLabel "Cubism"@en;
   skos:broader :sh85001441, :sh85007461, :sh85007805,
                :sh85086445, :sh85096661;
   skos:narrower :sh85036235, :sh85039437, :sh85109192;
   skos:related :sh2001008665, :sh85105416;
   skos:closeMatch <http://d-nb.info/gnd/4165855-3>;
   skos:exactMatch
<http://stitch.cs.vu.nl/vocabularies/rameau/ark:/12148/cb119361753>;
   skos:changeNote [
       a ch:ChangeSet;
       ch:changeReason "new"^^xsd:string;
       ch:createdDate "2001-06-22T00:00:00"^^xsd:dateTime;
       ch:creatorName org:dl;
       ch:subjectOfChange :sh85034652
     ],
     [
       a ch:ChangeSet;
       ch:changeReason "revised"^^xsd:string;
```

```
    ch:createdDate "2001-07-19T13:07:56"^^xsd:dateTime;
    ch:creatorName org:dlc;
    ch:subjectOfChange :sh85034652
].
```

4.4 SKOS and pre-coordinated vocabularies

When discussing subject headings in the previous section, we described the use of subdivisions. The use of topical (e.g. 'Economics'), geographical (e.g. 'Russia'), chronological (e.g. '21st century') or form subdivisions (e.g. 'Dictionaries') allows the creation of complex headings. SKOS provides a very generic approach to the representation of authority data at large and leaves aside the specificities of pre-coordinated systems, which concatenate independent terms in a specific order. To support the individual components of pre-coordinated subject labels, the Library of Congress has proposed the Metadata Authority Description Schema in RDF (MADS/RDF, Library of Congress, 2011). Since its publication in 2010, the MADS/RDF initiative has attracted a fair amount of criticism. Commentators suggest giving priority to addressing well known issues with the syndetic structure of LCSH due to the errors in the automated process, which converted undifferentiated SeeAlso relationships to Broader, Narrower, or Related relationships in 1987, before making the error-prone semantics available as SKOS formatted data (Spero, 2008). More importantly, the fact that the data model issued its own classes and properties without reaching out to existing ontologies has been criticized.[5]

5 Enabling interconnections

How can we establish links between objects belonging to different collections, which have been indexed and catalogued with the help of different vocabularies? The technique of *vocabulary mapping* or *alignment* attempts to create connections between existing controlled vocabularies.

Until now every vocabulary has been presented and discussed in isolation. Even if vocabularies such as DDC, LCSH and AAT serve different purposes and are managed independently one from another, a significant overlap between the vocabularies exists. At some point they describe the same realities. If we want to connect collection holdings which have been described with different vocabularies, it would be of great use if links existed between the vocabularies indicating that they represent the same concept.

Two heterogeneity problems stand in the way of vocabulary interoperability (Isaac et al., 2008):

• Representational heterogeneity: vocabularies are often managed with the

help of in-house, customized tools or with very general software, such as
Excel, that does not offer any constraint checks. The result is that
vocabularies cannot easily be exchanged or merged automatically. Different
types of vocabularies, such as thesauri and classification schemes, contain
different structural elements which also causes interoperability issues.
* Conceptual heterogeneity: different vocabularies might refer to the same
  concept, but refer to different names or labels, or there might be
  differences regarding the hierarchical level.

Once the problem of representational heterogeneity is solved by having
vocabularies in a unified, structured format such as SKOS, we still need to solve
that of conceptual heterogeneity between vocabularies.

Let us use a simple example and look how the three vocabularies we have
presented accommodate the concept 'Cubism'. The DDC puts 'Cubism' under
the notation 709.04032; the same term is also present in LCSH under the
identifier sh85034652. The AAT offers, under the identifier 300021495, the
preferred term 'Cubist' and associates 'Cubism' as the non-preferred term.

DDC
* 7 Arts & recreation
* 70 – Arts
* 709 – History, geographic treatment, biography
* 709.04 – 20th century, 1900–1999
* 709.0403 – Cubism and futurism
* 709.04032 – Cubism

LCSH
* Preferred term: Cubism
* Broader terms: Aesthetics; Art, Modern – 20th century; Modernism (Art); Painting
* Narrower terms: Decoration and ornament – Cubism; Drawing, Cubist; Purism (Art)
* Related terms: Cubo-futurism (Art); Post-impressionism (Art)

AAT
* Styles and Periods
  * European
    * Modern European styles and movements
      * Cubist
        * Analytical Cubist
        * Synthetic Cubist

On first sight, the mapping across the three vocabularies seems straightforward.
If one has a closer look, it can be noted that the DDC and LCSH consider

Cubism as an art form from the 20th century, independently from a geographical area. However, the AAT puts Cubism in a specific European context. More importantly, the LCSH brings in 'Purism (Art)' as a narrower term under 'Cubism'. In the AAT, this term sits independently from Cubism under 'Modern French fine arts'. These are subtle but important differences in between the three vocabularies.

The alignment process in between vocabularies is a highly complex endeavour, as illustrated through our simple example described above. In 1998, four European national libraries established the Multilingual Access to Subjects (MACS) project in the context of the Conference of European National Librarians (CENL). The manual alignment process between RAMEAU, LCSH, and SWD took ten years and is now implemented at the Swiss National Library and the Deutsche Nationalbibliothek (Landry, 2009). Another important alignment project has been conducted in the scope of the CATCH/STITCH project (van der Meij, Isaac and Zinn, 2010). A service has been developed to perform semi-automated vocabulary alignment between large vocabularies, such as RAMEAU, ICONCLASS, and LCSH.[6] Several vocabularies from the cultural heritage domain are imported, matched, and published using SKOS matching relations. Attention is paid to the evaluation of machine-created mappings between interlingual vocabularies derived from the above mentioned MACS project, leading to a hosting and alignment service for libraries that do not have the resources or the competencies to provide such infrastructure.

5.1 A low-cost approach: reconciling metadata records

Vocabulary alignment is an important but complex and very costly enterprise, which has to be managed in the context of large-scale projects across institutions. It should also be stressed that only a minority of institutions use well established controlled vocabularies. Very often, local vocabularies are developed to cater better to the specific needs of the institution. Due to the lack of time and resources, local vocabularies are often developed in an ad hoc manner and do not closely follow, for example, ISO standards regarding thesaurus construction. The case study based on the metadata of the Powerhouse Museum in this chapter is a good illustration of an in-house developed controlled vocabulary.

Instead of spending years on aligning a locally developed vocabulary with thesauri such as the AAT, we propose to adopt a more pragmatic approach. With minimal efforts, the terms used within metadata records, typically found in a metadata field such as 'Keywords', can be *reconciled* with existing and well established vocabularies. Instead of performing a lengthy and complex mapping process in between vocabularies, the reconciliation process bypasses that operation by checking whether a used keyword appears in an external vocabulary, considered as the *reconciliation source*. The success rate of this operation depends on multiple factors, as will be discussed in the case study. The advantage of this method is that it can also be applied on natural-language keywords that were assigned by curatorial staff, or even user-generated tags.

There are currently opportunities for every metadata practitioner to experiment with linking her or his own metadata to existing external vocabularies. By relying on string similarity, automated services can be used to verify whether terms from a local vocabulary, keywords expressed in natural language or even user-generated tags match terms from vocabularies such as DDC, LCSH or AAT. For example, experiments were carried out to reconcile tags from the bookmarking service Delicious to LCSH (Yi and Chan, 2009). The authors selected three sets of 100 tags, based on their frequency (high, mid, and low frequency) and analysed the possibilities of automatically linking the tags with LCSH. Each user tag was compared on the basis of 'complete-word matching', meaning that a tag is linked with a subject heading when the tag appears in the heading as a complete word. As the authors mention, this means that the tag 'computer' results in a match with the subject heading 'computer networks' but the tag 'network' is not considered to be a complete-word match with the same heading, as the tag is only a portion ('network' for 'networks') of the word in the subject heading, and 'not as a complete word' (Yi and Chan, 2009). This approach resulted in 60.9% of matches.

Different methods allow the augmentation of the string matching process. First of all, stemming can be applied to reduce variations of the same term by bringing them back to the stem or root form of a word. A stemming algorithm could for example reduce the words 'photograph', 'photographer' and 'photographs' to the root word 'photograph'. Secondly, non-preferred labels can be taken into account, as they help to find synonyms and variant spellings.

Running the reconciliation process used to require a lot of complex tools. Now metadata managers can use an interactive data transformation (IDT) tool such as OpenRefine, as will be demonstrated in the case study of this chapter.

6 Conclusion

We hope that by now you are no longer associating controlled vocabularies with underwear, as they are definitively a good idea, but also something we should share (the vocabularies, that is). When used for the indexing of a collection of documents, they allow greater precision and recall during search and retrieval within an information system. Within the context of linked data, they also allow connections to be created between collections.

However, their use and application is not as simple as it might seem. Re-using controlled vocabularies in a linked data context requires substantial knowledge of why and how they were constructed and how they evolved across decades. This chapter should made it clear that traditional controlled vocabularies are most certainly not 'a gate through which the mind is led into the recorded world of the human adventure' but, as in the case of a classification such as DDC, more to be considered as 'an address book for the library stacks' (Frické, 2012). This chapter made the differences between three types of controlled vocabularies (classification schemes, subject headings and thesauri) explicit by putting them in their historic background. Understanding why they were initially developed is necessary to understanding the possibilities and limits of them.

From a strict semantic web perspective, these vocabularies are poor performers. As discussed in this chapter, they lack both the expressiveness and the coherence of ontologies, making them inadequate for use as formal reasoning. Is this a bad thing? Apart from well delineated application domains with high stakes and sufficient resources, the semantic web enterprise has lost most of its appeal. Through a simple but illustrative example, we have seen the complexity of making statements in RDFS and OWL and putting together an ontology.

The failure of full-blown ontologies has created a new opportunity for controlled vocabularies in the context of linked data. As we have seen, traditional vocabularies have an important role to play for the realization of the third and fourth linked data principles: offer URIs which provide useful information accessible in a standardized format and which contain links to other URIs. Every vocabulary we have discussed (DDC, LCSH and AAT) has issued unique identifiers for its terms under the form of URLs. The uptake of SKOS as a standard format for the representation of relations between terms has helped over the last few years to solve the issue of representational heterogeneity, to which the third linked data principle refers. Even if ISO standards for thesaurus construction had already been published since the 1970s, this standardization effort was not reflected in the variety of tools and formats used to represent thesauri. The use of SKOS has paved the way to share and distribute thesauri more easily. The fourth linked data principle refers to the provision of extra URIs, which help to discover extra information. This brings us to the more challenging issue of providing links between vocabularies. The traditional approaches to solving the issue of conceptual heterogeneity between vocabularies have relied on complex alignment approaches. As it is not an option for most of the readers of this handbook to start such a complex and time-consuming operation, we propose to explore the opportunities of a reconciliation method based purely on approximate string matching. The following case study will describe in depth how to experiment with this reconciliation method, allowing you to assess on your own the potential added value of this low-cost approach to creating links between your metadata and established vocabularies.

7 CASE STUDY: Powerhouse Museum

In this case study, we will reconcile the Powerhouse Museum dataset against the Library of Congress Subject Headings (LCSH). However, before we dive into that, we will first obtain some hands-on experience with thesauri by building a small one ourselves from scratch.

7.1 Creating a modern art thesaurus using SKOS

7.1.1 Setting up a thesaurus file

In this part of the case study, we temporarily assume the role of a maintainer of a small modern art metadata collection. An export of this collection is available as a CSV file on this book's website.[7] If you download this file, you will see columns such as Title, Artist and Genre. This last column contains textual values such as Cubism, Impressionism and Pointillism. In order to add more structure to the data, we want to reconcile this column to a thesaurus of modern art genres, which we will create ourselves.

To create a thesaurus, we need an overview of the different concepts and how they are related to each other. Such an overview can come from many sources; for this exercise, we simply consulted a Wikipedia page.[8] We see the categories are organized in a more or less hierarchical way. 'Modern art' is at the top level, genres such as 'Neo-impressionism' and 'Cubism' are at the next level, and subgenres such as 'Divisionism' and 'Purism' are at the deepest level.

SKOS thesauri can be created in many ways, as several software packages exist to do so. The ontology editor Protégé has a special extension for SKOS, and specialized editors such as THManager are freely available. However, we will create the vocabulary by hand as a Turtle file, to obtain a full understanding how SKOS works at the lowest level. Create a new file named modern-art-skos.ttl and open it in your favourite editor. Any plain-text editor will do, such as Notepad on Windows or TextEdit on Mac, but be sure to save the file as text without markup.

Before we start adding triples to this empty Turtle file, it might be handy to set some prefixes for later use first. One is a prefix of our choice that will be used to identify our vocabulary. For instance, let's choose the art prefix with corresponding URL http://example.org/art#. This will make our concepts, such as art:Impressionism, expand to http://example.org/art#Impressionism. For all real-world use-cases, you will want to use existing URLs that you control, in order to conform to the linked data principle that any resource URL must return meaningful data. For the sake of example, we use the example.org domain, which has been made freely available by Internet Assigned Numbers Authority (IANA) for testing purposes. The other prefixes we need are skos, in which the SKOS vocabulary resides, and dc, which defines the Dublin Core terms. The first lines of our Turtle file will thus look like this:

```
@prefix art: <http://example.org/art#>.
@prefix skos: <http://http://www.w3.org/2004/02/skos/core#>.
@prefix dc: <http://purl.org/dc/terms/>.
```

Next, we must describe the thesaurus itself. We have to give it a name and a title, and indicate its top concepts. As a title, we choose 'Modern art periods thesaurus'. For the name of the thesaurus and top concept, we are free to choose anything we like, but for convenience, it is best to stick to the ASCII characters and to avoid white space and other special characters. Therefore, we will name the thesaurus art:ModernArtPeriodsThesaurus and the top concept art:ModernArt. Note that we shouldn't be concerned about name clashes, as we own the art namespace. Any concepts in the linked data cloud with the same name will have different identifiers. We can now add the following to our thesaurus file:

```
art:ModernArtPeriodsThesaurus a skos:ConceptScheme;
   dc:title "Modern art periods thesaurus"@en;
   skos:hasTopConcept art:ModernArt.
```

As a brief reminder of Turtle (for details, see section 5.5 in Chapter 2): above are three triples that share the same subject. The semicolon indicates the next triple will re-use the subject; the full stop at the end indicates the end of the triple (so the next one will need a subject of its own). Here, we state that our thesaurus is a SKOS concept scheme, with a given English title (in Dublin Core semantics). Its top concept is art:ModernArt. If you want, you can also indicate the thesaurus' author(s) with the dc:creator property.

7.1.2 Adding concepts to the thesaurus

The next task is to add concepts to the scheme. One concept in particular is different from the rest: the top concept, which does not have any concepts it depends on. We will therefore add it first:

```
art:ModernArt a skos:Concept;
   skos:prefLabel "Modern art"@en;
   skos:inScheme art:ModernArtPeriodsThesaurus.
```

The above three triples express that art:ModernArt is a SKOS concept in the thesaurus art:ModernArtPeriodsThesaurus, and that its preferred label in English is 'Modern art'. A concept can have only one preferred label per language. That means we could add labels for French and German:

```
art:ModernArt a skos:Concept;
    skos:prefLabel "Modern art"@en;
    skos:prefLabel "Art moderne"@fr;
    skos:prefLabel "Moderne Kunst"@de;
    skos:inScheme art:ModernArtPeriodsThesaurus.
```

However, alternative names for the concept must be encoded as skos:altLabel:

```
art:ModernArt skos:altLabel "Modern art (1860-1945)"@en.
```

Once the top concept has been described, we can move on to the underlying concepts. Their description is identical to that of the top concept, except that their relation to other concepts should be detailed. For instance, Impressionism is a refinement of Modern art, hence there should be a skos:broader link from the former to the latter:

```
art:Impressionism a skos:Concept;
    skos:prefLabel "Impressionism"@en;
    skos:broader art:ModernArt;
    skos:inScheme art:ModernArtPeriodsThesaurus.
```

We can add the other concepts in the list similar to the above. Sometimes, genres have subgenres. In that case, the skos:broader relation should go from the genre to the subgenre:

```
art:HeidelbergSchool a skos:Concept;
    skos:prefLabel "Heidelberg School"@en;
    skos:broader art:Impressionism;
    skos:inScheme art:ModernArtPeriodsThesaurus.
```

In the case of special characters, it is a good idea to find an ASCII name for the concept (even though most systems support UTF-8 encodings):

```
art:DieBrucke a skos:Concept;
    skos:prefLabel "Die Brücke"@en;
    skos:broader art:Expressionism;
    skos:inScheme art:ModernArtPeriodsThesaurus.
```

Note that, in addition to a skos:broader link, we might also add skos:narrower links in the opposite direction. However, be careful about consistency if you decide to do so. For instance, the top concept art:ModernArt would have a lot of incoming links. Furthermore, the skos:broader links can be inferred from the skos:narrower links (and vice-versa) by a semantic web reasoner.

Following the examples above, you can encode the remaining genres on the Wikipedia page. In case you don't want to try this right now, we have created a partial thesaurus at http://book.freeyourmetadata.org/chapters/3/modern-art-skos.ttl, which you can use for the next step. Before you try your Turtle file with OpenRefine, it might be a good idea to check it for validity, for instance with http://www.rdfabout.com/demo/validator/. Additionally, you can visualize the thesaurus with SKOS Play (http://labs.sparna.fr/skos-play/) to check if the hierarchical structure is right. Our partial thesaurus structure as generated by SKOS Play looks like this:

- http://example.org/art#ModernArtPeriodsThesaurus
  - Modern art
    - Art Nouveau
      - ★ Jugendstil
      - ★ Modernisme
      - ★ Vienna Secession
    - Cubism
      - ★ Analytic Cubism
      - ★ Orphism
    - Expressionism
      - ★ Der Blaue Reiter
      - ★ Die Brücke
    - Impressionism
      - ★ American Impressionism
      - ★ Cos Cob Art Colony
      - ★ Heidelberg School
    - Neo-impressionism
      - ★ Divisionism
      - ★ Pointillism
    - Post-impressionism
      - ★ Cloisonnism
      - ★ Les Nabis
      - ★ Synthetism

7.2 Reconciling a dataset against our thesaurus

7.2.1 Installing the RDF extension

While OpenRefine comes with reconciliation support 'out of the box', RDF features have to be added through an extension. Installing extensions can be rather complex, so be sure to closely follow the steps below:

1 Download the RDF extension from the list at
   https://github.com/OpenRefine/OpenRefine/wiki/Extensions, or directly
   from the book website at
   http://book.freeyourmetadata.org/chapters/3/rdf-extension.zip.
2 The extension is currently packed into a compressed file. Unpack it into a
   folder of your choice.
3 Start the OpenRefine application. At the bottom of the starting page,
   click the link **Browse workspace directory**. This will take you to
   OpenRefine's main folder.
4 This folder will contain several others. Among them should be a folder
   named extensions. If not, create this folder yourself.
5 Drag the folder you unpacked during step 2 into the extensions folder.
   The folder structure should now look like this: the extensions folder
   contains an rdf-extension folder (or similar), and this folder in turn
   contains folders such as MOD-INF and scripts.
6 Close OpenRefine, not only by closing the browser window but also by
   closing the application itself by right-clicking its icon and choosing **Close**
   (or the equivalent for your operating system).
7 When starting OpenRefine again and opening a project, an **RDF** button
   should appear at the top right. This indicates the installation was successful.

Detailed instructions can also be found at the RDF extension website,
http://refine.deri.ie/installationDocs.

7.2.2 Creating a project for the dataset

Now that we have created a thesaurus and installed the RDF extension, we
will load the example collection dataset into OpenRefine. Start OpenRefine
and from the main page, choose **Create Project**. OpenRefine now asks where
the data should be loaded from, so choose **Web Addresses (URLs)** and enter
the collection URL http://book.freeyourmetadata.org/chapters/3/modern-art-
collection.csv, confirming with **Next**.

   We now see a preview of what the data will look like. The header row has
been recognized, showing **Title**, **Artist**, **Year**, **Genre** and **Location**. However,
the first row of the data already reveals some encoding problems: the accented
character in the genre *Die Brücke* does not display as expected. To fix this, we
have to tell OpenRefine the encoding of the original file. Click inside the
Character encoding field at the bottom and select **UTF-8**, the encoding used
for the dataset. All 50 rows of the data now display correctly, so we can click
the **Create Project** button.

The familiar OpenRefine view now appears. Perhaps it is handy to select **Show 50 rows** at the top, so we can see the entire collection. As we have learned in the previous chapter, we can now create facets on the data. For instance, by clicking the **Year** triangle and choosing **Facet | Numeric Facet**, we can see that the artworks date from 1876 to 1939. However, our main focus is the **Genre** column, which contains elements of our thesaurus.

7.2.3 Importing the thesaurus

Before we can reconcile against the thesaurus, it needs to be added to OpenRefine as a reconciliation source. This needs to happen only once per thesaurus, so once a thesaurus is added, it can be used on multiple projects. Click the **RDF** button (which is part of the RDF extension) at the top right and choose **Add reconciliation service | Based on RDF file**. In the dialog that pops up, name the new reconciliation source 'Modern art periods'. If you have created the thesaurus file yourself, you can upload it here. Select the **Upload file** option and locate the file. If you haven't created it, you can download the pre-made version from the website first.[9] Make sure to select **Turtle** as file format.

It is of utmost importance to tick the skos:prefLabel checkbox, as we have modelled the thesaurus using SKOS. The **Label properties** are used to tell OpenRefine for which values it should look inside the thesaurus. Since we did not use rdfs:label, the reconciliation process would not work with it. Once those settings are made, click the **OK** button. The thesaurus can now be used for reconciliation.

7.2.4 Reconciling the Genre column

Now that the reconciliation service has been set up, reconciling the values of the **Genre** column is straightforward. Click the **Genre** triangle and select **Reconcile | Start reconciling**. The reconciliation dialog lists the different services on the left, as indicated in Figure 4.1.

When you select our own **Modern art periods** thesaurus, OpenRefine will automatically try to reconcile some of the records to determine whether the data matches the entries of the chosen reconciliation service. In this case, it finds that some of the entries of the **Genre** column have the type skos:Concept in the thesaurus, which is indeed correct. Therefore, click the **Start Reconciling** button. OpenRefine will now try to match each of the entries of the **Genre** column to a concept in our thesaurus.

The results with the pre-made thesaurus are displayed in Figure 4.2. They might be slightly different from yours, since you might have added different terms to your thesaurus. The green bar below the **Genre** column header indicates the percentage of successfully reconciled values. The automatically

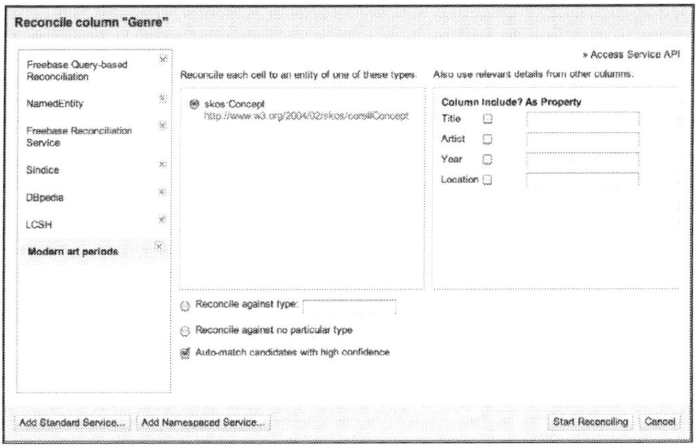

Figure 4.1 The reconciliation dialog

created facets on the right provide a numerical overview of the matches.

If you performed the reconciliation with the example thesaurus, you will see that 46 values have been reconciled with a match score of 1.0, indicating full similarity. Four values have not been found; we can click the none link in the judgement facet to show which ones they are. Three records have the Bauhaus genre; one record belongs to Dadaism. However, we can try to find a manual match by clicking the Search for match link on one of the topics. When you start typing into the field, you will notice that the subjects of our thesaurus start appearing. As you will find out, the reason these records have not been reconciled is that these genres were not included in our example thesaurus. So at this point there's nothing we can do with the current thesaurus. Yet we can click the New Topic button. While this does not alter the original

Figure 4.2 The results of the reconciliation

thesaurus, it marks those values as new topics, as can be seen in the **judgement** facet on the left. That way, we can easily collect improvement suggestions for the thesaurus. When you're done, you can remove the reconciliation facets by clicking the **Remove All** button on the left.

7.2.5 Interpreting the results

The obvious question now is: how has reconciliation enhanced this small dataset? What value does it have that was not in there before? To understand this, we will contrast the possibilities of the initial versus the enhanced dataset. In the initial dataset, the values of the **Genre** column are, to a computer, meaningless text strings. For instance, the value 'Art Nouveau' does not constitute any more meaning than 'Aae Nortuuv', which is the same set of letters but in a different order. Therefore, if we asked to list all artworks that belong to the 'Art Nouveau' genre, we would only retrieve those works where the value for **Genre** is character-by-character identical to Art Nouveau. This would not include works where there is a slight difference in spelling or expression (such as 'Art nouveau' or 'Art-nouveau'), and neither works of subgenres such as 'Jugendstil' or 'Modernisme', even though they all belong to Art Nouveau. As an extreme example, searching the works for 'Modern art' would reveal no results, even though all of them clearly are modern art!

By reconciling these strings of characters to elements from our thesaurus, we transform them into a universal identifier that can make sense to machines when combined with the thesaurus itself. The value is no longer 'Art Nouveau', but http://example.org/art#ArtNouveau, which is indicated by the fact that this value has been turned into a blue hyperlink that you can click. Even though there is nothing on this page yet, the URL itself is important for unique identification. Besides, a real-world thesaurus would be published online, so the URLs of its elements would correspond to actual information about that art period. When a machine looks up the URL in the thesaurus, it will find the following information:

```
art:ArtNouveau a skos:Concept;
skos:prefLabel "Art Nouveau"@en;
skos:broader art:ModernArt;
skos:inScheme art:ModernArtPeriodsThesaurus.
```

So art:ArtNouveau is a concept labelled 'Art Nouveau' in English, and a refinement of the broader concept with the label 'Modern Art'. Furthermore, the thesaurus contains other concepts with labels 'Vienna Secession', 'Jugendstil', and 'Modernisme' that are refinements of 'Art Nouveau'. Therefore, by turning the string of characters Art Nouveau into the term identified by the URL http://example.org/art#ArtNouveau, it becomes a *concept* that relates to others. This can be used to return more complete search results. Additionally, if this dataset would be published online (as linked data and/or webpages), then *Art Nouveau* would be a link that facilitates the discovery of related information.

This simple example has illustrated how to create your own thesaurus and how to reconcile a small collection of metadata against it. You can adapt the thesaurus for use with your own dataset, or create an entirely new one that fits your purpose. Any textual field that identifies a concept can thereby be transformed into an actual link to that concept instead.

While this example has given us an understanding of the basic principles, the reconciliation itself was relatively easy because we controlled both the dataset and the thesaurus. In the next sections, we will reconcile an existing dataset against an existing thesaurus, and have a look at the problems that occur in such real-world cases.

7.3 The Powerhouse Museum collection

The Powerhouse Museum in Sydney provides a freely available metadata export of its collection on its website.[10] The museum is one of the largest science and technology museums worldwide, providing access to more than 100,000 objects, ranging from steam engines to fine glassware and from haute couture to computer chips. The Powerhouse has been very actively disclosing its collection online and making most of its data freely available. From the museum website, a tab-separated text file can be downloaded. The file contains basic metadata (17 fields) for these objects, released under a Creative Commons Attribution Share Alike licence.

The reconciliation process specifically focuses on the Categories field, which is populated with terms from the Powerhouse Object Names Thesaurus (PONT).[11] This thesaurus was created by the museum and first published in 1995. As of September 2009, the thesaurus consists of 6504 preferred terms and 2091 non-preferred terms. The controlled vocabulary is currently available as a downloadable PDF file,[12] but an online thesaurus browser should be published shortly on the museum's website. PONT recognizes Australian usage and spelling, and reflects in a very direct manner the specificity of the collection. This results, for instance, in a better representation of social history and decorative arts, whereas only a minimal number of object names exist in the domains of fine arts and natural history. According to Sebastian Chan, former Head of Digital, Social and Emerging Technologies at the Powerhouse Museum, the staff of the museum responsible for the Categories field are trained registrars, whereas curators provide the metadata regarding significance, history, and provenance of the collection.

7.4 Reconciling the Powerhouse Museum collection with LCSH

7.4.1 Importing the dataset into OpenRefine

To ensure that we obtain the same results in every step, we have made the March 2012 version of the dataset available on the book's website.[13] From the OpenRefine main page, select **Create Project** and load the data either from the local file you have downloaded or directly from the dataset URL. OpenRefine automatically detects that the file format is tab-separated value.

However, automatic format detection is error-prone: if you scroll down, you will note some anomalies. On row 21, the object with identifier 7650 seems to have an overly large description. Upon closer inspection, it is revealed this is due to an incorrect interpretation of field boundaries. To remedy this, untick the checkbox with the label **Quotation marks are used to enclose cells containing column separators**, located at the bottom right. You might remember from Chapter 2 that quotation marks can have different meanings in a delimited file; here, OpenRefine's heuristics made the wrong guess. The data preview now looks better. Name the project 'Powerhouse Museum Collection' and click the **Create Project** button at the top right.

You should now have a new project with 100,170 rows. Feel free to use facets and filters to get acquainted with the data. There might also be some quality issues you would like to fix using the techniques from the last chapter. However, we will now focus on the **Categories** column. It might be handy to click the **Categories** triangle and to select **View | Collapse all other columns**, so that other fields do not distract you while performing reconciliation.

7.4.2 Preparing the data values

The **Categories** column has been used as a multi-valued field. Each object can belong to several categories, and the values have been separated by a pipe character '|'. It is not meaningful to inspect the combined values; instead, we will split the values over different rows so that each record can have one or more single values. Click the **Categories** triangle and choose **Edit cells | Split multi-valued cells . . ..** In the dialog, enter the vertical bar. If you are unsure how to produce this character on your keyboard, you can first copy it from one of the cells and then paste it into the dialog. After clicking **OK**, OpenRefine splits the data into 204,648 rows. You can switch between **Show as rows** and **Show as records** to verify that the number of records is still 100,170. This means that, on average, every record has 204,648/100,170 ≈ 2 categories per row.

To get an overview of the used categories, click the **Categories** triangle and select **Facet | Text facet**. On the left, we will see an alphabetically sorted facet with the 5036 different categories and the number of records that have this category. Select **Sort by count** to have an overview of the most popular categories, as shown in Figure 4.3.

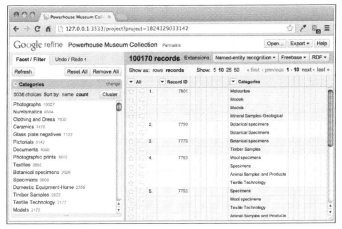

Figure 4.3 Using a text facet to find the most popular categories

However, in this first few rows, we already note an inconsistency: the value **Botanical Specimens** occurs with and without a capital letter S. This makes us wonder whether there might be more inconsistencies inside the data. It is important to settle this before we start the reconciliation process: first, we achieve uniform identity *within* the dataset, then we can connect this identity to an external source. Therefore, click the **Cluster** button in the **Categories** panel, which will bring up the **Cluster & Edit** dialog we have already used in the previous chapter. The standard method **key collision** with the keying function **fingerprint** already finds the capitalization mismatches. Click **Select All** and **Merge Selected & Re-Cluster** to repair those. You can try other methods to find more different spellings that belong together. For instance, the keying function **ngram-fingerprint** finds

Table 4.4 Most popular categories	
Name	Items
Photographs	10027
Numismatics	8505
Clothing and Dress	7636
Ceramics	7478
Glass plate negatives	7122
Pictorials	5143
Documents	4681
Photographic prints	3870
Botanical specimens	3435
Textiles	2695
Specimens	2608
Domestic Equipment – Home	2359
Timber Samples	2322
Textile Technology	2177
Models	2172
Animal Samples and Products	2069

Mailbags and **Mail bags**. Be careful not to cluster too aggressively: the ngram-fingerprint also groups **Shirts** and **T-Shirts** together, but they are clearly different things. The **nearest neighbor** doesn't seem to find any actual groups, apart from singular/plural variations such as **Sculpture** and **Sculptures**. Select the **Close** button to return to the dataset view. After this preparation step, 5002 different categories are left, the most popular ones being those shown in Table 4.4.

7.4.3 Setting up the LCSH reconciliation service

The LCSH thesaurus is available for download in SKOS format at the Library of Congress website, http://id.loc.gov/. However, as this file contains more than 400,000 distinct SKOS concepts, we will not be able to load it as a file into OpenRefine directly, as we did with our custom thesaurus. Instead, these concepts need to be made available in a triple store, which can search them more efficiently. Then, OpenRefine can query the triple store using SPARQL to retrieve only the concepts it needs. We have set up such a SPARQL endpoint for you at http://sparql.freeyourmetadata.org/.

Before we start the reconciliation, you might be curious to see what's in this triple store. By visiting http://sparql.freeyourmetadata.org/, we can issue some SPARQL queries. This triple store contains various datasets, so we first have to specify the one we will use.

In the *Default Graph URI* text box, enter `http://id.loc.gov/authorities/subjects`. This identifies the graph that contains all LCSH triples. Enter the following query:

```
SELECT COUNT(?concept) WHERE { ?concept a skos:Concept. }
```

This will count the number of SKOS concepts in the LCSH graph. The current answer is 406,629, but that can evolve if the underlying dataset changes. To see a sample of some of the headings, enter the following query:

```
SELECT ?concept, ?label
WHERE { ?concept skos:prefLabel ?label. } LIMIT 100
```

This will select 100 random preferred labels.

Before we can use this SPARQL endpoint, we must add it to OpenRefine as a reconciliation service. To do this, click the **RDF** button at the top right and choose **Add reconciliation service | Based on SPARQL endpoint….** This dialog looks familiar to the one we used to add our own thesaurus, except that it now asks for a remote SPARQL endpoint rather than a local file. Enter the following details:

- **Name:** LCSH
- **Endpoint URL:** http://sparql.freeyourmetadata.org/
- **Graph URI:** http://id.loc.gov/authorities/subjects
- **Type:** Virtuoso
- **Label properties:** tick only `skos:prefLabel`

Please understand the difference between the **Endpoint URL** and **Graph URI**. We have already made use of these when issuing SPARQL queries manually.

The endpoint URL is the address of the web service. You can visit it in your browser, and will be greeted by a SPARQL form in which you can insert a query. Under the hood, the query processor will send requests to this URL. Each endpoint can have millions (or even billions) of triples, partitioned into different graphs. For instance, one graph could be DBpedia, another graph could be an art collection, yet another graph could be a previous version of this art collection. Graphs thus roughly correspond to datasets, as they group triples together.

Within the endpoint, each graph is identified by a URI. To tell the endpoint which graph you want to query, you need to send the correct URI along – otherwise, it will query a graph of its choice, or perhaps even all graphs at once. While many graph URIs are actually HTTP URLs, it's important to understand that they are only identifiers, i.e., they will never be visited during query processing. Instead, the URL of the endpoint will be used to send the query and the graph URI on which this query should be executed.

During reconciliation, OpenRefine will also issue SPARQL queries, but then in an automated way. The Type setting allows OpenRefine to communicate in an optimized way with the endpoint through some vendor-specific extensions. Since the database we offer runs on top of Virtuoso, this is the best setting. Finally, as with our own thesaurus, we have to indicate what property name is used to indicate the concept's value. Since this is a SKOS thesaurus, the correct setting is skos:PrefLabel. Click the OK button to add the new reconciliation service.

7.4.4 Reconciling the data against the LCSH

Now that the data has been prepared and the reconciliation service has been set up, we can start the reconciliation process. Again, if you want to reconcile multiple datasets, the reconciliation service has to be set up only once. To start the reconciliation, click the Categories triangle and select Reconcile | Start Reconciling.

Reconciling 100,000 records might take a long time, e.g., depending on your connection, 20 minutes to several hours. If you don't plan to wait, you can either let the reconciliation run unattended, or try reconciliation on a subset of the data instead. For instance, you can first create a Text filter on the Record ID column and fill in the value '99'. This will start reconciliation on only those records with an ID that contains '99', just 3% of the entire collection.

Choose the LCSH service from the left. OpenRefine will try reconciliation with a few of the records, and then determine that they are instances of skos:Concept. Click the Start Reconciling button to begin the process. After

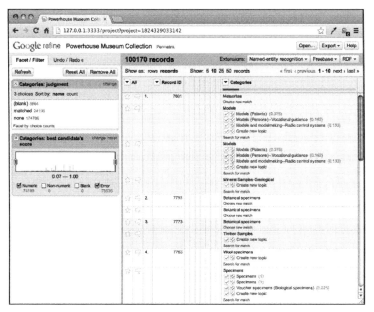

Figure 4.4 A first reconciliation attempt on the Powerhouse Museum
collection metadata

some time, you will obtain results similar to those depicted in Figure 4.4. We
observe several things here.

First, the **judgement** facet indicates that reconciliation has been rather
disappointing. Out of the 204,648 category values (of which 5,004 are unique),
only 24,196 have been matched to an LCSH concept. Creating an additional
text facet on **Categories**, and filtering on those rows that were matched
reveals that only 809 categories out of 5,004 have been found. In addition to
21,198 blank values (i.e., records without any category), 174,786 values could
not be reconciled automatically.

Next, the **best candidate's score** facet provides an overview of the matching
scores between values and subject headings. A score of 1 means that the value
and the subject heading's label are identical; the lower the score, the larger
the difference. OpenRefine has automatically accepted the match only those
in cases where (a) there exists a match with a high score and (b) the other
matches have significantly lower scores. So each value that has the **matched**
status in the **judgement** facet had a single high-score match from this value to
LCSH. None of the others received an automatic judgement. The **score** facet
indicates that 74,199 values received *some* score (e.g., there is at least one topic
with a similar label in LCSH). For all other 99,275 values, no resembling label
could be found. Using a **Categories** text facet, we can see that the largest such
categories are **Glass plate negatives** (7,122 objects), **Pictorials** (5,243 objects),

and **Photographic prints** (3,870 objects).

Inspecting the reconciliation results on the right, we see three different cases, as also indicated by Figure 4.4. The best situation is of course when the corresponding heading in the LCSH has been matched. This has happened for the **Meteorites** value. Note how it has turned into a blue link; if we click it, we arrive at the LCSH page.[14] The previous literal text Meteorites has thus been replaced with a unique identifier that points to the concept, which has semantics associated with it. Indeed, from the **Meteorites** page, we can click through to the broader term **Meteors**, then to **Solar system**, and so on. Furthermore, this information is also available in a machine-interpretable format, so machines can make sense of it. This is how we can fulfil the fourth linked data principle in an automated way: reconciliation adds links to other datasets.

Unfortunately, the second case is when no match has been found, and no suggestions were available either. This has happened to the categories **Mineral Samples-Geological**, **Timber Samples**, and **Wool specimens** in Figure 4.4. Here, we will have to find a match ourselves, using the **Choose new match** link. For instance, if we click this link below **Wool specimens**, we can start typing possible suggestions. As you enter letters, OpenRefine will contact the SPARQL endpoint and find labels that match your search. If you type wool into the field, you will see a list of suggestions such as **Wool fabrics**, **Wool-carding**, and **Wool-fat**. This indicates why OpenRefine didn't find a match: the PONT term 'Wool specimens' and LCSH term 'Wool fabrics' are too different. However, you can select the match manually by clicking it in the list. This will match all 1822 cells that had **Wool specimens** as a value to the LCSH term **Wool fabrics**. You could perform this operation with the help of a **Categories** text facet, in order to find matches for those values that occur must frequently.

The third case is also quite unfortunate, albeit a bit less so: when OpenRefine was not able to make an automated match, but it has found some suggestions for which it needs your judgement. This has happened to **Models** and **Specimens** in Figure 4.4. For **Models**, the found suggestions are **Models (Patents)** (score: 0.375), **Models (Persons)–Vocational guidance** (score: 0.162), and **Models and modelmaking–Radio control systems** (score: 0.133). None of these matches actually covers the meaning of *Models*, so we cannot accept them. (Also note that the same **Models** category was assigned twice to the same object; this is a quality issue you might want to tackle during the cleaning process.) A strange mismatch occurs with **Specimens**, where the suggestions are **Specimens** (score: 1), a second **Specimens** (score: 1), and **Voucher specimens (Biological specimens)** (score 0.225). So while a perfect fit was found, OpenRefine couldn't match it . . . because there were two. If we click both **Specimens** links, we see that they indeed refer to different pages. One is http://id.loc.gov/authorities/subjects/sh87006764.html and the other is http://id.loc.gov/authorities/subjects/sh99001749.html. At first sight, this doesn't make sense: why have a thesaurus if it does not uniquely identify concepts? Don't worry about that for now; we will arrive at a solution to this soon.

Summarizing, the initial reconciliation was able to link 24,198 values to LCSH. These values are spread across 22,261 records, which is 22.2% of the entire collection. So roughly one-fifth of the dataset was connected to the linked data cloud automatically. While not a tremendous success, it is already a good start, especially given the limited manual effort that was necessary. Yet we hope to do better than that, so we will try reconciliation again with slightly different settings.

7.5 Issues with LCSH reconciliation

As we were surprised by the rather low matching percentage, we have studied the causes for mismatches and devised a method to vastly improve this (van Hooland et al., 2013).

A first problem is the existence of *term qualifiers*. The fact that two distinct **Specimens** matches were found can be explained because one of them refers to the subject heading (http://id.loc.gov/authorities/subjects/sh87006764.html), whereas the other is a term qualifier, i.e., a subdivision. The use of qualifiers is an established practice within thesauri in order to address the issue of homonyms, by disambiguating a term through the inclusion of one or more words enclosed within parentheses following the term. Qualifiers may also be used to facilitate the understanding of an obscure term. Their use can make the application of a thesaurus more cumbersome and may cause problems within automated systems. Therefore ISO 25964 states that 'their use (especially in preferred terms) should be avoided. Multi-word term should be preferred to a single-word term with a qualifier, as long as the compound form occurs in natural language' (ISO, 2011, 22). However, the ISO also acknowledges that it is 'often difficult and subjective' (p. 40) to decide whether to include a compound term or not, so not opting for a qualifier often results in equally complex discussions.

Throughout the collection of the Powerhouse Museum, only 127 records – representing 0.1% of all records – are described with terms containing a qualifier. Out of these records, only one term with a qualifier, **Blowpipes (Weapons)**, exists in LCSH as an alternate label (sh85015049). As the presence of qualifiers within the categories is almost negligible, the cost/benefit relation does not justify the development of automated actions to potentially enhance the reconciliation success. Throughout the LCSH itself, 24.6% of the terms (consisting of both preferred labels and alternate labels) make use of qualifiers. Over time, qualifiers have not only been used within LCSH to disambiguate homonyms or to clarify obscure or foreign terms, but also to render a heading more specific, e.g. *Olympic games (Ancient)*, to specify the genre of a proper name, e.g. *Banabans (Kiribati people)*, and to indicate the medium used to perform music, e.g. *Concertos (Violin)* (examples taken from Chan, 2005). Svenonius (2000b) points out that 'the use of a single device for more than one function can be problematic, particularly in times of technological change', as the inconsistent use of qualifiers makes potential post hoc automated processing complex. There is not only a large variation in the functions the qualifiers perform, there is also a considerable variation in the number of words used for a qualifier. ISO (2011) states that 'qualifiers should be as brief as possible, ideally consisting of one word', but only 51.5% of the LCSH qualifiers consist of one word. 33.5% are made up of two and 10.7% of three words, the rest being spread out from 4 to 11 words.

Another issue is that we only considered SKOS *preferred labels*. Some of the terms that are preferred labels for PONT are actually alternate labels for LCSH. Since we indicated we only wanted to use skos:prefLabel, not all possible matches were included. Yet this was done on purpose: OpenRefine does not differentiate between different types of labels. So if one concept uses a label as its preferred label, and another uses the same label as alternate label, OpenRefine will not be able to choose between the two. A quick search on http://sparql.freeyourmetadata.org reveals this happens in many cases:

```
SELECT ?a, ?b, ?label
WHERE { ?a skos:prefLabel ?label. ?b skos:altLabel ?label }
```

For instance, the label *Skating* is an alternate label of the term with preferred label *Ice skating* (sj96005713), even though a separate term with preferred label *Skating* (sh85123105) already exists. As long as this issue stands, alternate labels can do more harm then good.

7.6 Reconciling the data against the pre-processed LCSH

As a solution to the issues identified above, we have created a pre-processed version of the LCSH that is optimized for reconciliation. In this version, the following has been changed:

- Subdivisions are only present if they did not conflict with an existing main heading with the same heading.
- Alternate labels were added, to the extent they did not cause clashes with other labels.

These changes were applied automatically by a script, which we made freely available for use with your own thesauri.[15] This data has then been appended to a separate graph in the triple store.

Let's try the reconciliation with the pre-processed LCSH thesaurus. First, add a new reconciliation service by clicking the **RDF** and choosing **Add reconciliation service | Based on SPARQL endpoint . . ..** Now enter the following details instead:

- **Name**: LCSH (pre-processed)
- **Endpoint URL**: http://sparql.freeyourmetadata.org
- **Graph URI**: http://sparql.freeyourmetadata.org/authorities-processed
- **Type**: Virtuoso
- **Label properties**: tick only skos:prefLabel, then tick **other** and enter the *alternate label* URI: http://www.w3.org/2004/02/skos/core#altLabel

Note in particular how the graph URI is different. We are no longer accessing the full LCSH version, but the processed version that is available in the same endpoint. Also, skos:altLabel has been indicated as a possible label property. Be sure to choose **Virtuoso** as the type, as this speeds up the reconciliation process. Then click **OK** to add the new reconciliation service.

In order to remove the initial reconciliation results, you can go back in the undo/redo history to the stage before reconciliation happened. However, you can also duplicate the column values so the results can be compared side-by-side. To do this, select the **Categories** triangle, **Edit column | Add column based on this column . . ..** In this dialog, choose a new column name such as **Categories (LCSH pre-processed)** and confirm with **OK**. Before you start, it might be a good idea to remove the existing reconciliation facets by clicking the **Remove All** button on the top left.

Begin the reconciliation process by clicking the **Categories** triangle and selecting **Reconcile | Start reconciling . . .,** this time choosing the **LCSH (pre-processed)** service from the left. Click **Start Reconciling.**

Again, you might want to try this on a subset of your data first, especially given the fact that the database must now search to skos:prefLabel *and* skos:altLabel.

The results are much better this time: 95,183 category values have been matched. If we click the **matched** value in the **judgement** facet, we see only those rows with a matching value. If we now switch to records mode with the **shows as records** option, we will see all records that contain at least one matching value. In total, there are 69,758 out of 100,170 records that have at least one link to LCSH. This means that, with careful pre-filtering of the initial thesaurus, almost 70% of all records were automatically linked to the linked data cloud.

In particular, note the **Specimens** value, which was not reconciled at the first attempt because a subdivision with the same name existed. Since that concept has been filtered, reconciliation with the actual main heading succeeded. Despite this optimism, we have to remain careful. For instance, the object on row 1 is a meteorite cast, as explained by its title. While it has correctly been reconciled with the **Meteorites** heading, it also has the incorrect **Models** heading. This is only discovered by following the **Models** link, leading to the page http://id.loc.gov/authorities/subjects/sh00006390.html, which explains that this heading serves as 'a topical subdivision under types of objects and organs and regions of the body'. We could have avoided this particular mismatch by simply excluding all subdivisions. Yet automated matching will always introduce errors, no matter how hard we try to tweak the settings. This is yet another reminder that metadata is always a work in progress. On the bright side, having a significant percentage of the collection connected to the linked data cloud is more important.

One more thing: to obtain the URL of the reconciled entity, apply the following trick. Click the **Categories (pre-processed LCSH)** triangle and choose **Edit column | Add column based on this column . . ..** Name this column **Category URL** and enter the expression cell.recon.match.id. This will transform the cell value into the identifiers of the reconciliation match. After you click **OK**, a new column with the URLs of the LCSH identifiers is generated. This column can then be part of your export.

The finalized OpenRefine project is available for download.[16] You can open it in OpenRefine after you have downloaded it by choosing **Import Project** from the start page. This gives you the opportunity to inspect the reconciled dataset without having to follow all the steps and waiting for the reconciliation service.

If you want to try reconciliation with other thesauri, you can configure their SPARQL endpoints as well. For instance, a Dewey Decimal Classification (DDC) endpoint is available at http://dewey.info/sparql.php. At the time of writing, the Art and Architecture Thesaurus (AAT) was not available publicly, but Getty is in the process of opening up its vocabularies as linked data. We have evaluated reconciliation of the Powerhouse Museum with AAT in van Hooland et al. (2013).

Notes

1 http://www.getty.edu/research/tools/vocabularies/aat/.
2 http://poolparty.biz.
3 http://www.isotopicmaps.org/.
4 http://zthes.z3950.org/.

 5 Jeffrey Beal has presented an overview of different comments formulated regarding the MADS/RDF initiative.
 6 http://www.cs.vu.nl/STITCH/repository/.
 7 At http://book.freeyourmetadata.org/chapters/3/modern-art-collection.csv.
 8 http://en.wikipedia.org/wiki/Art_periods#Modern_art.
 9 http://book.freeyourmetadata.org/chapters/3/modern-art-skos.ttl.
 10 http://www.powerhousemuseum.com/.
 11 http://www.powerhousemuseum.com/collection/database/thesaurus.php.
 12 http://www.powerhousemuseum.com/pdf/publications/phm-thesaurus-sept09.pdf.
 13 http://book.freeyourmetadata.org/chapters/3/powerhouse-museum.tsv.
 14 http://id.loc.gov/authorities/subjects/sh85084315.html.
 15 https://github.com/RubenVerborgh/Vocabulary-Processing.
 16 http://book.freeyourmetadata.org/chapters/3/powerhouse-museum_reconciled.openrefine.tar.gz.

References

Alistair, M., Matthews, B., Beckett, D., Brickley, D., Wilson, M. and Rogers, N. (2005) *SKOS: a language to describe simple knowledge structures for the web*, http://epubs.cclrc.ac.uk/bitstream/685/SKOS-XTech2005.pdf.

ANSI/NISO (2005) *Guidelines for the Construction, Format, and Management of Monolingual Controlled Vocabularies (Z39.15)*, Technical report.

Baker, T., Bechhofer, S., Isaac, A., Miles, A., Schreiber, G. and Summers, E. (2013) Key Choices in the Design of Simple Knowledge Organization System (SKOS), *Web Semantics: science, service and agents on the world wide web*, **20**, (May),1–68 .

Berners-Lee, T., Hendler, J. and Lassila, O. (2001) The Semantic Web, *Scientific American*, **284** (5), 34–43.

Boydens, I. (2013) *Documentologie*, Université libre de Bruxelles.

Broughton, V. (2004) *Essential Classification*, Facet Publishing.

Chan, L. M. (2005) *Library of Congress Subject Headings: principles and application*, Libraries Unlimited.

Clarke, S. D. (2008) The Last 50 Years of Knowledge Organization: a journey through my personal archives, *Journal of Information Science*, **34** (4), 427–37.

Fischer, K. (2005) Critical Views of LCSH, 1990–2001: the third bibliographical essay, *Cataloging & Classification Quarterly*, **41** (1), 63–109.

Frické, M. (2012) *Logic and the Organization of Information*, Springer.

Isaac, A., Schlobach, S., Matthezing, H. and Zinn, C. (2008) Integrated Access to Cultural Heritage Resources Through Representation and Alignment of Controlled Vocabularies, *Library Review*, **57** (3), 187–99.

ISO (2011) *Information and Documentation – Thesauri and interoperability with other vocabularies (ISO 25964-1) – Part 1: Thesauri for information retrieval*, Technical report.

ISO (2013) *Information and Documentation – Thesauri and interoperability with other vocabularies (ISO 25964-1) – Part 2: Interoperability with other vocabularies*, Technical report.

Landry, P. (2009) Providing Multilingual Subject Access Through Linking of Subject Heading Languages: the MACS approach. In Bernardi, R. and Chamers, S. (eds) *Proceedings of the Workshop on Advanced Technologies for Digital Libraries*, Bolzano University Press, 34–7.

Library of Congress (2011) *MADS/RDF Primer*, http://www.loc.gov/standards/mads/rdf/.

Miles, A. and Bechhofer, S. (2009) *SKOS Simple Knowledge Organization System Reference*, W3C Recommendation, World Wide Web Consortium.

Moravec, H. (1988) *Mind Children: the future of robot and human intelligence*, Harvard University Press.

Pariser, E. (2011) *The Filter Bubble*, Penguin.

Pastor-Sanchez, J.-A., Mendez, F. J. M. and Rodríguez-Muñoz, J. V. (2009) Advantages of Thesauri Representation with the Simple Knowledge Organization System (SKOS) Compared with Other Proposed Alternatives for the Design of a Web-Based Thesauri Management System, *Information Research*, **14** (4), http://informationr.net/ir/14-4/paper422.html.

Petersen, T. (1990) Developing a New Thesaurus for Art and Architecture, *Library Trends*, **38** (4), 644–58.

Pinker, S. (1994) *The Language Instinct*, William Morrow and Co.

Soergel, D. (1995) The Art and Architecture Thesaurus: a critical appraisal, *Visual Resources: an international journal of documentation*, **10**, 369–400.

Spero, S. (2008) LCSH is to Thesaurus as Doorbell is to Mammal: visualizing structural problems in the Library of Congress Subject Headings. In *Metadata for Semantic and Social Applications: Proceedings of the International Conference on Dublin Core and Metadata Applications*, Humboldt University Berlin, 203.

Steiner, T., van Hooland, S. and Summers, E. (2013) MJ No More: using concurrent Wikipedia edit spikes with social network plausibility checks for breaking news detection. In *Proceedings of the 22nd International Conference on World Wide Web Companion*, International World Wide Web Conferences Steering Committee, 791–4, http://dl.acm.org/citation.cfm?id=2488029.2488049.

Svenonius, E. (1986) Unanswered Questions in the Design of Controlled Vocabularies, *Journal of the American Society for Information Science*, **37** (5), 331–40.

Svenonius, E. (2000a) *The Intellectual Foundations of Information Organization*, MIT Press.

Svenonius, E. (2000b) LCSH: semantics, syntax and specificity, *Cataloging & Classification Quarterly*, **29** (1–2), 17–30.

Turing, A. (1950) Computing Machinery and Intelligence, *Mind*, **59** (236), 433–60, http://mind.oxfordjournals.org/content/LIX/236/433.short.

van der Meij, L., Isaac, A. and Zinn, C. (2010) A Web-Based Repository Service for

Vocabularies and Alignments in the Cultural Heritage Domain. In *Proceedings of the 7th European Semantic Web Conference (ESWC)*, vol. 6088, 394–409.

van Hooland, S., Verborgh, R., De Wilde, M., Hercher, J., Mannens, E. and Van de Walle, R. (2013) Evaluating the Success of Vocabulary Reconciliation for Cultural Heritage Collections, *Journal of the American Society for Information Science and Technology*, **64** (3), 464–79, http://freeyourmetadata.org/publications/freeyourmetadata.pdf

Will, L. (2012) The ISO 25964 Data Model for the Structure of an Information Retrieval Thesaurus, *Bulletin of the American Society for Information Science and Technology*, **38** (4), 48–51.

Yi, K. and Chan, L. M. (2009) Linking Folksonomy to Library of Congress Subject Headings: an exploratory study, *Journal of Documentation*, **65** (6), 872–900, http://www.emeraldinsight.com/journals.htm?articleid=1823651&show=html.

Young, H. (1959) The Enduring Qualities of Dewey. In *The Role of Classification in the Modern American Library: papers presented at an institute conducted by the University of Illinois Graduate School of Library Science, November 1–4, 1959*, 62–75.

5

Enriching

Learning outcomes of this chapter

- Getting value out of non-structured metadata
- Understanding current possibilities and limits of named-entity recognition
- Being aware of the information versus non-information debate
- Case study: enriching the British Museum metadata

1 Introduction

As a metadata enthusiast, one may be struck with a sense of nostalgia when looking at catalogues from the 19th or early 20th century. The aesthetics of wooden cabinets and the beautiful handwriting make us realize how our profession has evolved over the last century. Apart from the physical appearance of the catalogue, it is interesting to take some time to read a couple of the entries. Very often, you will notice how lengthy some of the descriptions are, when compared with our contemporary descriptive practices.

With the professionalization of documentation practices in libraries, archives and museums, the entry forms for metadata became increasingly structured. Gradually, the lengthy narratives were sliced up in smaller information units, allowing a more standardized approach. The development of controlled vocabularies, as described in the previous chapter, is a good example of how a more structured approach towards subject access was rolled out across institutions.

This process of the increasing structuring of metadata illustrates well the gradual move from the narrative towards the database, as described by Manovich (2001) in his seminal work *The Language of New Media*. As humans, we make sense of the world through stories, told through lengthy descriptions. This explains why museums often offer audioguides, which explain in detail the context of a specific object.

Unfortunately, a computer cannot do much with a narrative. The more structured and well delineated metadata are, the better we can manage them with our IT tools. For example, the previous two chapters focused on how more value can be derived from metadata through cleaning and reconciliation. Both operations allow you to leverage your existing metadata. They do have one important constraint: they can only be applied upon *structured* metadata.

One can only apply cleaning and reconciliation to strings of characters with well delineated boundaries. Data cleaning can be very powerful once you know the specific format of a field. For example, if you know that an address has to be encoded by first mentioning the street name and only afterwards the house number, you can check whether this condition is met. If the range of possible values for a field is known, you can again easily use this constraint to check for example whether the content of the field 'Age' falls within the logical boundaries of the age of a person (anywhere between 0 and 120 years). These examples illustrate the importance of imposing clear boundaries on how metadata are encoded. In the world of databases we use the term *integrity constraints* to refer to a set of rules which help to ensure the consistency of data.

There is therefore a tendency to create highly structured input forms which contain a maximum of pre-selected values. The effort and desire to reduce the ambivalence of natural language in order to facilitate metadata management by automated applications is well illustrated in the following quotation from a Library of Congress report on the future of cataloguing:

> The library community will realize that bibliographic data need to support a variety of user management, and machine needs. In particular, it will be recognized that human users and their needs for display and discovery do not represent the only use of bibliographic metadata; instead, to an increasing degree, machine applications are their primary users. Data will be designed and developed with this in mind.
>
> Library of Congress, 2008, 26

Cataloguers such as David Bade have reacted quite fiercely against the view of considering IT applications as the primary users of metadata (Bade, 2012). The enthusiasm for metadata automation is seen as a smokescreen for cutting costs by reducing the input of trained cataloguers, leading to intellectually poorer metadata. The debate is complex. As a professional community, we should remain critical and not fall into the trap of putting technology too quickly on a pedestal.

However, we also need to be pragmatic and make the most of our limited resources. In the context of large-scale digitization projects, institutions are currently facing the challenge of providing access to the high-volume output of scanning operations. Manually annotating and creating metadata for the output of massive digitization projects is in most cases simply not an option. Automated means to provide access need therefore to be explored. The quality of OCR has made important progress, providing the opportunity to perform full-text searches through a scanned corpus. Even if search engines are very powerful, they also have serious limitations, which we discussed in Chapter 4.

Originally developed for the press and media industry, named-entity recognition (NER) is now increasingly considered as a logical extra step to be applied after the conversion of a scanned textual document from an image format into an indexable text document. NER currently provides the easiest and cheapest method of identifying and disambiguating topics in large volumes of unstructured textual documents. By doing so, NER can provide extra access points for a user confronted with a large collection of documents. This chapter will provide an introduction to the use of NER for enriching existing metadata. More specifically, we will analyse how NER can identify important concepts in lengthy and unstructured descriptive fields. As we mentioned, the cleaning and reconciliation techniques of Chapters 3 and 4 cannot be applied upon this type of unstructured metadata field. The use of NER will demonstrate how to derive more value computationally out of a field which has traditionally been hard to handle in an automated way.

1.1 Overview of the chapter

Before describing NER in detail, it is important to situate this method within the larger context of how we are currently trying to grasp and make sense of the tremendous numbers of digital objects being created. It is interesting to confront shifts in thinking and emerging practices from the library and information science field with current tendencies from the digital humanities. The DH community has a long-standing interest in the automated handling of unstructured textual documents and has strong ties with the field of computational linguistics. Instead of perceiving the explosion of digitized information as a threat or an impossible burden to carry ('how on earth can we catalogue all of this?'), digital humanists have started to discover the possibilities offered by the new scale on which digital documents have become available. More and more projects in the Digital Humanities are actually embracing the arrival of 'Big Data'.

Confronted with the same flood of digitized resources, the LIS community and cultural heritage institutions have in parallel undergone an important shift in thinking. The traditional model of only publishing heavily curated metadata evolved into thinking about metadata as a permanent work in progress. Within this new way of thinking about metadata, the new scale at which users can engage with cultural heritage through the social and mobile web plays an important role. The practices which are currently emerging from both the LIS and DH community are complementary and help to understand the extent to which NER can offer an added value for metadata management. In the following sections, we will first discuss the opportunities for the augmentation of existing metadata through crowdsourcing and the debate that has been initiated around the topic of Big Data in the humanities. Throughout the rest of the chapter, the focus will lie on the possibilities of automatically mining large volumes of unstructured text with NER services. Both opportunities and challenges are presented. A case study provides a hands-on overview of what type of results can be expected when applying NER on a collection of descriptive fields from the British Library.

2 The potential of crowdsourcing

Over the last decade, libraries, archives and museums have started to experiment on a large scale with the possibilities of user-generated content. Museums, for example, initially explored the web to implement the vision of the *virtual museum*. Three-dimensional tours, accompanied by heavily curated and edited documentation, were very much in line with the traditional aura of authority. Now the role of museums on the web is gradually shifting towards becoming a *data provider*.[1] Collections and their metadata are expected to be accessible on the web, even if the metadata are incomplete or at times incorrect.

Institutions increasingly reach out to the user community to give feedback and share their knowledge. The social and mobile web has made this possible on a completely new scale. Within the web 2.0 context, two different forms of user-generated content have emerged: tags and comments.

2.1 The social tagging hype

Social tagging quite rapidly became, around 2002–4, one of the most popular forms of user-generated content on the web. The rise and subsequent fall of Delicious, a service to manage and share bookmarks through user-generated tags, well illustrates the hype cycle of social tagging. Founded in 2003, the service was bought by Yahoo! in 2005 during a period of frenzy for social tagging. Initially, the application maintained its popularity but gradually lost its appeal. In 2011, Yahoo! sold Delicious to another company.

Within the cultural heritage context, the STEVE project attracted some visibility.[2] As a whole, social tagging has lost some of its initial appeal for both users and institutions. Even if tags hold value to facilitate browsing through a collection, their semantic value tends to be quite low, as users apply tags to describe low-level characteristics such as colours, for example.

2.2 User comments to correct and enrich metadata

Many institutions have also experimented over the years with user comments. For example, organizations such as the Library of Congress have been very successful at gathering public interest in their holdings by making selections of the holdings available through applications such as Flickr, where users can easily add comments and make annotations. Increasingly, collection managers allow users to add comments on the front-end of their own websites.

This practice does raise a question about the type of comment and their relevance. Surprisingly few studies have actually analysed the content of user comments in order to get a better understanding of the type of information users are contributing (van Hooland, Mendez and Boydens, 2011). Based on a randomly collected sample of 355 comments, an analysis was made of user comments sent to the image database of the National Archives of the Netherlands, which contains approximately 500,000 images. A manual and iterative analysis of the sample of comments resulted in the following categories:

- *correcting* the displayed metadata (regarding spelling, identification of persons, event/action and geographical and temporal location): 45.58%
- including *narrative elements* in relation to the image: 31.09%
- linking of the user's *personal history* regarding the image: 8.95%
- mentioning a *false or inadequate display* of the image: 3.14%
- stating an *opinion* or *judgement*: 2.86%
- engaging in a *dialogue* with the institution or other users, under the form of a question: 1.15%.

These categories are neither exclusive or inclusive, meaning that a comment can belong to more than one category, but does not necessarily belong to any of them. Although the process of categorizing is subjective, we do believe it allows a deeper understanding of the nature of user comments and their relevance towards the public.

Based on these figures, we can say that the biggest incentive for users to send comments is to correct the existing metadata published by the institution. 34% of the comments criticize the existing metadata and propose a correction. Within this type of comment, as shown in Figure 5.1, 40.34% is relevant to incorrect spelling of the metadata (with the larger part being spelling of names of persons and locations), 10.92% to the identification of persons, 24.37% to the identification of

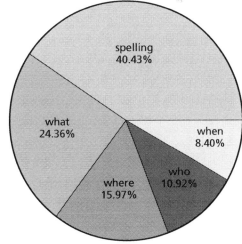

Figure 5.1 Categories of user proposals to correct existing metadata

an object, 15.97% to geographical location and 8.40% relevant to time. The National Archives recognize on the website that some image descriptions may be incomplete or contain errors, and therefore explicitly invite users to indicate potential errors and to send possible corrections. We do not possess precise information regarding the validation of the corrections, but according to the National Archives, more than half of this type of comment is effectively used to correct the existing metadata.

3 Embracing scale

We have seen in the previous section how the idea of issuing only a small subset of authoritative and heavily curated objects is starting to lose ground to publishing a maximum of data and metadata that an institution has available electronically. Within this changing mindset, the focus shifts from the quality of individual objects and their metadata to the possibilities the aggregation offers.

The digital humanities have had a long-standing interest in applying quantitative methods, such as lexicometrics, to answer research questions which normally involve qualitative methods. The rise in popularity of Big Data has given a boost to the use of quantitative methods in the humanities. Opportunities exist to apply some of these methods in the cultural heritage sector and make the most out of what one might call 'Big Metadata'.

First of all, let us look at the source of the massive arrival of digital documents within our institutions. The digitization frenzy of the last decade has produced huge numbers of digital images. A large portion of these image files represent scanned texts, which need to be converted to textual files before we can search inside the documents.

3.1 Converting scans into text

When users are confronted with scans of historical textual documents, they often do not realize they are looking at an image and not a text. The reality of the limitations of the graphical format only becomes clear when the user tries to use the Ctrl-F button to perform a full-text search across the .pdf or .jpg document he or she has on the screen. As long as scanned text remains in the image format, there is very little we can do to facilitate the access to and use of the scanned documents. Historic newspapers, for example, only have minimal item- or collection-level metadata, often limited to the newspaper title, the date of publication and some copyright information.

Fortunately, substantial progress has been made with optical character recognition (OCR) over the last few years. OCR now makes it possible to convert scans of printed materials into full text which can be queried with a search engine. Typical OCR accuracy rates currently go beyond 99% for printed text in good condition. The cost for the conversion process has also significantly decreased due to the arrival of mature open-source solutions. However, the success rate can radically drop when confronted with damaged or deteriorating materials. Frustratingly, the losses are largest when the need is most pressing: older documents typically have fewer metadata than new ones, yet the digitized versions of these old documents are usually less legible due to ageing, making OCR algorithms struggle to get accurate recognition. Newer documents typically yield higher success rates, yet these documents usually have more metadata available already.

The recognition of handwritten materials is still very much at an early stage. For these materials, other alternatives have been introduced. Projects such as Old Weather and Transcribing Bentham have successfully relied on crowd-sourcing to transcribe handwritten historical documents.[3] However, it is not always possible to engage a sufficient number of volunteers. Increasingly, users are given small financial incentives via platforms such as Amazon's Mechanical Turk to perform the encoding of handwritten texts. For example, the Written Rummage project has experimented with this model to transcribe and proofread a test collection of scans from the Frederick Douglass Papers (Lang and Rio-Ross, 2011).

Even if full-text search is a tremendously powerful feature, it requires the user to already have a specific term or name in mind, and to take into account problems of polysemy and synonymy. Converting scans into digital texts and making them indexable is therefore only a first basic step towards providing access. The following sections will give an overview of the initiatives which illustrate the supplementary steps currently taken to make sense of large amounts of unstructured text.

3.2 Introducing Big Data

Chris Anderson launched the term Big Data in the media and stirred a vivid debate with the premise that it could imply 'the end of theory' (Anderson, 2008). Within this line of thinking, the application of statistical analyses upon data of a previously unimagined volume allows you to detect patterns in the data which reflect trends and outliers. According to Anderson, once you have enough data at your disposal there is no longer a need for preconceived theory or hypothesis to interpret the data, as the data start to speak for themselves through data mining. One famous example which is frequently cited to underline this assumption is the Google Flu Trends project. Over an extended period of time, a relationship has been observed between where, when and how many people search for flu-related topics in a search engine and the actual outbreak of flu.[4] In this specific context, the aggregation of a massive dataset of user queries to a search engine outperforms traditional research regarding flu surveillance.

This vision has charmed many and is being applied across various disciplines such as science and research, marketing and financial services. However, its overly simplistic way of relying on statistical properties to make assumptions about what has happened in the world or to make predictions about future processes has been also been criticized. Let us illustrate the debate by examining how the Big Data approach is being discussed and applied in the humanities.

3.3 Quantifying the humanities

If the Flu Trend project brought Big Data on the radar of the general audience, it was the Google N-Gram viewer which gave the humanities a direct feel of the potential of Big Data. The N-Gram viewer allows you to perform comparative queries across the millions of books which have been digitized in the context of the Google Books project. A 1-gram is a succession of characters uninterrupted by a space, whereas an n-gram is a succession of 1-grams. Within the phrase 'We had a great weekend outdoors', 'outdoors' is a 1-gram, 'great weekend' a 2-gram and 'a great weekend outdoors' a 4-gram.

The thrill of the Google N-gram viewer is that it lets you visualize the evolution of the presence of a word or an expression over time through the Google Books corpus, which offers access to scans of around 4% of all books ever printed, from as early as the 16th century and in multiple languages, representing over 500 billion words. In a couple of seconds, it lets you visualize the evolution in time of the use of a specific word or expression and compare that with the evolution of a set of other terms. Never before has it been so easy to analyse, for example, the impact of censorship during Nazi Germany by visualizing the presence, or more particularly the absence, of condemned artists such as Marc Chagall in the German corpus. By launching parallel queries on ice cream, steak and sushi for example, one can trace the evolution of the American diet (Michel et al., 2011).

The Big Data approach in the humanities is not limited to textual data. The ImagePlot toolkit from the Software Studies Institute at UC San Diego demonstrates how visual data such as images and video can be data mined in order to discover patterns and relationships between objects, uniquely based on quantifiable properties such as brightness, saturation, textures and shapes.[5]

3.4 Going beyond the canon

The underlying assumption of all these projects is that variations of quantifiable low-level properties (user queries, n-grams, visual features) lead to higher-level insights. One of the important conditions underlying this method is to have access to a critical mass of data. The more data that can be aggregated and mined, the higher the statistical significance of patterns which might result. This characteristic ('the more data, the better') clashes with one of the central pillars of humanistic scholarship: the canon. The canon represents a list of well identified and selected works used as the primary sources for scholarly work. The Shakespeares and Picassos only represent a minimal subset of the totality of cultural production, but this small subset can be analysed over time by generations of scholars in all of their details through a practice known as *close reading*.

As a community, scholars need to share a common ground in order to allow a critical debate. Especially in fields like literature, that common ground has been built up over decades and even centuries. The notion of the canon has been heavily criticized over recent decades and contemporary scholars are increasingly making use of more diverse primary materials. Unfortunately, our cognitive capabilities have not expanded, so we are still limited to study in detail a very limited portion of the materials available.

With 'Graphs, maps, trees', Moretti (2005) wrote an engaging plea for the concept of *distant reading*. Instead of solely reading in a detailed manner a small selection of texts, Moretti proposes the use of computational techniques to go beyond the study of the uniqueness of a specific text written by an author at a particular point in time in order to reveal cycles and genres based on formal characteristics. Since its introduction by Moretti, the concept of distant reading has been embraced by the digital humanities community. Unfortunately, the nuanced discourse and method of Moretti is sometimes represented as a simple rejection of close reading in favour of relying on computation tools.

This has lead to strong reactions from more traditional scholars. Within a series of opinion pieces in the *New York Times*, Stanley Fish criticized the way digital humanities reverse the traditional research method. Instead of first establishing an interpretative hypothesis and subsequently trying to find empirical evidence to prove or invalidate the hypothesis, digital humanists simply 'run the numbers, and then see if they prompt an interpretive hypothesis. The method, if it can be called that, is dictated by the capability of the tool' (Fish, 2012).

Fish particularly targets the article 'Canons, Close Reading, and the Evolution of Method' by Matthew Wilkens. In this piece, Wilkens automatically extracted all place names from the Wright collection, which contains every work of long-form fiction known to have been published in the USA between 1815 and 1875. Based on the observation of more international place names than expected, Wilkens makes the assumption that 'American fiction in the mid-nineteenth century appears to be pretty diversely outward looking in a way that hasn't received much attention' (Wilkens, 2011). Fish makes the point that without knowing the specific context in which the name of an international city is mentioned in a text, it is troublesome to draw conclusions merely based on their presence in the text. In a style which typifies the digital humanities, Wilkens emphasizes the hit-and-miss character of this type of research method: 'There is no guarantee that we'll be able to explain what we find or that it will fit neatly with what we have seen so far, but that's a feature and not a bug'.

This 'let us run the tool on top of the data and be surprised' approach characterizes many applications of text mining software in the humanities. Let us, therefore, focus in the following section on understanding more about how some of these tools function, what kind of results we can reasonably expect and what their limits are.

4 Gold mining for semantics

One technique has attracted a particular amount of attention over the last years, and is especially well suited for the treatment of descriptive non-structured metadata fields which we were unable to handle with previous methods of data cleaning and reconciliation. Originally developed by computational linguists as an information extraction subtask, *named-entity recognition and disambiguation* has subsequently attracted the attention of researchers in various fields such as biology and biomedicine, information science and the semantic web. Named-entity recognition (NER) is the task of searching full texts in natural language for identifiable entities. For instance, consider the following sentence:

On 25 September 2006, we visited Washington to see the White House.

An NER algorithm could find the following entities: '25 September 2006', 'Washington', and 'White House'. At this stage, these terms are simple strings of characters: beyond the fact that they constitute *some* entity, the algorithm doesn't perform any interpretation. It merely points to the entities inside the text, without knowing what they are or how they relate to each other.

When the algorithm additionally performs disambiguation, each term is associated with a meaning as well. In this case, '25 September 2006' would become the date *2006/09/25*, and 'Washington' and 'White House' could become http://dbpedia.org/resource/White_House and http://dbpedia.org/resource/Washington,_D.C. respectively. This reminds us of reconciliation, where a string of text was also transformed into a URI to enable the unique identification of the concept it represents. However, with NER, the algorithm has additional context information at its disposal that can significantly improve the quality of the match. In the example sentence, 'Washington' points to the city and not to the person, as evidenced by the presence of 'White House'. If, by contrast, the sentence would mention 'the statue of Washington', then a match to http://dbpedia.org/resource/George_Washington would be correct instead. Disambiguation thus completes recognition by offering the interpretation of the entities. However, it is important to make the conceptual distinction: recognition is about *finding* the entities in a text fragment, whereas disambiguation is about *mapping* those entities to a universal identifier.

4.1 What is a named entity?

The original concept of a 'named entity' (NE), proposed by Grishman and Sundheim (1996), covered names of people, organizations, and geographic locations as well as time, currency and percentage expressions. Similarly, named entities were defined for the 2002 Conference on Computational Natural Language Learning shared task as 'phrases that contain the names of persons, organizations, locations, times, and quantities' (Tjong Kim Sang, 2002).

As a result of the diversification of NER applications, this rather loose definition was further extended to include products, events, and diseases, to name but a few types recognized today as valid named entities, although Nadeau and Sekine (2007) note that the word 'named' in 'named entity' is effectively restricting the sense to entities referred to by rigid designators, as defined by Kripke (1982): 'a rigid designator designates the same object in all possible worlds in which that object exists and never designates anything else'.

There is, nonetheless, no real consensus on the exact definition of a (named) entity, which remains largely domain-dependent. A useful approach was adopted recently by Chiticariu et al. (2010), who proposed a list of criteria for the domain customization of NER, including entity boundaries, scope and granularity. They observe, for instance, that some NER tools choose to include generational markers (e.g. 'IV' in 'Henry IV'), whereas other do not. The definition of a named entity, according to them, is never clear-cut, but depends both on the data to process and on the application. In this chapter, we chose to use *entity* to refer to any type of entity, whether a named entity (in Kripke's sense) or a plain term. Similarly, we will use the well known acronym NER to cover both named-entity recognition and term extraction.

The NER task is strongly dependent on the knowledge bases used to train the NE extraction algorithm. Leveraging resources such as DBpedia, Freebase, and YAGO, recent methods have been introduced to map entities to relational facts exploiting these fine-grained ontologies. In addition to the detection of an NE and its type, efforts have been made to develop advanced methods for disambiguating information units with a URI. Disambiguation remains one of the key challenges in natural language processing, giving birth to the field of word-sense disambiguation (WSD), since natural languages (as opposed to formal or programming languages) are fundamentally ambiguous (Bagga and Baldwin, 1998; Navigli, 2009). As we discussed before, the term 'Washington' may refer to George Washington or to Washington DC, depending on the surrounding context. Similarly, people, organizations and companies can have multiple names and nicknames, but the algorithm can be guided by clues in the surrounding text for contextualizing the ambiguous term and refining its intended meaning. Therefore, an NE extraction workflow consists of analysing input content for detecting named entities, assigning them a type weighted by a confidence score and by providing a list of URIs for disambiguation.

4.2 Services and knowledge bases

NER algorithms often require a substantial knowledge base and constant updates to ensure new entities are recognized. As such, they are not offered as downloadable software packages, but rather as online services. An NER service takes a text fragment as input, performs named-entity extraction on it, and then disambiguates the entities with linked data identifiers. Different services vary in the algorithm they use for entity extraction, and the sources of the URLs they use for disambiguation. Initially, the web mining community harnessed Wikipedia as the linking hub where entities were mapped. A natural evolution of this approach, mainly driven by the semantic web community, consists of disambiguating named entities with data from the Linking Open Data cloud.

The following list details the characteristics of several well known NER services, as adapted from Steiner (2013).

- **AlchemyAPI** (http://www.alchemyapi.com/api/entity) is capable of identifying people, companies, organizations, cities, geographic features, and other typed entities within textual documents. The service uses statistical algorithms and NLP to extract semantic richness embedded within text. AlchemyAPI differentiates between *entity extraction* and *concept tagging*. The concept-tagging API is capable of abstraction, i.e. understanding how concepts relate and tag them accordingly ('Hillary Clinton', 'Michelle Obama' and 'Laura Bush' are all tagged as 'First Ladies of the United States'). In practice, the difference between named-entity extraction and concept tagging is subtle. As a consequence, we treat entities and concepts in the same way. Overall, AlchemyAPI results are often interlinked to well known members of the LOD cloud, among others with DBpedia and Freebase. AlchemyAPI offer free use of their services for research and non-profit purposes. On registration, users receive an API key allowing a default amount of 1000 extraction operations per day. Upon request, non-profit users receive 30,000 operations per day.
- **DBpedia Spotlight** (https://github.com/dbpedia-spotlight) is a tool for annotating mentions of DBpedia resources in text, providing a solution for linking unstructured information sources to the Linking Open Data cloud through DBpedia. DBpedia Spotlight performs named-entity extraction, including entity detection and disambiguation with adjustable precision and recall. It allows users to configure the annotations to their specific needs through the DBpedia Ontology and quality measures such as prominence, topical pertinence, contextual ambiguity, and disambiguation confidence. DBpedia Spotlight can be used free as a web service.
- **Zemanta** (http://developer.zemanta.com/docs/) allows developers to query the service for contextual metadata about a given text. The returned

components currently span four categories: articles, keywords, photos, and in-text links, plus optional component categories. The service provides high-quality identification of entities that are linked to well known datasets of the LOD cloud such as DBpedia or Freebase. Zemanta also offer free use of their services for research and non-profit purposes. Upon registration, users receive an API key allowing a default amount of 1000 operations per day. Upon request, non-profit users receive 10,000 operations a day.

- The **OpenCalais** web service (http://www.opencalais.com/) automatically creates rich semantic metadata for textual documents. Using Natural Language Processing, machine learning, and other methods, OpenCalais analyses documents and finds the entities within, and also returns the facts and events hidden within them. OpenCalais is the only one of the examined web services that provides details on occurrences in concrete sections of the submitted coherent text. This allows for the exact matching of the location in the text where a certain entity is detected. This is especially useful, as OpenCalais is also often capable of recognizing references within the text, such as pronouns, to previously discovered entities. A major problem with the extracted entities is that they are not always uniquely disambiguated. OpenCalais uses its own URLs for identified concepts, sometimes returning different URLs for the same things. Furthermore, the resources identified by URLs often don't contain meaningful information beyond the entity type. In particular, few links to other entities are included.

Other services are also available, such as **Evri**, **Extractiv**, and **Yahoo! Term Extraction**. Most NER services are proprietary, with a closed-source code base, so their algorithms cannot be inspected and compared on a conceptual level. In contrast, DBpedia Spotlight is open-source, which has the advantage that it can be used to implement NER with custom vocabularies.

A number of research projects and cultural institutions have experimented with NER services in recent years. The Powerhouse Museum has implemented it within its collection management database in order to browse related topics based on the extracted entities (Chan, 2008). It has used it in combination with user input to correct mistakes made by the algorithm. While such features have been appreciated both by the professional museum world and end-users, it is rare to find a concrete analysis of the added value of NER.

4.3 Evaluating the quality of NER

At the beginning of this chapter, we referred to scholars' criticisms of digital humanities practices, which express concerns regarding the dependence upon the capabilities of a tool and an uncritical acceptance of the results it produces

(Fish, 2012). Due to the commercial and closed-source character of the NER services described above, we are obliged to work with *black boxes*: data are ingested, and results come out. However, we should be wary of taking the output of NER services at face value. Because these services can be applied in a quick and low-cost manner, we should not assume they offer an added value.

This section will therefore introduce a generalizable methodology to assess the quality of NER results. The marketplace for NER services is growing and evolving at a fast pace. Therefore, be prepared to compare the performance of competing NER services and to analyse what the qualities and weak spots of each service are. Let us run through the general principles of the methodology.

4.4 Gold Standard Corpus

More precisely, we propose an evaluation which will help us to measure the *precision* and *recall* of various NER services. We have already defined these terms in Chapter 4, but let us quickly recapitulate. Precision is the proportion of retrieved results which are actually relevant to the search. The more irrelevant results the search system provides, the lower the precision. Recall is the proportion of relevant results to the search that were successfully retrieved. The more relevant results that are not returned by the search system, the lower the recall. How do you know what the precise number of relevant results for a query should be? To give an answer to this question, the method of the Gold Standard Corpus (GSC) has been developed. It might seem complex, but this method is actually quite simple. The central idea is to ask different people to indicate manually where in a document they find relevant results in answer to a specific query. The annotations of different individuals are then compared, in order to produce a perfectly annotated corpus, hence the reference to the adjective 'gold'. By comparing the results of an automated information retrieval system upon the same corpus, the precision and recall can be calculated.

For different application domains GSC have been constructed and can be reused. There is, to the best of our knowledge, no freely available corpus that can be used as a GSC for the evaluation of NER in the cultural heritage sector. Making the same observation, Rodriquez et al. (2012) built their own GSC for the evaluation of NER on raw OCR text, but they used specific data for the corpus, such as testimonies and newsletters, which do not compare with object descriptions. Even if museum-oriented GSC existed, it would still be useful to develop a manually annotated corpus based on a representative sample of your own metadata. The task of NER being largely domain-dependent means that results may vary significantly from one collection to another. The more institutions do this and share their GSC and their evaluation results, the easier it will become to identify well performing services. For these reasons we propose a method to annotate your own sample corpus, but to do this in a standardized manner, which will allow others to understand how you created the sample and re-use your evaluation work of an NER service.

What are the different steps to be taken? First of all, a concrete set of named entity (NE) types needs to be defined in order to perform the annotation. In other words, you need to describe exactly what you are looking for in a text, so that the annotations can be applied in a consistent manner. An analysis of your metadata needs to demonstrate what types of NE are particularly present. For example, the Dutch SoNaR corpus (Oostdijk et al., 2008) divides NE into six categories: PER (Persons), LOC (Locations), ORG (Organizations), EVE (Events), PRO (products), and MISC (Miscellaneous) (Buitinck and Marx, 2012). Based upon an analysis of your own metadata, an assessment has to be made to decide what types of entities are the most relevant. If you know by default that a specific NE type almost never appears within your metadata, there is little use in including the type, as it would make the annotation process more complex then needed. Keep things as simple as possible. In our experience, PER, LOC and ORG have been the most relevant entity types.

Once the categories are determined, they need to be used during the manual annotation process. As this is a lengthy process, it is impossible to annotate an entire export of your metadata, which may consist of tens of thousands of records. You therefore need to create a sample, which will allow you to limit the annotation time but which will still deliver statistically significant results. Simple formulas can be used to calculate the sample size, based on the total number of metadata records and two extra parameters which closely interact: the *confidence interval* and the *confidence level*. The confidence interval is the margin of error which you take as acceptable. For example, with a confidence interval of 5, you can assert that when 13% of your sample population has characteristic A, between 8% (=13-5) and 18% (=13+5) of the entire population has characteristic A. A confidence interval of 5 is a generally accepted standard across different domains. The confidence level, mostly expressed in a percentage, represents the level of trust you have. A generally accepted standard is 95%. So if we bring together a confidence interval of 5 and a level of confidence of 95% and you observe within your sample corpus that 20% of the descriptive fields contain two or more personal names, you are 95% sure that within the entire population between 15% and 25% contain two or more personal names.

Once the sample is selected, the descriptive metadata consisting of several phrases need to be converted into a text file with one word per line, in order to facilitate the annotation process. This operation is referred to as *tokenization* and can be performed with software such as the Natural Language Toolkit's WordPunct Tokenizer. The sample then has to be annotated by at least two distinct persons in order to reduce errors. The following format, based on (Ramshaw and Marcus, 1995), can be used:

```
James B-PER
Smith I-PER
delivered O
a O
speech O
in O
Washington B-LOC
for O
the O
members O
of O
Congress. B-ORG
. O
```

Once the entire sample has been annotated in this manner, the different versions are compared in order to weed out potential errors. This comparison can be done in an automated manner. In order to calculate the level of agreement between different annotators the Kappa coefficient (K) is used (Carletta, 1996). The value of K ranges between 0 (zero agreement) and 1 (total agreement). A value of K greater than 0.8 shows that the annotation is reliable for drawing definite conclusions. This type of annotated sample can then be used as a GSC, allowing the computation of the precision and recall by service and category. Our previous research can be consulted for a more detailed description of this evaluation method, allowing you to create your own GSC if needed (van Hooland et al., 2014).

4.5 Limitations of the GSC approach

However, the GSC method has clearly some major limitations. The rigorously defined and limited number of NE types allows us to obtain an objective assessment, but excludes an important number of terms identified by the NER services, such as *epigraphy* or *gold*, for example. The terms hold a potential value for users but do not appear in our GSC since they are common nouns or adjectives.

In order to assess the overall quality of the outcomes of the entity extraction services, we propose some other elements that can be taken into account when evaluating the added value of entity recognition in the cultural heritage sector, but by doing so we leave the realm of objectivity.

4.6 Assessing relevance, specificity and disambiguation

A first question which could be asked on the totality of the retrieved entities is whether they are *relevant* with regard to the description. A manual inspection of retrieved entities within a sample allows an assessment of whether an entity is closely connected or appropriate to the description, but at the end of the day relevance is context-dependent. The same applies to an analysis of the discriminatory value of retrieved entities. Variance of the application domain, but also of the type of use, makes it impossible to differentiate in an absolute manner low- from high-level semantics. For example, words considered as stop words in one context can be considered to be useful in others, as 'the' and 'who' could be discriminatory in the music domain when querying for 'The Who'.

One of the main selection criteria for the inclusion of the three specific NER services we work with (DBpedia Spotlight, Alchemy and Zemanta) is their ability to disambiguate through the provision of URIs. A manual inspection of the concepts retrieved within a sample allows an assessment of how well the different NER services disambiguate, and more particularly what the impact of polysemy is. In our experience, cases of polysemy rarely rise. When this happens, the literal sense of an entity (for example 'Blue flower', i.e. a flower which has the colour blue) is often mistaken for the figurative sense ('Blue flower' as the symbol of the joining of human with nature, rendered popular by German romanticism).

You will be able to look for yourself for these types of problems in the sample data we will use for the case study. Let us focus for now on the bigger picture and climb a bit higher up the conceptual ladder. When disambiguating named entities through URLs, how do we actually identify things on the web? This is a fundamental question which will become increasingly present in the years to come.

5 Managing ambiguous URLs

If you come across a link such as http://en.wikipedia.org/wiki/Jeff_Koons, how should you interpret this URL? Does the link point to an HTML document, an article, or a person – or something else? URLs and URIs have been introduced in Chapter 2, but this section will go deeper into unique identification on the web and, by extension, in the world or even the universe.

5.1 URLs provide identification and location

The first and most well known identifier on the web is the Uniform Resource Locator or URL. The purpose of a URL is actually twofold: *identification* and *location*. To understand the difference, we will look at two other types of identifiers that perform only one of those functions:

- A *social security number* uniquely identifies a person. So given this number, there will be at most one individual who corresponds to it. However, a social security number does not provide the means to locate a person directly.

• In contrast, a *home address* allows one to locate a person. Yet, several people might live at any given address, so the address alone is insufficient to identify a single person. Furthermore, addresses can change over time, whereas identity does not.

One of the major contributions of the web was to couple universal identification and location through URLs. A URL can indeed serve as an identifier for something on the web, as is the case with http://en.wikipedia.org/ wiki/Jeff_Koons. Additionally, the URL will detail how to retrieve this resource because of its special structure. A URL starts with a *protocol* name (e.g., http or https), followed by the hostname of the machine on which the thing resides (e.g., en.wikipedia.org). The remaining portion of the URL indicates the local path on the host (e.g., /wiki/Jeff_Koons). To retrieve a representation of the thing, we need to translate the hostname into an IP address (using the DNS protocol) and then issue an HTTP request to that host with the local path.

This explains how a URL can locate a concrete document, but still leaves the question of what exactly it identifies. We could be tempted to say that the URL identifies the retrieved document, but this is not true. Indeed, at different points in time, the URL http://en.wikipedia.org/wiki/Jeff_Koons locates different documents, because Wikipedia is constantly edited by volunteers. However, the URL http://en.wikipedia.org/w/index.php?title=Jeff_Koons&oldid=569081712 points to a specific revision of the document that should not change. Another angle would be to say that it identifies the person Jeff Koons, but then we would be unable to distinguish between the two. Clearly, the distinction is important: the person has a birth date, which is different from the article's creation date. As its name already indicates, the web's solution is that a URL identifies a *resource*, which is a *conceptual* relationship. For instance, http://en.wikipedia.org /wiki/Jeff_Koons points to 'the latest revision of the Wikipedia article on Jeff Koons', whereas http://en.wikipedia.org/w/index.php?title=Jeff_Koons&oldid= 569081712 points to 'the revision created on 18 August 2013 at 13:52 of the Wikipedia article on Jeff Koons'. URLs thus allow one to uniquely identify a concept and to locate a document that represents it.

5.2 URIs provide identification

While Uniform Resource Identifiers (URIs) do not allow location, they can still be useful to incorporate in descriptions. Very broadly speaking, any distinguishable concept in the universe can be assigned a URI. In particular, any URL is a URI, but infinitely many others exist. For instance, ISBN numbers can be written as URIs, with the ISBN number 978-0062515872 corresponding to urn:isbn:978-0062515872. Note how this number indeed identifies a book, but does not directly allow you to retrieve a copy of it.

More recently, the concept of URI has been generalized to IRI, the Internationalized Resource Identifier. URIs are limited within the ASCII character set, whereas IRIs allow the inclusion of Unicode characters. IRIs also serve as XML namespaces, as they can precisely give a unique name to any entity.

5.3 URLs can identify real-world concepts

When we said earlier that a URL identifies a resource, we didn't specify whether this resource should be electronic-only, or whether real-world objects can also be identified. This is the issue of *information* resources, which are representable in electronic format, versus *non-information* resources, which are not. Clearly, a Wikipedia article about Jeff Koons is an information resource, because it can be represented in electronic form. Its URL thus identifies the article, locates it, and allows the sending an electronic representation of it. However, Jeff Koons is a non-information resource, as we cannot represent him electronically. Sure, we can represent a document *about* Koons, but this would be a different resource than the artist himself.

You might remember from the linked data principles discussed in Chapter 2 that HTTP URLs should be used to identify concepts. Hence, we should be able to use an HTTP URL to identify Jeff Koons, even if he cannot be transferred electronically. Therefore, data sources such as DBpedia have taken a pragmatic approach. The URL http://dbpedia.org/resource/Jeff_Koons identifies the artist, whereas the URL http://dbpedia.org/page/Jeff_Koons identifies the document *about* the artist. Thus when Jeff Koons is mentioned in the document, the first URL will be used. Furthermore, if we visit the first URL in the browser, DBpedia is not able to represent Jeff Koons, so it *redirects* you towards the page about Jeff Koons instead. As a result, if you want to describe Jeff Koons, you could do this as follows:

```
<http://dbpedia.org/resource/Jeff_Koons> a foaf:Person.
```

In contrast, the page about Jeff Koons can be described like this:

```
<http://dbpedia.org/page/Jeff_Koons> a foaf:Document.
```

Furthermore, the relation between the two can be made explicit by:

```
<http://dbpedia.org/resource/Jeff_Koons> foaf:primaryTopicOf
    <http://dbpedia.org/page/Jeff_Koons>.
```

5.4 Identity and named entities

Understanding what a URI is actually referring to is conceptually probably the most challenging question. Before referring to examples of the case study, the topic needs to be positioned within the broad debate in the web community on whether a URI should be understood as a reference to a document or a resource. For example, does the URI http://en.wikipedia.org/wiki/Richard_Nixon identify the former US president, or does it identify a document *about* this person? Clearly, they are distinct entities: they can have separate values for the same property (e.g. the age of a person is different from the age of a document about that person) and one entity can evolve independently of the other. Since one URI can only identify a single resource (Berners-Lee, Fielding and Masinter, 1994; Berners-Lee, Masinter and McCahill, 2005), a concept and its describing document(s) should necessarily have different identifiers. The question of what is identified by a URI has been a long-standing issue for the W3C's Technical Architecture Group (TAG), and has been known as 'HTTP-range 14' (Berners-Lee, 2002c). The conceptual difficulty arises because HTTP URIs serve a double purpose: on the one hand, they identify a resource, and on the other hand, they can provide the address to obtain a representation of that resource. The linked data principles (Berners-Lee, 2006) demand that both functions are effectuated to ensure all URI-identified resources have a representation at their own address.

Berners-Lee (2002a; 2002b) initially suggested a distinction between URIs without and with fragment identifier. The former (e.g. http://en.wikipedia.org/wiki/Richard_Nixon) would identify documents, and the latter (e.g. http://en.wikipedia.org/wiki/Richard_Nixon#richard) would identify a concept (within that document). This distinction is also referred to as the difference between *information resources* and *non-information resources*. The compromise ultimately chosen by the TAG was to make this distinction by inspecting the return code when the URI is dereferenced (Fielding, 2005). While this is an acceptable solution for some, the debate still goes on (Rees, 2012).

This issue and the discussion surrounding it is very relevant for the digital humanities community, because it determines how identifiers for documents and concepts should be used. In particular with NER, we should be careful not to consider a link to a document *about* a resource as an identifier for that resource.

Unfortunately, not all APIs make this distinction. While AlchemyAPI and Zemanta differentiate between various link types and sources (attaching labels such as 'dbpedia', 'yago', and 'website'), there is no explicit indication whether the link points to an information or a non-information resource, although any given link type should consistently produce one or the other. DBpedia Spotlight returns DBpedia URIs, which always point to the concept. Still, it is important that distinct extracted entities have a unique URI to determine whether two pieces of content refer to the same entities. Continuing the earlier example, a text about Richard Nixon and a text about a document that describes President Nixon handle a different topic. However, if an NER service assigns the document's URI as an identifier of the person, that URI cannot be used to identify the document itself, leading to a paradoxical situation.

6 Conclusion

How should we respond to the massive arrival of digital documents? With this question in mind we started this chapter on the automated creation of metadata through NER. Chapters 3 and 4 had a strong focus on methods for metadata cleaning and reconciliation which were developed within the LIS community, and which can be put to a good use within the digital humanities. In this chapter, the tables have turned.

Experience with the development of electronic editions and a global focus on handling full-text documents from the literary and historical community has given digital humanists a strategic advantage in the dealings with large amounts of unstructured data. Instead of the traditional LIS focus on what Cheryl Ball has called 'boutique data', digital humanists quite rapidly embraced 'Big Data'. Instead of being driven by an angst of no longer being able to index and catalogue resources manually, the DH community has taken the arrival of large digital corpora as an opportunity to renew quantitative methods within the humanities. Initiated by Moretti, the concept of distant reading has attracted a lot of attention and has not always been welcomed warmly, as we illustrated with the discussion between Fish and Wilkens. Unfortunately, the proposition to go beyond the canon with methods of distant reading is often interpreted as an abandonment of the traditional close reading. In reality, the two approaches complement and enrich one another. This is also the case with the use of NER for enriching metadata.

Despite the popularity of NER services in recent years, there is surprisingly little information or consensus on what we actually consider to be a named entity. This by and large is context-dependent and we therefore choose in this chapter to use the term 'entity' to refer to any type of entity, whether a named entity or a plain term. Term extraction has been an important topic for decades within computational linguistics. It is therefore fundamental to understand that NER services not only identify specific terms within unstructured text, but also disambiguate these terms through the use of knowledge bases such as Freebase or DBpedia. We illustrated this with the example of Washington, which could refer to either a state, city or a person. By choosing between http://en.wikipedia.org/wiki/Washington,_D.C., http://en.wikipedia.org/wiki/Washington_(state) or http://en.wikipedia.org/wiki/George_Washington, an NER service provides us information on how to interpret the identified entity.

Currently, NER services very much remain closed black boxes. DBpedia

Spotlight is an open-source tool, but performs quite badly when compared to commercially available solutions. Most commercial NER providers offer free use of their service within a pedagogical or non-commercial domain, such as the cultural heritage sector. However, this domain evolves very rapidly and new services and products are constantly being launched on the market. How can an institution evaluate different products and actually measure the quality of NER?

In order to give cultural heritage institutions the means to independently test the relevance of NER services, we described how to build and use a GSC to measure precision and recall. This standardized approach allows an objective assessment but only applies to well identified categories of named entities, such as locations, person and organization names. If we want to go further with the assessment of the quality of NER services, by for example analysing their level of specificity or relevance, we inevitably enter into a subjective realm, as these aspects are very much context-dependent. Instead of entering that debate, we have focused on the sometimes problematic character of URLs. If we are going to give URLs a fundamental role to play within our information society, we had better understand them, or at least develop more of a consensus on how we should use and interpret them. Not knowing exactly whether http://en. wikipedia.org/wiki/Jeff_Koons identifies an HTML document, an article, a person – or something else – seriously undermines the pivotal role URLs have to play within a linked data world. This issue, better known as HTTP-range 14, has long been an open-standing issue in the computer science and semantic web domain. Simply ignoring its existence will not solve it, and it is typically a problem area where the LIS and DH communities can deliver an original input.

The case study of this chapter will now allow you to have your own go at the use of NER services, through an extension for OpenRefine which was specifically developed for this handbook.

7 CASE STUDY: the British Library

In order to demonstrate the use of NER on descriptive, unstructured metadata fields, we decided to use a set of metadata from the British Library which have also been made available through Europeana. This data set is mainly composed of metadata describing the Asia, Pacific and Africa Collections, containing images of the landscape and architectural heritage of South Asia from the late-18th to mid-20th centuries. From the website http://pro.europeana. eu/web/guest/datasets, we downloaded the dataset available in RDF/XML for the United Kingdom and converted it into a CSV file. As we will only focus within this case study on the application of NER on the description field, we will not give an overview of the other metadata fields. Before we start with the dataset from the British Library, we will first introduce you to an online NER service. Then we will load the dataset into OpenRefine and perform NER in an automated way. After a short discussion of the results, we will propose a method to formally analyse the recall and precision of the NER services by making use of a Gold Standard Corpus.

7.1 Manual named-entity recognition

To get a grip on named-entity recognition services, we will manually execute a service on an example text fragment. In addition to the service for machines, which is based on XML, DBpedia Spotlight also offers a user-friendly interface in the browser. To test it, navigate to http://dbpedia-spotlight.github.io/demo/, and you will see a sample text and various settings you can adjust. You can try the service with the text provided or choose a text of our own, perhaps from a news or encyclopedia article. Let's choose the summary text from Pablo Picasso's DBpedia page:

> Pablo Ruiz y Picasso, known as Pablo Picasso (25 October 1881–8 April 1973) was a Spanish painter, sculptor, printmaker, ceramicist, and stage designer who spent most of his adult life in France. As one of the greatest and most influential artists of the 20th century, he is widely known for co-founding the Cubist movement, the invention of constructed sculpture, the co-invention of collage, and for the wide variety of styles that he helped develop and explore. Among his most famous works are the proto-Cubist Les Demoiselles d'Avignon (1907), and Guernica (1937), a portrayal of the German bombing of Guernica during the Spanish Civil War. Picasso, Henri Matisse and Marcel Duchamp are commonly regarded as the three artists who most defined the revolutionary developments in the plastic arts in the opening decades of the 20th century, responsible for significant developments in painting, sculpture, printmaking and ceramics.
>
> http://dbpedia.org/page/Pablo_Picasso

Replace the example fragment in the large textbox by the above summary, and click the **Annotate** button. Within a few seconds, DBpedia Spotlight scans the text for named entities and disambiguates them. The recognized concepts have been turned into coloured and underlined links. You can click or hover over them to see to which concept they have been disambiguated. When we tried the service on the above sample, 20 concepts were recognized. This number may be slightly different if you try it yourself, as the algorithm behind Spotlight is in constant evolution, and the number of topics in DBpedia continuously grows.

The recognized concepts are listed in Table 5.1, in the order by which they occur in the original text.

entity	URL
Table 5.1 Recognized entities in the Pablo Picasso abstract	
Pablo Ruiz	http://dbpedia.org/resource/Pablo_Ruiz_(Argentine_singer)
Picasso	http://dbpedia.org/resource/Pablo_Picasso
Pablo Picasso	http://dbpedia.org/resource/Pablo_Picasso
Spanish	http://dbpedia.org/resource/Spain
printmaker	http://dbpedia.org/resource/Printmaking
ceramicist	http://dbpedia.org/resource/Ceramic_art
stage designer	http://dbpedia.org/resource/Scenic_design
France	http://dbpedia.org/resource/France
Cubist	http://dbpedia.org/resource/Cubism
constructed sculpture	http://dbpedia.org/resource/Assemblage_(art)
Les Demoiselles d'Avignon	http://dbpedia.org/resource/Les_Demoiselles_d'Avignon
Guernica	http://dbpedia.org/resource/Guernica_(painting)
German	http://dbpedia.org/resource/Germany
Guernica	http://dbpedia.org/resource/Guernica_(painting)
Spanish Civil War	http://dbpedia.org/resource/Spanish_Civil_War
Picasso	http://dbpedia.org/resource/Pablo_Picasso
Henri Matisse	http://dbpedia.org/resource/Henri_Matisse
Marcel Duchamp	http://dbpedia.org/resource/Marcel_Duchamp
plastic arts	http://dbpedia.org/resource/Plastic_arts
ceramics	http://dbpedia.org/resource/Ceramic_art

We note several interesting things there:

- All recognized entities are also disambiguated: for each found entity, DBpedia Spotlight also suggests a unique identifier of the concept. This is not the case for all NER services; some entities might be recognized but not disambiguated.
- All disambiguation URLs are resources on DBpedia. This is part of the Spotlight algorithm; services such as Zemanta use URLs from different sources.
- Entities can be recognized multiple times: Pablo Picasso is found on the words 'Picasso', 'Pablo Picasso', and a second occurrence of 'Picasso'.
- A strict one-to-one mapping from the concept in the text to the URL's concept is not necessary. For instance, the adjective 'Spanish' has been disambiguated to the URL http://dbpedia.org/resource/Spain, corresponding to the concept of the proper noun 'Spain'. Similarly, 'ceramicist' and 'ceramics' are both mapped to http://dbpedia.org/resource/Ceramic_art. This illustrates the flexibility of the disambiguation process. It also shows that relationships created by NER services should not be interpreted as *corresponds to the concept* but rather as *refers to the concept*.

- The recognition algorithm does inadvertently make mistakes. For instance, the fragment 'Pablo Ruiz y Picasso' is not recognized as a single entity, but rather as two entities: 'Pablo Ruiz' and 'Picasso'. While the latter is properly disambiguated (even though only the last name was recognized), the former is incorrectly mapped to the singer Pablo Ruiz.
- The first mention of 'Guernica' is correctly disambiguated to the artwork. However, the second mention actually refers to the city, yet Spotlight disambiguates it again to the artwork. This indicates the difference between proper recognition and proper disambiguation. However, the algorithm *is* context-sensitive. If we try the service with the fragment 'I lived in Guernica, Spain.', it will correctly disambiguate the concept to http://dbpedia.org/resource/Guernica_(town).
- Several entities have not been recognized. For instance, while 'printmaker' and 'ceramicist' were found, 'painter' and 'sculptor' were not. Also, DBpedia seemingly does not find time-based entities, such as '25 October 1881' or '20th century' – presumably because there are no DBpedia pages about them.

7.2 Named-entity recognition with OpenRefine

As we saw in the last chapter, OpenRefine has basic native support for reconciliation, the mapping of fields with single- or multi-word terms to a unique identifier. With the RDF extension, its support can be extended to RDF and SPARQL datasources. However, it does not come with out-of-the box support for NER on full-text fields. Several third-party companies provide web services that offer NER functionality, but those services can be difficult to access without a technical background, and each service has a different, proprietary interaction model. Furthermore, it is impractical to invoke them repeatedly on multiple text fragments. An ideal solution would be to integrate NER services into an existing workflow, saving users from repetitive, low-level interactions.

To this end, we have developed an open-source extension for OpenRefine, which is freely available for download at https://github.com/RubenVerborgh/Refine-NER-Extension. The NER extension provides an integrated front-end that gives access to multiple NER services from within OpenRefine, thereby providing three levels of automation:

- The interaction with NER services happens transparently.
- A single user interaction can apply NER on an entire dataset.
- Each record can be analysed by multiple NER services at the same time.

It also allows users to manage their service preferences, ensuring consistency between NER operations on different datasets. The extension makes NER part of a common toolkit of data operations, offering the full potential of NER in a single, accessible operation. Furthermore, the implementation of the extension abstracts NER services into a uniform interface, minimizing the amount of code necessary to support additional services.

The initial version of the extension supports three services: AlchemyAPI, DBpedia Spotlight, and Zemanta. Despite the excellent results delivered by Stanford NER (Rodriquez et al., 2012), we decided not to include this service, as it limits itself to standard recognition and does not provide disambiguation with URIs. For similar reasons, it was decided not to include OpenCalais, as the URIs it provides are unfortunately proprietary ones and only a fraction of the returned entities link to other sources from the linked data cloud.

7.2.1 Installing the NER extension

The installation of the NER extension is analogous to that of the RDF extension. However, for completeness, we list the full steps below:

1 Download the NER extension at
   http://software.freeyourmetadata.org/ner-extension/.
2 The extension is currently packed into a compressed file. Unpack it into a folder of your choice.
3 Start the OpenRefine application. At the bottom of the starting page, click the link **Browse workspace directory**. This will take you to OpenRefine's main folder.
4 This folder will contain several others. Among them should be a folder named extensions. If not, create this folder yourself. If you have installed the RDF extension, you will see it in there as well.
5 Drag the folder you unpacked during step 2 into the extensions folder. The folder structure should now look like this: the extensions folder contains a named-entity-recognition folder, which in turn contains folders such as MOD-INF and scripts.
6 Close OpenRefine, not only by closing the browser window but also by closing the application itself by right-clicking its icon and choosing **Close** (or the equivalent for your operating system).
7 When starting OpenRefine again and opening a project, a **Named-entity recognition** button should appear at the top right. This indicates the installation was successful.

Detailed instructions can also be found at the NER extension website, http://freeyourmetadata.org/named-entity-extraction/.

7.2.2 Importing and navigating the Europeana dataset

As the Europeana dataset of the British Library is in RDF format, we have converted it into a CSV file so you can easily import it into OpenRefine. The converted version can be downloaded.[6] Start OpenRefine and choose **Create Project**. Choose the downloaded file and click **Continue**. The default importing options work fine, so continue through the **Click Project** button. OpenRefine now shows you the 31,088 rows in the dataset.

This export only contains a few fields: **title, types, subjects, description, spatial, extent,** and **uri**. The **types** and **subjects** fields are multi-valued; if you split them, they could be used for reconciliation. The **spatial** and **extent** columns contain metadata about the location and dimension of the object, respectively. The **uri** field links back to the Europeana portal, which displays the item in a visual layout. The **title** and **description** fields are the most interesting for named-entity recognition, as they contain full-text. Since the **description** field contains significantly more text, we will use it in this use case. To focus more clearly on this field, click the **description** triangle and choose **View | Collapse all other columns**.

7.2.3 Selecting part of the dataset

First a word of caution: *NER services take a considerable amount of time*. It's not uncommon for a dataset of this size to take several hours or even days to complete. Therefore, we will try NER on a *subset* of the data for now. As an example, we will take the first 100 rows. To do this, click the **description** triangle and select **Facet | Custom text facet**. In the **Expression** text box, enter row.index < 100 and click **OK**. The resulting facet divides the dataset into the first 100 rows (true) and the remaining rows (false). For simplicity, we will just remove those remaining rows, so select **false** in the facet you have just created and then go to the **all** triangle, choosing **Edit rows | Remove all matching rows**. Finally, remove the **description** facet by clicking its close button at the top left. You now see 100 rows, ready for experimenting.

This might be a good time to remind ourselves of the fact that OpenRefine has a flexible undo function, which can bring back those rows anytime. If you are curious about the results, you can retry the following steps on the entire dataset. However, this can take some time, so you might want to run this task on an idle computer at night or over the weekend. Alternatively, we have done this for you on the Europeana dataset, as we will explain later.

7.2.4 Performing NER with DBpedia Spotlight

Now that the dataset has been brought back to a manageable number of rows, we can start the NER process. Double-check that you've installed the NER extension (if you see a **Named-entity recognition** button at the top right, you're fine) and go to the **description** triangle, choosing **Extract named entities**. OpenRefine lets you choose between several NER services you can invoke at the same time. However, only **DBpedia Spotlight** is enabled for now, as the other services require a prior configuration step. Therefore, select **DBpedia Spotlight** and click the **Start extraction** button.

Behind the scenes, OpenRefine will now call the DBpedia Spotlight service with each of the text fragments, similar to how we did manually before. Depending on the current occupation of the service, the results are delivered in a couple of minutes. The progress indicator at the top of the window keeps you informed about the progress.

When the service returns, you will notice that the number of rows has increased. This is because the NER extension puts each extracted entity on a separate row. In our case, OpenRefine now reports 633 rows, but this can slightly differ depending on the current algorithm behind Spotlight. To group the entities to the item they belong to, switch to records mode by activating **Show as: records** at the top. Now OpenRefine shows you again 100 items, each of which can have multiple entities with it. This result is shown in Figure 5.2.

How do we interpret the results? Let's start by understanding exactly what has happened during the NER process. First, the NER extension created a new column called **DBpedia Spotlight**. Then, it went through all of the rows'

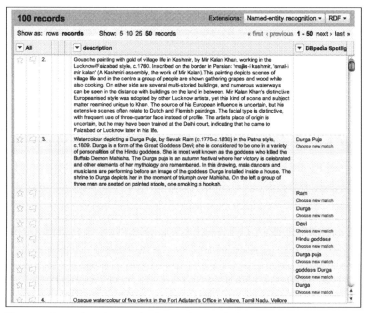

Figure 5.2 Results of executing DBpedia Spotlight: disambiguated terms appear as links

description fields. If no entity was found in a field of a certain item's row, then its NER column is left empty. If one entity was found, it is placed in its NER column. If several entities are found, new rows are created right below the item's row to accommodate for all entities. This is why we recommend switching to records mode, as it groups the results per item.

To see how successful the extraction has been, let's see for how many of the items an answer was found; in other words, we are looking for those records without an empty NER column. Click the **DBpedia Spotlight** triangle and select **Facet | Customized facets | Facet by blank**. A new facet appears on the left hand side. The numbers we got were 24 rows that are empty (true) and 598 rows that are not (false). As you can see, OpenRefine displays the number of *rows* in the facet, not the number of records. However, clicking on the false facet while in records mode, shows that those non-empty rows are distributed over 76 items. This was to be expected: the 24 empty rows belong to 24 items for which no entities have been found, whereas the remaining 76 items out of our total of 100 have at least one entity each. This brings the average to 7.9 entities per description (excluding those that had no matches).

We can now investigate the individual items to see what entities have been found. Figure 5.2 shows the matches for the description text in the third row: **Durga Puja**, **Ram**, **Durga**, **Devi**, **Hindu goddess**, **Durga puja**, **goddess Durga**, and **Durga** once more. Indicated by a blue colour on screen, these entities are links to the disambiguated concept. For instance, if we click **Durga Puja**, we arrive at the page for the concept http://dbpedia.org/resource/Durga_Puja. This page details various properties about Durga Puja, including the fact that it is an Indian festival. Therefore, if we were to export the dataset at this stage, people looking for 'Indian festival' could still find this artwork, even though this term is not literally mentioned inside the description. Furthermore, the artwork could be related to others that depict related events. This illustrates the power of named-entity recognition, even with freely available services such as DBpedia Spotlight.

However, there is also some noise in the entities. For instance, while **Ram** was correctly identified as part of an entity, the full entity is actually **Sevak Ram**. Furthermore, the entity has been disambiguated to http://dbpedia.org/resource/Rama, which is a topic within Hinduism rather than the artist of the painting. This indicates that we should always be careful with automatically suggested entities. However, premium services such as AlchemyAPI or Zemanta will probably perform better. Furthermore, the settings of the DBpedia Spotlight service can be tweaked through the **Configure services . . .** option of the **Named-entity recognition** toolbar button, which influence the confidence threshold of the algorithm.

One final thing to note is that the NER service might identify multiple occurrences of the same entity, either under the same or under a different form. This is the case with **Durga** and its variations.

7.3 Performing NER with AlchemyAPI and Zemanta

Now that we have tried NER with Spotlight, we might be curious to see the results of other services. However, as AlchemyAPI and Zemanta are not freely available, you need an account in order to use them. Then the credentials of this account must be added to the NER extension settings so the extension can access them. Fortunately, both services offer trial accounts, so you can test them to see if they perform well on your dataset.

The steps to register for an account are linked from within the extension. Click the **Named-entity recognition** toolbar button and choose **Configure services**. You see a list of all supported services. If you want to set up AlchemyAPI, click the **configuration instructions** link next to it, which will take you to the registration page. The same applies to Zemanta. Once you have received your credentials, fill out the *API key* field of the NER extension's configuration window and click **Update**.

Before you try other services, we strongly recommend to remove the DBpedia Spotlight results. As this first use of the NER extension has lead to new rows being created, it might become difficult to understand which extraction belongs to what item. In fact, if you want to perform NER with different services on the same dataset, it is better to select the services you want in a single operation, as we'll show shortly. For now, go to the **Undo/Redo** tab to revert to step 1 where we trimmed the dataset to 100 rows.

Click the **description** triangle and choose **Extract named entities**. Choose both **AlchemyAPI** and **Zemanta** (if you have accounts for them) and click **Start extraction**. The NER extension will now find entities in all rows using both services at the same time. One thing you will notice already in comparison to DBpedia Spotlight is that the extraction process proceeds a lot faster. This is due to the fact that these are commercial services.

When the results appear, we see new columns called **AlchemyAPI** and **Zemanta**, which contain the recognized entities by the respective services. Note that these columns are independent, i.e., the fact that an AlchemyAPI and a Zemanta term appear on the same row does not imply any connection. All entities are, however, connected to the **description** field of the corresponding record. Our results for the first item are displayed in Figure 5.3.

This nicely illustrates the complementarity of different NER services. While DBpedia Spotlight was not able to find any match for this item, AlchemyAPI finds several and Zemanta even more. While AlchemyAPI was not able to disambiguate all found terms, it still was able to identify some of them such as **Delhi, Major-General**, and **Azajour**. Non-disambiguated terms do not have

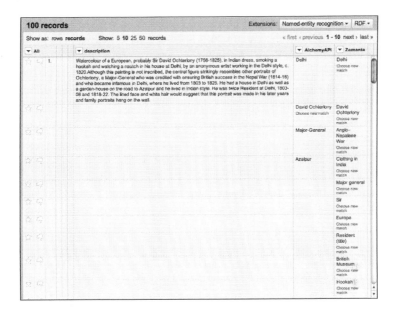

Figure 5.3 Results of executing the AlchemyAPI and Zemanta. Not all terms have been disambiguated, as indicated by missing hyperlinks.

a hyperlink to a concept, but they can still be used to identify important terms in a full-text field.

An interesting thing to note is that both services can find multiple identifiers of the same concept. By default, the first identifier is chosen for the hyperlink, but other identifiers become visible as you click the **Choose new match** link on an entity. For instance, AlchemyAPI suggests the following identifiers for **David Ochterlony**:

- http://yago-knowledge.org/resource/David_Ochterlony
- http://dbpedia.org/resource/David_Ochterlony
- http://rdf.freebase.com/ns/m.06sb31.

Zemanta, on the other hand, suggests the following:

- http://en.wikipedia.org/wiki/David_Ochterlony
- http://rdf.freebase.com/ns/en/david_ochterlony
- http://dbpedia.org/resource/David_Ochterlony.

Surprisingly, both lists include DBpedia identifiers, even though DBpedia Spotlight itself was not able to identify David Ochterlony. The Zemanta results also bring us back to the issue about URL identification raised in section 4.5.

Zemanta identifies Ochterlony by a DBpedia URL and a Wikipedia URL. However, the former identifies a person, whereas the latter identifies an article about that person. Even though the results are valid if we apply this interpretation, software will likely not be able to automatically make the distinction between the person and the article. This is one more reason to be cautious with the integration of entities.

7.4 Analysing the complete NER results

As it might take some time to run NER on the entire dataset, we have made our results available as an OpenRefine project which you can download.[7] As loading the complete NER information with all identifiers for all cells demands considerable memory, we have only maintained the first identifier and its URL. In order to easily analyse this dataset, we will start by creating some facets.

Switch to 'rows' mode by clicking the **Show as rows** link at the top; this will provide granular access to the individual entities as opposed to the records to which these entities belong. Then create a blank facet on the **description** column by clicking the **description** triangle and selecting **Facet | Customized facets | Facet by blank**. Do the same for the **AlchemyAPI, DBpedia Spotlight** and **Zemanta** columns. If you now select false in the **description** facet, you will only see those rows that have a description. As a result, the other facets will show the number of cases where at least one entity was found. This facet configuration is shown in Figure 5.4.

Concretely, we see that there are 31,052 items with descriptions. In 29,738 of those, AlchemyAPI found at least one entity; for DBpedia Spotlight, this count is 30,370; and 30,520 for Zemanta. (Of course, that does not say anything about the accuracy of those entities.) We can also check the complementarity of the services. To see how Spotlight and Zemanta performed on those rows that AlchemyAPI missed, activate the true option of the **AlchemyAPI** facet, which will find those 1314 entity fields that are empty. It turns out that, 1285 of Alchemy's unsuccessful attempts were solved by DBpedia Spotlight, and 1221 were solved by Zemanta. We can continue the analysis by activating true in the **DBpedia Spotlight** facet, which reveals that Zemanta found entities for 23 items that did not yield any results with either AlchemyAPI or DBpedia Spotlight. Trying out these selections on parts of your dataset can give you insights on what NER algorithms work best in your particular situation.

Again, the data quality of the underlying dataset is of utmost importance. This becomes visible if we look at those descriptions for which services were unable to find entities. To inspect this, reset the **AlchemyAPI** and **DBpedia Spotlight** facets by clicking their **reset** link, and set the **Zemanta** facet to true,

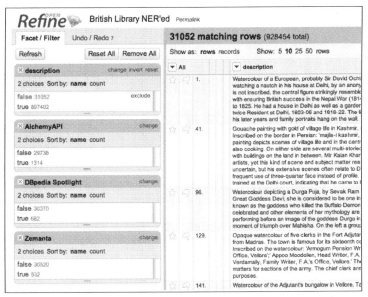

Figure 5.4 By viewing only the rows with descriptions, we can see in how many cases each of the algorithms found at least one entity

showing all descriptions for which Zemanta found no solutions. We notice that several of the descriptions that fail to yield results contain severe OCR errors. For instance, one of the rows contains the following description:

> Photogr&h of sowy e&ks e&r G&gotri fro Bh&irogh&ti, t&ke by S&uel Boure i the 1860s.

As fragments like these pose a challenge for humans, it's not hard to imagine that automated algorithms have even more trouble with them. As always, data quality is a prerequisite for further enhancement steps.

By glancing through the results, one quickly has the impression that Zemanta delivers the most interesting results, as all of the entities are disambiguated. Alchemy is very good at detecting names of persons and locations, but most often does not provide an URL to a knowledge base. DBpedia provides a lot of results, but they are often not relevant. On the whole, Zemanta provides the most interesting results, as its disambiguation process works surprisingly well. Zemanta sometimes even provides a URL of the actual resource, and by doing so goes beyond the provision of a URL from a knowledge base. For example, based on the description 'Acquired with the assistance of the Heritage Lottery Fund', Alchemy provides http://dbpedia.org/page/Heritage_Lottery_Fund but Zemanta actually points straight to http://www.hlf.org.uk, the website of the organization.

However, if you look closely you will also find some disambiguation issues. If you perform a text filter on the descriptions for 'Prince Philip', you will find a record about Philip of France, who is also mentioned in the description as Prince Philip and therefore gets mixed up with Prince Philip, Duke of Edinburgh. Fortunately, these types of errors are rather exceptional.

7.5 Evaluation of the results

This case study illustrated how easy it is to start experimenting on your own with NER. Before implementing the outcomes of NER on a large scale you might want to get a clear understanding of the quality differences between NER services and whether it makes sense, for example, to use them in parallel. In previous research we described a quantitative method to assess the precision and recall of three different services upon a corpus which is quite similar to the corpus used within the case study (van Hooland et al., 2014). If you want to conduct a quality assessment for your own collection, we recommend you to repeat the procedures outlined in the mentioned paper.

Unfortunately we cannot go into a detailed analysis in this case study, but we can end with some global remarks. The results show that, on our 390 records sample, Zemanta performed best, followed by AlchemyAPI, while DBpedia was firmly lagging behind. Overall, precision is better than recall. As a reminder, precision is the fraction of retrieved instances relevant to a search criterion, whereas recall is the fraction of the instances relevant to the query that are retrieved. The fact that precision scores higher than recall could be surprising, since many common terms found by the services (e.g. watercolour, portraits, etc.) were tagged as incorrect since they did not fit one of the strict categories (such as person, localization or event) used for the calculation of precision and recall. In this respect, DBpedia was more affected than the two others. Recall does not hit the 50% mark for any service, which means that they failed to identify more than half of the named entities we judged relevant. To sum up, while these results show that silence overbears noise, AlchemyAPI and Zemanta provide a meaningful input for cultural heritage metadata. This case study therefore has the merit of showing that a decent number of entities can be retrieved relatively easily by using general-purpose tools. For cultural institutions with limited budgets, we are confident this could prove a simple and efficient way of gaining extra semantic value from existing metadata.

Notes

1 See Sebastian Chan's blog post, which describes these evolutions in more detail: http://www.freshandnew.org/2011/10/culture-heritage-digital-at-web-directions-south-2011/.
2 http://www.steve.museum.
3 http://www.oldweather.org and http://blogs.ucl.ac.uk/transcribe-bentham/.
4 http://www.google.org/flutrends/.
5 http://lab.softwarestudies.com/p/imageplot.html.
6 At http://book.freeyourmetadata.org/chapters/4/british-library.csv.
7 At http://book.freeyourmetadata.org/chapters/4/british-library_reconciled.openrefine.tar.gz.

References

Anderson, C. (2008) The End of Theory: the data deluge makes the scientific method obsolete, *Wired Magazine*, http://www.wired.com/science/discoveries/magazine/16-07/pb_theory.

Bade, D. (2012) IT, That Obscure Object of Desire: on French anthropology, museum visitors, airplane cockpits, RDA, and the next generation catalog, *Cataloging & Classification Quarterly*, **50** (4), 316–34.

Bagga, A. and Baldwin, B. (1998) Entity-based Cross-document Coreferencing Using the Vector Space Model. In *Proceedings of the 36th Annual Meeting of the Association for Computational Linguistics and 17th International Conference on Computational Linguistics, ACL '98*, vol. 1, Association for Computational Linguistics, Stroudsburg, PA, 79–85, http://dx.doi.org/10.3115/980845.980859.

Berners-Lee, T. (2002a) *The Range of the Http Dereference Function*, Mailing list of the W3C Technical Architecture Group, http://lists.w3.org/Archives/Public/www-tag/2002Mar/0092.html.

Berners-Lee, T. (2002b) *What Do HTTP URIs Identify?*, http://www.w3.org/DesignIssues/HTTP-URI.html.

Berners-Lee, T. (2002c) *What is the Range of the HTTP Dereference Function?*, Issue of the W3C Technical Architecture Group, http://www.w3.org/2001/tag/group/track/issues/14.

Berners-Lee, T. (2006) *Linked Data*, http://www.w3.org/DesignIssues/LinkedData.html.

Berners-Lee, T., Fielding, R. T. and Masinter, L. (1994) *Uniform Resource Identifier (URI): generic syntax*, IETF Request for Comments, http://tools.ietf.org/html/rfc3986.

Berners-Lee, T., Masinter, L. and McCahill, M. (2005) *Uniform Resource Locators (URL)*, IETF Request for Comments, http://tools.ietf.org/html/rfc1738.

Buitinck, L. and Marx, M. (2012) Two-stage Named-entity Recognition Using Averaged Perceptrons. In Bouma, G., Ittoo, A., Métais, E. and Wortmann, H. (eds), *NLDB*, Vol. 7337 of *Lecture Notes in Computer Science*, Springer, 171–6.

Carletta, J. (1996) Assessing Agreement on Classification Tasks: the kappa statistic, Journal of *Computational Linguistics*, **22** (2), 249–54, http://dl.acm.org/citation.cfm?id=230386.230390.

Chan, S. (2008) *OpenCalais Meets Our Museum Collection: auto-tagging and semantic parsing of collection data*, http://www.freshandnew.org/2008/03/opac20-opencalais-meets-our-museum-collection-auto-tagging-and-semantic-parsing-of-collection-data/.

Chiticariu, L., Krishnamurthy, R., Li, Y., Reiss, F. and Vaithyanathan, S. (2010) Domain Adaptation of Rule-based Annotators for Named-entity Recognition Tasks. In *Proceedings of the 2010 Conference on Empirical Methods in Natural Language Processing*, MIT, 1002–12.

Fielding, R. T. (2005) *The Range of the HTTP Dereference Function*, Mailing list of the W3C Technical Architecture Group, http://lists.w3.org/Archives/Public/www-tag/2005Jun/0039.html.

Fish, S. (2012) Mind Your P's and B's: the digital humanities and interpretation, 'Opinionator', *New York Times*, 23 January 2012.

Grishman, R. and Sundheim, B. (1996) Message Understanding Conference-6: a brief history. In *16th International Conference on Computational Linguistics*, The Association for Computer Linguistics, 466–71.

Kripke, S. (1982) *Naming and Necessity*, Harvard University Press.

Lang, A. and Rio-Ross, J. (2011) Using Amazon Mechanical Turk to Transcribe Historical Handwritten Documents, *Code4Lib*, **15**, http://journal.code4lib.org/articles/6004.

Library of Congress (2008) *On the Record: report of the Library of Congress working group on the future of bibliographic control*, Technical report.

Manovich, L. (2001) *The Language of New Media*, MIT Press.

Michel, J.-B., Shen, Y. K., Aiden, A. P., Veres, A., Gray, M., Brockman, W., Team, T. G. B., Pickett, J., Hoiberg, D., Clancy, D., Norvig, P., Orwant, J., Pinker, S., Nowak, M. and Aiden, E. L. (2011) Quantitative Analysis of Culture Using Millions of Digitized Books', *Science*, **331** (6014), 176–82.

Moretti, F. (2005) *Graphs, Maps, Trees: abstract models for a literary history*, Verso.

Nadeau, D. and Sekine, S. (2007) A Survey of Named Entity Recognition and Classification, *Linguisticae Investigationes*, **30** (1), 3–26.

Navigli, R. (2009) Word Sense Disambiguation: a survey, *ACM Computing Surveys*, **41** (2), 10:1–10:69, http://doi.acm.org/10.1145/1459352.1459355.

Oostdijk, N., Reynaert, M., Monachesi, P., Noord, G. V., Ordelman, R., Schuurman, I. and Vandeghinste, V. (2008) From D-Coi to SoNaR: a reference corpus for Dutch. In Chair, N. C. C., Choukri, K., Maegaard, B., Mariani, J., Odijk, J., Piperidis, S. and Tapias, D. (eds), *Proceedings of the Sixth International Conference on Language Resources and Evaluation (LREC'08)*, European Language Resources Association (ELRA), Marrakech.

Ramshaw, L. A. and Marcus, M. P. (1995) Text Chunking Using Transformation-based

Learning. In *ACL Third Workshop on Very Large Corpora*, ACL, 82–94.

Rees, J. (2012) HTTP-range 14 webography, *W3C Wiki pages*, http://www.w3.org/wiki/HttpRange14Webography.

Rodriquez, K. J., Bryant, M., Blanke, T. and Luszczynska, M. (2012) Comparison of Named Entity Recognition Tools for Raw OCR Text. In *Proceedings of KONVENS 2012*, Vienna, 410–14.

Steiner, T. (2013) *Enriching Unstructured Media Content About Events to Enable Semi-Automated Summaries, Compilations, and Improved Search by Leveraging Social Networks*, PhD thesis, Universitat Politècnica de Catalunya.

Tjong Kim Sang, E. F. (2002) Introduction to the CoNLL-2002 Shared Task: language-independent named entity recognition. In *Proceedings of CoNLL-2002*, Taipei, 155–8.

van Hooland, S. De Wilde, M., Verborgh, R., Steiner, T. and Van De Walle, R. (2014) Exploring Entity Recognition and Disambiguation for Cultural Heritage Collections, *Literary and Linguistic Computing*, http://llc.oxfordjurnals.org/content/early/2013/11/29/llc.fqt067.

van Hooland, S., Mendez, E. and Boydens, I. (2011) Between Commodification and Sense-making: on the double-sided effect of user-generated metadata within the cultural heritage sector, *Library Trends* **59**, (4), 707–20.

Wilkens, M. (2011) Canons, Close Reading, and the Evolution of Method. In Gold, M. (ed.), *Debates in the Digital Humanities*, University of Minnesota Press.

6

Publishing

Learning outcomes of this chapter

- Issuing URLs and managing them in the long term
- Designing representations for manual and automated consumption
- Understanding the role of REST for global architecture of your database
- Case study: Cooper-Hewitt National Design Museum, New York

1 Introduction

Do you still remember those websites with shiny Flash intros? As with regular fashion, looking back on past IT hypes may sometimes result in painful memories. Just as you have a hard time understanding why you needed a massive Madonna-like fringe in the 1980s, you now might wonder why on earth you spent time and money on having an entire website programmed in Macromedia Flash. As it turned out, Flash was not the best choice for the current hetero-geneous web, where an increasing number of visitors use mobile devices that make a complete redevelopment necessary. We bet that in five years' time, you will have the same thought about the APIs you are currently building to publish JSON and RDF.

What does IT fashion have to do with publishing your metadata? With this chapter we come full circle. Chapter 2 focused on the production of metadata *upstream*, after which we discussed successive methods to streamline and augment the quality of existing metadata in the following three chapters. This chapter will focus on the dissemination of metadata situated *downstream*.

Throughout the various chapters, the notion of change has played a central role. Technological evolutions affect every stage of the lifecycle of metadata, but there is a noticeable difference between the pace at which things evolve up- or downstream. Typically, the administrative back-end of a software service is replaced or updated at a slower pace than the publicly available front-end. The relational databases which manage all the tables containing metadata, controlled vocabularies and links with media assets generally have a longer lifespan than the tools responsible for the publication of objects and metadata on a public front-end. The design-by-buzzword context in which web applications are developed is illustrated by the rapid rise – and disappearance – of must-have applications and formats. However, we forget all too often that in a distributed network such as the internet, innovation through fast-paced technological changes comes at a cost. The expense of *adapting* how we publish on the web considerably drives up the costs of our information industry as a whole. As the cultural heritage sector is typically one of the first victims of budget cuts, we should think critically about how we can minimize these adaptation costs.

At the same time, the need to provide automated access to structured metadata is rising. Metadata interoperability has been one of the consistent topics throughout the different chapters. As we already mentioned at the very beginning of the handbook, the automated exchange of metadata between collection registration databases has been in a sense the search for the Holy Grail ever since the automation of collection registration in the 1970s. Chapter 2 referred in detail to the difficulties in sharing metadata between databases.

Different methods have been developed over the years to automate the communication of metadata between databases. Unfortunately, a lot of confusion exists about the exact functionalities of these different techniques. Shortly after 2000, *web services* were the hot topic. This term is not mentioned as often any more, but it will be important to explain what exactly these services involve and the ideas behind *service-oriented architecture*. Within the library automation world, protocols such as Z39.50 and SRU/SRW offer a good example of web services.

Interestingly, web services also brought attention to *application programming interfaces* (APIs). This concept, especially, has been misunderstood and abused over the years. That is why we will talk here of the *multi-API fallacy*. There is no point in building multiple APIs next to one another, as this results in an information architecture which is difficult to maintain. We will come back to the basic principles of HTTP and demonstrate how the architectural style known as REST can help you develop an information architecture which is more resistant to technological change.

Publishing your own metadata and leaving the narrow boundaries of your collection registration database has been just one part of the story. After all, the end-goal of linked data is to make the links between collections and objects explicit, right? You therefore not only want to publish your metadata, but also to immediately make it clear where the user may find similar objects. When two metadata records point to the same authority file, the connection between the two objects seems straightforward. However, you need to bear in mind the *unidirectional* character of links. This feature of the web has played a decisive role in the successful way a network can be rolled out in a distributed and decentralized manner. But it also means that the LCSH URL http://id.loc.gov/authorities/subjects/sh85034652.html describing Cubism is agnostic of all the different cubist objects contained in collections across the world that point to this URL. The case study at the end of chapter will therefore look at options to embed links across collections within your collection registration database. In order to provide practitioners with hands-on experience of these techniques, an example metadata publishing application has been developed. Additionally, this application will allow you to understand the benefits of a REST information architecture.

The chapter will start by explaining the decisions involved in URL design, in order to enable long-term validity of URLs. As URLs are the most important interface of any web application and the outside world, it is important to know which factors play a role – and which ones are commonly believed to do so, but actually don't. Once we have an insight into how to address resources through URLs, we should decide how to represent them for human and machine consumption. While we described several structured formats earlier on, this chapter will detail how to apply those formats to capture the content of resources. One of the red threads over the years is how we have shifted from human to computer consumption. The publication of metadata in HTML pages offered both human users and search engines access, but quickly more elegant approaches were looked for. Therefore, we will investigate how specialized HTML annotations can enable machine-interpretation.

The desire for new applications continues to grow, particularly for rich web and mobile applications. The re-use of web content in these contexts requires an automated access to the content in a more rigidly structured format than HTML, such as JSON. If the incentives are important enough, the owner of the web content typically invests in developing a JSON application programming interface (API). As will be discussed in this chapter, we need to think about how we can independently manage resources and how they are represented for human or machine consumption.

2 Identifying content with URLs
2.1 What URLs are (and what they're not)

The very first step when publishing is to assign appropriate URLs to each piece of content. The question of what a URL identifies has been discussed in Chapter 5 in the context of named entities. Here, we will look at URLs from the other side instead: how to design an appropriate URL structure. The fact that this is necessary might come as a surprise, because it used to be the case (and unfortunately still is) that the software that publishes the data determined the URL structure. For instance, we commonly spot .php or .aspx in URLs of software written in PHP or ASP.Net respectively.

Consider the following URL:

http://example.org/index.php?option=com_blog&view=blog&lang=en.

It shows that the underlying server software is PHP and reveals a specific Content Management System (CMS) with an internal com_blog module, even though those volatile details are of no relevance to the information consumer. If we allow software packages to have this influence on our information, then unavoidable future migrations will be painful. In the example application we referred to, the switch from PHP to ASP, or even to a different CMS within PHP, would invalidate all existing URLs. Although it is possible to forward those existing URLs, where does that end? If one software package has specific URL rules, so might another. Therefore, URLs should be designed *solely* based on the underlying content. In his inimitable style, Tim Berners-Lee (1998) captured the deliberate design of URLs – and excuses not to do so – in the document *Cool URIs Don't Change*. The excuses illustrate several myths about URLs, some of which are still alive today. When designing URLs, it is crucial to know what is factual.

To debunk perhaps the most persistent myth: there is *no* coupling between the path of a URL and the location of a file on the server. For instance, if we see the URL http://www.example.org/cubism/artists/picasso.jpg, it would be tempting to assume that the server has a folder cubism somewhere, with a child folder artists containing the file picasso.jpg, like so: C:\Websites\www.example.org\cubism\artists\picasso.jpg.

However, this assumption is completely erroneous. There is no hard-coded mapping whatsoever between a URL and some file on the server. We're partly misguided by the .jpg extension, which seems to suggest that picasso.jpg is a JPEG file that resides somewhere in a file system. Again, this is wrong – did you know that the URL http://www.example.org/cubism/artists/picasso.jpg could in fact even lead to something in HTML or CSV format? This is because a URL is an *opaque* (as opposed to a *transparent*) identifier for every consumer of that URL. It is invalid to make any assumption on how a server will treat a URL, and in particular, none of the constraints that hold for a file-based system hold for URLs in general.

Given our day-to-day experience with file-based systems, we are inclined to break down the URL into parts and give meaning to each of them. It's perfectly fine to do that for yourself, as long as you're aware that this is a human interpretation only. When the client sends a URL to the server, the identifier arrives as a whole; more precisely, it arrives as an indivisible domain name (http://www.example.org/) and an indivisible path (/cubism/artists/picasso.jpg). Together, these two parts form an indivisible identifier to the server, meaning: 'for the domain http://*www.example.org*, find the piece of content identified by */cubism/artists/picasso.jpg*.' When we see the slashes, we might think the server will regard the parts they separate as distinct entities, but this is not true. For example, the server treats all of the following URLs in a similar way:

- http://example.org/cubism/artists/picasso
- http://example.org/cubism:artists:picasso.jpg
- http://example.org/images?name=picasso
- http://example.org/CubismArtistsPicasso.abc.def
- http://example.org/236346189GH2
- http://example.org/.

Note how none of the characters have a special status (apart from the mandatory slash separating the path from the domain name) and how extensions make no difference. A server is free to decide how it treats any URL; as a consequence, there is nothing we can infer from a URL's structure. This also explains why one URL can point to a document and another to a concept, as we discussed in the previous chapter.

That said, some server software packages do have internal rules for how URLs are treated, and perhaps these do give a particular interpretation to slashes or extensions, or any other characters. However, it is crucial to understand that this is a choice and limitation of that specific software package, and by no means an obligation on the web. Fortunately, developers of many software packages understand this and offer flexible URL options.

The independence of URLs and files makes it possible to move files around while still maintaining the same URLs to the outside world. Even more, the independence of URLs and the underlying software makes it possible to completely change the implementation while still offering the same URLs. As Berners-Lee (1998) indicates, the stability of URLs is of utmost importance, no matter how much technology changes in ten years. If you still offer the same resources, they should remain accessible through the same URL, regardless of the numerous design changes your website will undoubtedly have undergone. There are only two real excuses for not having a resource at a URL anymore: either you no longer have ownership of the domain name, or the resource no longer exists. In the latter case, make sure not to re-use the same URL for a different resource, as this will lead to undesired side-effects.

2.2 Future-proof URL design

If the software doesn't constrain URLs, they can be defined by what they are most closely tied to: the content and its structure. The question thus becomes how we can assign URLs to pieces of content in a future-proof way. As the goal is for URLs to stay stable for the entire lifecycle of their domain name, we must ensure they are based on *invariant* and *unique* properties of the content they point to. Invariant properties for works of art are title and author; but these are of course seldom unique. The combination of both might be unique for some authors, but others have different works with the same title. The best option is to rely on deliberately assigned unique identifiers. For instance, VIAF uses unique numbers to identify artists. As a result, its URLs contain this number (e.g., http://viaf.org/viaf/15873/ for a page about Pablo Picasso) and because of this, these URLs will never require any modification.

Another mechanism is to use semi-unique properties such as full names. While this yields subjectively nice identifiers like http://en.wikipedia.org/wiki/Pablo_Picasso, some items cannot have their preferred URL. For instance, http://en.wikipedia.org/wiki/Nicos_Nicolaides has been reserved for the Greek painter Nicos Nicolaides, whereas the Greek politician with the same name has the alternative URL http://en.wikipedia.org/wiki/Nicos_Nicolaides_(politician). This again illustrates that no external assumptions about the URL may be made: as the server remains responsible for assigning URLs, we cannot assume that any DBpedia topic can be found by appending its name to a base URL.

In many cases, concepts can be organized in a hierarchy. It can then be convenient to organize URLs in the same way, giving each URL human-interpretable clues about its destination. The most common way on the web to indicate such a hierarchy is to use slashes, but as we explained above, this is only a human convention and no special meaning of these characters should be assumed. For example, the Greek painter could be given the URL http://greece.example.org/people/artists/nicos_nicolaides, whereas the politician could have http://greece.example.org/people/politicians/nicos_nicolaides. This also creates the expectation that the different levels of the apparent hierarchy can be accessed separately. For instance, /people/artists can have a (partial) list of all artists, and /people a (partial) list of all people mentioned on the site. However, recall that this is purely a convention for humans; for servers, a URL is just an ordinary list of characters, none of which has special significance. Therefore, we should never solely rely on URL structure to navigate from one resource to another. Hyperlinks remain the primary navigation source on the web, and they can be generated by the server that knows the underlying hierarchical structure. This avoids 'guessing' the correct URL. Once this URL has been communicated by the server, it can be used in external hyperlinks as well.

The primary purpose of URL design is to obtain identifiers that give some guidance to people, but most importantly, they should be sustainable in the long term so that hyperlinks to them never break. The concept pointed to by the URL should be unambiguous: a URL to a page about a certain writer should continue to point only to that page, even though its contents might evolve and even though a politician with the same name might be added later on. Take special caution to avoid time-sensitive information URLs. In particular, no references to technology should be made, as the concept the URL points to will probably survive the software currently used to deliver it. Ideally, even extensions should be left out, as HTML (.html) and JPEG (.jpg) might become obsolete one day, just like Flash (.swf). It's not that the extensions have a meaning to the server; as we discussed, they don't. On the contrary, precisely because they do not have a meaning related to the identified concept, it's better not to include them at all. URLs should focus on the resource they point to, not on the technology that happens to publish that resource.

3 Marking up content

Once we have decided how to address content, it must be represented in a format that can be interpreted at the client side. In the early years of the web, the client landscape was quite homogeneous: desktop computers with a typical screen resolution and a single browser. Nowadays, content is consumed by several different types of clients. This still includes many human consumers, but they use vastly different devices ranging from small-screen smartphones and tablets to high-resolution laptop or desktop computers. Additionally, content is consumed by software, mainly in the form of in-browser applications, but the possibilities are endless if machines can interpret content. Therefore, we'll have a look at presenting content. The makeup/markup distinction has been introduced in Chapter 2; here, we will distinguish further between *structural markup* that describes the document and *semantic markup* that describes its contents.

Your challenge as a content publisher is to serve all different clients with the least amount of effort possible. One part of this is designing the representations of your content. Depending on the clients you aim to support, there might be one format or multiple ones. The other part consists of serving the right format to the right client, which is detailed in section 4 of this chapter. In the following sections, we will discuss the design of representations in HTML, JSON (JavaScript Object Notation), and RDF. Table 6.1 shows an overview of these formats and their uses.

Table 6.1 Different representation formats and their uses

type	consumed by	example use cases
HTML	humans; some annotations can be interpreted by machines	displaying text and media in a browser, navigating through hyperlinks
JSON	machines; format is application-dependent	access data in dynamic web applications or mobile applications
RDF	machines; application-independent format	automated data access and processing; linked data

3.1 HTML

HTML has two central features: marking up structural units within a text, and referring to other pieces of content by either embedding them or linking to them.

In Chapter 2, we discussed the role of HTML by contrasting *markup* and *makeup*. The purpose of HTML is to mark up text structurally, whereas CSS stylesheets can add visual styling corresponding to that markup. The benefit of this is that the same HTML markup can be used with different stylesheets to result in a different representation. Thereby, the same content can be displayed differently on small or large screens, avoiding the need to create separate versions for mobile clients. This was one of Flash's major drawbacks, as the layout was directly embedded into the content, without an explicit indication of content structure. HTML allows you to create and maintain only a single representation for all human consumption of a single piece of content.

Even though HTML documents were originally targeted at human consumers and not at machines, this separation is somewhat artificial. Already in the early days search engines that crawled HTML pages were using structural markup tags to infer the important parts on a page. People started wondering whether they could put more markup into a page to explicitly indicate certain pieces of content, which could then be parsed automatically. This first happened rather informally with *Microformats*, until RDFa introduced the possibility to embed RDF in regular HTML pages. However, RDFa's complexity lead to the creation of *Microdata*, which has a similar goal but simpler markup.

There are various good reasons for adding semantic annotations to your pages. First, it allows search engines to better interpret your contents (as opposed to only the structure), and thus to index it in a more efficient way, which leads to people finding your content faster when they need it. Second, your pages can be parsed automatically by other information-gathering clients, which do not need special guidance to understand the contents of your pages. Third, browsers can enhance a user's visiting experience with these annotations. For instance, if contact details are detected they can be added to the user's address book, or if events are detected, they can be added to a calendar. In a sense, it's the best of both worlds: it makes the multi-device and human-targeted HTML format also machine-interpretable.

Interestingly, such annotations can be automatically generated based on structured metadata. In fact, the purpose of semantic annotations is precisely to re-use as much as possible of the existing HTML content. For instance, if the title of a work is already mentioned in a document, there is no need to encode it again. Instead, an annotation is added to the element containing the title, so machines can interpret to what entity this title belongs. Other metadata that we take for granted (such as 'this is a person', 'this is an artwork') need to be explicitly encoded if we want automated processing. By enhancing a template within a CMS to use the extra markup, automated interpretation of resources comes at low cost. The next subsections will introduce you to the different annotation formats. When examining the code fragments, take a close look at the small amount of additional markup that is required to support them.

3.1.1 Microformats

Started as a grassroots initiative, Microformats are a set of conventions for marking up specific things such as contacts, events, and tags. These conventions are detailed at the web page http://microformats.org/. For example, *vCard* is the Microformat to mark up contact details, and it consists of special values for class attributes:

```
<aside class="vcard">
  <h2>
    <a class="fn org url" href="http://www.cooperhewitt.org/">
      Cooper-Hewitt, National Design Museum
    </a>
  </h2>
  <p class="adr">
    <span class="street-address">2 East 91st Street</span><br>
    <span class="locality">New York</span>,
    <abbr class="region" title="New York">NY</abbr>,
    <span class="postal-code">10128</span><br>
    <span class="country-name">USA</span>
  </p>
  <p>
    Telephone: <span class="tel">(+1) 212.849.8400</span><br>
    Email: <span class="email">cooperhewittpress@si.edu</span>
  </p>
</aside>
```

3.1.2 RDFa

The model underlying RDF has many serializations. In this book, we already mentioned Turtle and RDF/XML, and RDFa is another serialization. Unlike the two others, RDFa is embedded in another representation format, namely (X)HTML. Originally targeted at XML documents, RDFa became also compatible with HTML5 in version 1.1. RDFa offers the full power of RDF and can thus be used to describe any piece of content using any vocabulary. For instance, we can describe Picasso's *Guernica* as follows:

```
<div prefix="dbpedia: http://dbpedia.org/resource/ dbpedia-owl:
http://dbpedia.org/ontology/"
       resource="#Guernica" typeof="dbpedia:Painting">
    <p>Title: <span property="rdfs:label">Guernica</span></p>
    <p>Artist:
```

```
        <span property="http://dbpedia.org/property/artist"
typeof="dbpedia:Person"
              resource="dbpedia:Pablo_Picasso">
          <span property="rdfs:label">Pablo Picasso</span>
        </span>
      </p>
    </div>
```

As you can see, the syntax resembles what we've seen with Turtle. Subjects are identified by the resource attribute, properties by the property attribute, and objects as element values in the HTML code. typeof is used as a shortcut for rdf:type triples. There are prefix declarations to allow for shorter URIs (e.g., dbpedia and dbpedia-owl) and some prefixes such as RDFs are built in. The above fragment translates to the following Turtle:

```
:Guernica a dbpedia:Painting;
          rdfs:label "Guernica";
          dbpprop:artist dbpedia:Pablo_Picasso.

dbpedia:Pablo_Picasso a dbpedia-owl:Person;
                      rdfs:label "Pablo Picasso".
```

3.1.3 Microdata

As the syntax of RDFa was rather complex when it was still in XML-only stage, an HTML5 alternative named Microdata was created. Related to this, a vocabulary named *Schema.org* was launched by Bing, Google, and Yahoo! (and later Yandex). The Schema.org vocabulary aims to be a comprehensive list for most needs, featuring properties for books, events, people, organizations, and others. This example shows a Microdata version of the metadata of James Joyce's *Ulysses*:

```
<div itemscope itemtype="http://schema.org/Book">
  <h1 itemprop="name">Ulysses</h1>
  <p>Written by
    <span itemprop="author" itemscope
itemtype="http://schema.org/Person">
      <span itemprop="name">James Joyce</span>
    </span>
  </p>
</div>
```

The itemoscope attribute groups a subject's properties, indicated by itemprop.

Additionally, itemtype gives the subject one or many types. The Turtle equivalent would be:

```
:book1 a schema:Book;
       schema:name "Ulysses"
       schema:author _:person1.
:person1 a schema:Person;
         schema:name "James Joyce".
```

Even though in theory, any vocabulary could be used (as the model is nearly identical to that of RDF), only the Schema.org vocabulary occurs in practice. The idea is that people can create new items within the vocabulary as needed, and Schema.org will incorporate them if they become popular. However, such a centralized control is precisely what linked data tends to avoid, as it puts constraints on the flexibility.

3.1.4 Which markup to use?

Now that we apparently have three methods to semantically mark up HTML content, we face the problem of deciding which one(s) to use. In theory, all three approaches could be used in combination, but this would lead to bloated markup that is hard to maintain. The main argument in the decision is usage. Microformats are the oldest and have the smallest domain; hence, it does not make much sense to apply them anymore, except perhaps for contact or event data. Microformats 2 has recently been launched with several improvements, but it is perhaps too late to turn the tide. HTML5+RDFa 1.1 has been a W3C recommendation[1] since August 2013, and its suggested use for Facebook-indexable markup has persuaded many publishers to adopt it. The functionally equivalent Microdata has the main benefit of being endorsed by major search engines, but it is not clear to what extent the data is actually used nowadays. It overlaps almost entirely with RDFa, and the W3C is unlikely to adopt a second standard without significant difference (Sporny, 2013).

Statistics from Bizer et al. (2013) show that 29.75% of the top 10,000 domains use Microformats, 30.47% RDFa and 7.20% Microdata. This number drops significantly when looking at an increasing number of websites, where Microformats are still more popular than RDFa. The far most popular Microformat is hCard, the most RDFa-annotated resources are articles, blogs, and websites, and Microdata is most used for blog posts, navigational paths ('breadcrumbs') and addresses. So for generic markup, RDFa is recommended; perhaps contact details and events can also be marked up with Microformats. The future of Microdata is unsure – but then again, how sure can we be on the future of the web?

3.2 JavaScript Object Notation (JSON)

HTML5 has brought even more JavaScript web applications than ever before. Whereas JavaScript was used in the early days for effects and interface improvements, it has now become an integral part of how may websites function. JavaScript development has matured, and part of this is because of its access to data through JSON. HTML pages are created for human consumption, and perhaps, if they have semantic annotations, also for interpretation by a machine. However, JavaScript applications mostly don't seek to interpret data, they just need to be able to process it fast and display it.

Unlike HTML but analogous to XML, JSON has no predefined tags, so there is a lot of freedom involved in creating JSON representations. However, don't reinvent the wheel: if existing applications already use JSON for similar purposes, try to see if you can re-use their structure to some extent. Keep things simple; JSON doesn't strive for verbosity but for efficiency. For instance, we could present Guernica as follows:

```
{
  "title": "Guernica",
  "artist": {
    "firstName": "Pablo",
    "lastName": "Picasso"
  },
  "type": "painting"
}
```

Another guideline is to avoid surprise; don't force consumers of your JSON file to read your manual. For instance, users might want to find out more information about Picasso. One way to achieve this is to add an identifier:

```
{
  "title": "Guernica",
  "artist": {
    "id": "15873",
    "firstName": "Pablo",
    "lastName": "Picasso"
  }
}
```

Unfortunately, the code 15873 doesn't tell us how to proceed. Probably this number must be filled out in a URL template, but to find out which template, the documentation must be consulted. Instead, aim to be concrete and practical:

```
{
  "title": "Guernica",
  "artist": {
    "id": "http://viaf.org/viaf/15873/",
    "firstName": "Pablo",
    "lastName": "Picasso"
  }
}
```

By exposing an external identifier (a URL) instead of an internal one (a proprietary code), the above fragment becomes much more accessible. The structure remains as simple, but the values contain more 'meaning' (even if only in the human sense of the word).

3.2.1 JSON-LD

Speaking of meaning, it is also possible to add a semantic layer to JSON, just as we did for RDF. JSON for Linking Data (JSON-LD)[2] adds annotations to JSON in order to enable an RDF-compatible interpretation. Note how the following fragment of JSON-LD adds an @context element defining the mapping from JSON attribute names to RDF property URIs, and the @id element to mark a subject's URI.

```
{
  "@context": {
    "dbpprop": "http://dbpedia.org/property/",
    "title": "http://www.w3.org/2000/01/rdf-schema#label",
    "firstName": "dbpprop:firstName",
    "lastName": "dbpprop:lastName",
    "artist": "dbpprop:artist"
  },
  "title": "Guernica",
  "artist": {
    "@id": "http://viaf.org/viaf/15873/",
    "firstName": "Pablo",
    "lastName": "Picasso"
  }
}
```

The above translates to the following Turtle fragment:

```
<http://viaf.org/viaf/15873/> dbpprop:firstName "Pablo";
                              dbpprop:lastName "Picasso".
```

```
_:p dbpprop:artist <http://viaf.org/viaf/15873/>;
    rdfs:label "Guernica".
```

JSON-LD can be accessed as JSON by regular applications, although applications that do support semantics benefit from the extra layer of meaning.

3.3 RDF

Finally, to serve machine-targeted semantic representations, RDF is the best choice. As we explained in Chapter 2, RDF comes in different serializations. However, the XML representation is hardly relevant any more; Turtle is the *de facto* way to serve RDF content.

Like XML and JSON, there is no rigid structure for RDF. However, RDF itself is of course constrained to the triple model. Furthermore, following the linked data principles, you should link to other data, i.e., re-use vocabularies that others have created. Otherwise, automated clients will not be able to infer meaning from your data. As a general guideline, always add at least a label to your application's resources, using rdfs:label and/or dcterms:title. This will at least help a machine to make the information understandable for humans.

Also, categorize the data by adding rdf:type relations to broadly used vocabularies of the linked data cloud. When publishing person data, do consider foaf:Person and related properties. In addition, dbpedia:Person and specific subtypes such as dbpedia:Painter, dbpedia:Writer can be very helpful. The same goes for works of art. Have a look at the linked data cloud, starting with DBpedia or Sindice, for resources similar to yours. See which vocabularies they (re)use, which properties they add and which they omit. Consider including the same type of information, and perhaps even linking to the resources you discovered. Also, a list of popular vocabularies are those that RDFa parsers include by default: http://www.w3.org/2011/rdfa-context/rdfa-1.1.

As a last resort, define properties and classes of your own. After all, the open-world assumption is that 'anyone can say anything about anything'. However, things you define will only be useful to others if you include sufficient links. When in doubt, always remember that RDF publishing is an iterative process: you can't get it right the first time, but it is very important that you try hard. Good datasets not only link to others, but become linked themselves. Strive to publish re-usable data, and start by re-using yourself.

We purposely do not provide examples here, as there are many on the web. Use the techniques learned in the case study of Chapter 2 to explore examples within the linked data cloud.

4 A web for humans and machines

Now that we have discussed the formats that machines can interpret, the question that remains is: how to serve them? Where do we put them so that they don't interfere with the other formats, while still providing integration with the overall website? The traditional solution was to separate the human and machine sections of the site. HTML pages would be delivered in a regular way, whereas XML or JSON formats would be offered through a dedicated service with partly proprietary interaction mechanisms. This situation is what we call 'the old web for machines', which we will discuss next. After that, we will look into REST, an architectural style that integrates the human and machine web in a simple way.

4.1 The old web for machines

4.1.1 Web services

What happens when you ask developers to make something accessible for machines? The chances are that they will suggest to create an application programming interface (API), an entry point that enables them to program something. This is precisely what happened on the web at first: SOAP (Simple Object Access Protocol) was designed as a protocol to send programming instructions to the server in XML, and to retrieve an answer in XML. However, the fact that the protocol was standardized does not mean that any server that implements a SOAP service can automatically be called from a client; quite the contrary. Each server needs to define its own set of methods and messages, and clients need to be specifically programmed for a server. SOAP only fixes how messages are exchanged and interpreted.

While still used a lot in an enterprise context, SOAP did not really integrate well in the context of web applications. That is because SOAP is in fact not a web citizen as such; it just tunnels a messaging protocol through the underlying web protocol HTTP, but change the underlying protocol to something else and SOAP still works. SOAP does not make any attempt to reach out to other aspects of the web, and is therefore not a lasting solution. SOAP has its use for programming, but not for content distribution.

4.1.2 Lightweight APIs

When the XML hype was settling down, developers wondered whether they could simplify the messaging infrastructure imposed by SOAP. They started building HTTP APIs that functioned directly on the level of the web, instead of as a protocol on top of the web. At first, these APIs also worked with XML, but as JavaScript Web applications were gaining popularity, JSON became the content format of preference.

While this evolution towards lightweight APIs considerably simplified development on both the client and the server side, the interfaces remained separated. Concretely, humans would access resources through URLs like http://example.org/artists/15873, but the JSON API would have specific URLs like http://api.example.org/v1/getArtist?id=15873&format=JSON. There was no way to infer one from the other, as each developer chose other mechanisms. In essence, lightweight APIs are still programming over the web, albeit in a much more direct and straightforward way. Such HTTP APIs are still dominant today. Because of that, the human web and the machine web are still largely distinct, but as we'll see in the next section, this is not a necessity.

4.2 Representational State Transfer (REST)

Rather than a specific technology or standard, REST is an architectural style that 'has been used to guide the design and development of the architecture for the modern Web' (Fielding, 2000). REST will allow us to provide access for human and machine consumers in the same way, avoiding needless duplication and maintenance. It is important to note that REST is a *style* for system architectures, dictating several *architectural constraints*, rather than a technology or architecture in itself.

The most widespread architecture that is subject to these constraints is of course the world wide web itself, whose transfer protocol HTTP is governed by the REST principles. However, this does *not* imply that every website therefore conforms to the REST constraints *by default*. SOAP and HTTP APIs are notable exceptions, and consequently, they do not integrate well in the web.

The design considerations that make REST particularly special are its *uniform interface constraints*:

- identification of resources
- resource manipulation through representations
- self-descriptive messages
- hypermedia as the engine of application state.

To understand how a REST API works, how it integrates with the web and what its benefits are, we will guide you through these four constraints. They will be discussed via the main keywords they convey: namely *resources*, *representations*, *messages*, and *hypermedia*.

4.3 Resources

The essential unit of information in REST architectures is a *resource*, a conceptual entity that must be *uniquely identifiable*. On the web, this means that each resource must have its own unique URL. Even though this sounds trivial, this practice is not applied everywhere. A typical sign of not identifying resources by URLs is if the browser's 'Back' button is broken – clicking it does not bring you back to the page you visited previously. Resource identification starts with designing proper URLs (as we've seen in section 2 of this chapter) and using those URLs to refer to the things we publish about rather than the mechanisms we use to publish with.

How to identify resources

Non-REST compliant A link on a museum web page brings us to an object of its collection at the URL http://example.org/collection/ObjectViewer.aspx. If we follow a link to another object, the page's content changes, but the URL remains the same. As a result, the object has no URL to bookmark, nor can we share it with somebody else. The URL itself already indicates the problem: 'ObjectViewer' identifies a part of some system instead of the collection item we're looking at. The URL doesn't identify a resource.

REST compliant A museum web page shows a certain object of its collection at the URL http://example.org/objects/18353113/. Another object is accessible at /objects/35460799/, and similarly, each object has its own URL, which we can share or bookmark for later use. Each URL corresponds to what we are seeing and thus identifies a resource.

The important difference between resource identifiers such as URLs and traditional identifiers such as primary keys in databases is that the URL relation is *conceptual*. Figure 6.1 shows an example. The application domain entities are objects in a museum collection, indicated on top in white, they exist independently of web applications built on top of them. Resources and their corresponding URL are indicated in shaded boxes at the bottom. For instance, the conceptual mapping *Toy Theatre* will always correspond to the object with that name in the collection through the URL /objects/18353113/. Interestingly,

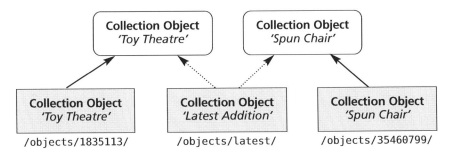

Figure 6.1 Resources (shaded boxes) are conceptual mappings, pointing to entities (white boxes). Which entity the resource points to can change and so can the entity itself; the semantics of the mapping, however, cannot.

while the conceptual mapping 'latest addition' is constant (it always corresponds to the most recently acquired object in the collection), the entity this points to changes as new items are acquired. This illustrates the conceptual nature of resources: constant mapping, possibly variable value.

4.4 Representations

Now that a shared concept of identification between client and server has been established, the next question is how information can be transferred between them. An essential property of REST architectures is that resources themselves are *not* transferred; instead, client and server exchange a *representation* of a resource. This is what we have learned in section 3 of this chapter: depending on the purpose, the same piece of content can be represented in different formats, such as HTML, JSON, or RDF. In the context of REST, the representation format is often called a *media type* and sometimes known as a *hypermedia type* if the document type natively supports hypertext controls such as links.

In REST platforms such as the web, identifiers address a piece of content and not a particular representation. This means that the URL http://example. org/objects/18353113/ refers to an object in the collection, and not the HTML or JSON version of that object. Consequently, the same identifier can be used, independent of whether the consumer is a person, a web application or a semantic application. This is possible through *content negotiation*: each client indicates what resource it wants and what media types it prefers, and the server sends a representation of that resource in a supported media type. For instance, a browser will ask for an HTML representation of http://example.org/objects/ 18353113/, while a JavaScript application will ask for JSON – using the same URL. This concept is illustrated in Figure 6.2.

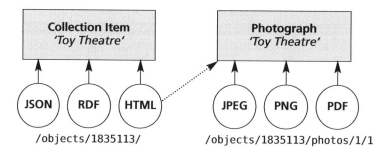

Figure 6.2 A representation *(circle)* captures the state of a resource *(rectangle)* and consists of data and metadata. Representations can include (links to) other resources, as is the case here with the HTML representation. Note how the target of the link is the *resource* (which is stable) and not any particular *representation* (which can be different).

This contrasts with file systems, wherein an identifier *(file name)* always corresponds to a specific physical representation *(the file)*. On the web, an identifier *(a URL)* corresponds to a conceptual entity *(a resource)*, which can have different representations, depending on the capabilities of the client.

How to provide access to resources through representations

Non-REST compliant A museum provides access to the HTML version of an object in its collection at http://example.org/objects/18353113/. However, the JSON version must be accessed through http://api.example.org/getObjectJson.php?id=18353113.

REST compliant The object is accessible through http://example.org/objects/18353113/ and, depending on the request, the server replies with HTML or JSON. In the future, RDF might be supported through this same URL.

Note how in the non-compliant example, the identification happens on the technical level instead of the conceptual level. The URL identifies 'the HTML representation of object 18353113' instead of 'object 18353113'. This makes the exchange of URLs between different systems difficult, as the choice for a specific representation is tied to the URL. This is the main issue with non-REST APIs: the 'human API' (regular HTTP) is different from the 'machine API'. Furthermore, the addition of new representation formats (such as RDF) would imply that a new API with new URLs has to be developed, which leads to unnecessary costs: the web already has an API for human *and* machine clients: the HTTP protocol. Without the resources-and-representations model, we indeed arrive at a *multi-API*: every type of client needs its own interface to the collection. The purpose of REST is exactly to provide a uniform interface through a single API, whose contract can be maintained in the long term.

4.5 Messages

The uniform interface of REST architectures is considerably simplified by requiring all messages to be self-descriptive. Concretely, this means that every message should contain all information necessary to understand and process it, independent of possible preceding messages (Fielding, 2000). Most of it happens on the protocol level and follows automatically if you follow the resource-oriented principles.

In order to have self-descriptive messages, interactions must be *stateless*. In general, the client should not assume the server remembered anything about the previous interaction and should therefore resend request details such as resource identifier, authentication details, media type preferences, etc.

How to send self-descriptive messages

Non-REST compliant A collection website provides a search function. When searching for 'Picasso', we see the first page of search results /objects?filter=picasso. To reach the second page, we have to click a button that submits the text nextpage to the server. The server can only answer the second request by looking again at the first.

REST compliant On the first page of search results /objects?filter=picasso, there is a link to the second page /objects?filter=picasso&page=2. Both requests contain all information the server needs to send a reply.

In the non-compliant example, we notice the message is not self-descriptive: the text nextpage does not fully define the request. To determine what to do, the server should remember the details of the previous request. This can get messy really soon if you use multiple browsing tabs simultaneously. It's not the server's task to remember where you were before; each request should fully indicate what you want. In contrast, the compliant example uses messages that fully define the request: the query is picasso and we require page 2. This also aligns with proper resource identification: only in the second case, an actual resource ('the second page of search results for "picasso"') is identified.

4.6 Hypermedia

If self-descriptive messages lead to stateless interactions, you might wonder how we transition from one state to another. Well, the *hypermedia constraint* indicates that all state changes should happen through hypermedia. So continuing the previous example, when you are on the result page /objects?filter=picasso, you don't need to type the full request for the second result page. Instead, there will be a link on the first page towards /objects?filter=picasso&page=2, so you can just click through. This is why the server doesn't need to remember your previous request. Inside the representation, it has put links and forms towards possible next steps, and since the server chooses those links, it is able to put in all information it needs to answer your next request. So this is where it all comes together: resources are identified by URLs and send through representations, inside those representations are the links that allow to go to the next state.

Now on the human web, hypermedia controls such as links and forms are common practice: nearly all HTML pages we visit provide links to others. We never have to use the browser's address bar to advance towards the next state (unless we want to go somewhere completely different). However, on the machine web, this is far less frequent in representation formats targeted at machines. However, as REST strives for the same interface for all types of clients, machine clients need those links as much as we do.

How to send hypermedia messages

Non-REST compliant Let's revisit the example on JSON representation design from section 3.2. The following representation does not contain links.

```
{
   "title": "Guernica",
   "artist": { "id": "15873" }
}
```

REST compliant The example below does incorporate a link and the client can just follow it. No documentation is necessary.

```
{
    "title": "Guernica",
    "artist": { "@id": "http://viaf.org/viaf/15873/" }
}
```

The non-compliant example is not driven by hypermedia but by *out-of-band information* that has to be interpreted separately, even though an HTML representation of the same resource would allow hypermedia interactions. Thereby, the web application gives a different *affordance* to people and software clients: the HTML representation affords navigating to the producer, whereas the JSON representation does not. When designing representations, developers often wrongly assume that software clients do not need these affordances. However, the hypermedia principle that any piece of information is linked to other pieces has been crucial to the success of the human web; we should therefore not underestimate its impact on the web for software clients.

Fielding (2008) captures this in the following definition: '[hypertext is] the simultaneous presentation of information and controls such that the information becomes the affordance through which the user (or automaton) obtains choices and selects actions'. The revolution of the web is indeed that information has become *actionable*; it is no longer a static piece of text but an interface that affords people and software clients the means to obtain more information of their choice. In order to enable this powerful mechanism, the fourth and last constraint of the uniform interface thus demands that *any* representation – HTML, JSON, and RDF – contains the links that lead to possible next steps. Not coincidentally, this is also the driver behind linked data: any piece of information should link to others that augment its context.

4.7 Providing access to your metadata

Now that you know about URLs, semantic annotations and REST, what is the most cost-effective strategy to publish your linked data? The answer to this question has multiple facets. However, be sure about one thing: no matter how badly your development team wants it, don't let them build a multi-API. Developers love to build APIs, and they charge huge amounts of money for it. The main message from the REST discussion in this chapter is that the web was built as a REST architecture, and so you need only a single API to serve many different types of clients. That API consists of your data items, exposed as resources through URLs with representations that link to other resources of your dataset and on the entire web. The underlying technology can be different at any institution; for instance, you could have a CollectiveAccess database with a Drupal CMS on top. However, the guiding principles for any such API are the same.

The effort in setting up and maintaining your API should be focused on (a) resource and URL design and (b) representation design. The first step therefore is to build an inventory of all resources, including all items of your collection but also auxiliary resources such as welcome and contact pages. Then, divide them into groups and/or a hierarchy, and determine their URL structure. For each group, decide which clients will access them. For example, your collection items could be accessible to humans on desktop computers and portable devices, to web and/or mobile applications (perhaps including your own), and to linked data aggregators. In contrast, your contact page is probably only interesting to human visitors.

As a second step, start the representation design. In most cases, this comes down to creating the relevant templates in your CMS, given use cases such as in Table 6.1. The case study at the end of this chapter will show example templates for different representation formats. Humans need HTML, so this is the most straightforward (and probably most important) media type. For web and mobile applications, JSON representations will be required. Provide them for those resources where they are needed, but be careful to re-use the *same* URLs for the same resources, regardless of their content type. Then, there are two choices for providing semantic data as well. The first is to augment your HTML representations with semantic annotations. This does not add another content type, but enriches an existing one, which can be great for lightweight semantic purposes. If you prefer to offer fully fledged documents, you can also provide complete Turtle representations of resources (again through the same URLs). If you are unsure what to decide, be aware that both options are possible: you can add some annotations to the HTML resource, and offer all of them in the Turtle representation. Thanks to the REST principles, clients will be able to parse the document of their preference.

5 Conclusion

5.1 Choose sustainability

This has been a chapter about best practices for sustainable publishing. Reflecting on what we have learned, it's time to look at the web and see how much of this is implemented as of today. It turns out the situation is rather disappointing. Even Berners-Lee (1998) remarks in his document about Cool URIs 'do what I say, not what I do'. It's a guarantee that out of the top 10 websites you visit, several will not obey the rules for proper URL design. You will still see much of the underlying technology slip through (watch out for those .aspx and .php extensions) and many of those URLs that are valid today will not be next year.

Consequently, it should not come as a surprise that the REST architectural style, which builds on proper resource and thus URL design, is also not implemented widely, despite the clear benefits this offers. We see three main reasons for that.

First, the knowledge about what REST exactly entails is fairly limited. A lot of incorrect information lives on the web, with prominent terms such as 'RESTful URLs' (which don't exist) and 'a REST service' (often used to indicate access to machine-readable representations through an interface separate from the main application, and hence not according to the REST uniform interface constraints). The term 'REST API' is seemingly used to label anything that does not use the SOAP protocol; even people considered experts in specific web technologies unwittingly give their plain HTTP API the incorrect label 'REST'. Hopefully, books such as this one will help to spread awareness of the correct meaning, but until then, 'hypermedia API' can be a distinguishing label.

Second, many people are unaware of the fact that URLs identify resources and not files. This misconception leads to the belief that HTML access *has* to be different from JSON or RDF access. This has created a false idea that it is necessary to build separate interfaces – and since there are going to be multiple interfaces anyway, they may as well be designed in a totally different way (for the exact same content, mind you). This has seemed to be justified by the perceived different needs of human and machine consumers, which are actually more the result of different habits acquired by application developers, who still have trouble abandoning the procedural world for resource-oriented thinking. Their reflex of doing getObjectById(35) and createObject(properties) is so strong, they have a hard time converting to GET /objects/35 and POST /objects/. Note that this difference is not purely cosmetic or syntactic; it's the difference between a proprietary, one-off system and a universally agreed-upon interface that integrates with everything else on the web. When publishing with the future in mind, we need to acknowledge the unique nature of the web, which is a collection of interconnected resources and not a file-based system we can misuse as a procedural interface.

Finally, the third cause is that programmers just get more fun and money out of building APIs. We're not saying that they would purposely deliver a system that is overly complicated; instead, it often just happens by accident (although often, it might well be due to laziness or greed). Imagine the following situation: somebody has an HTML-only website and asks an IT firm to build a JSON API. Is the firm going to say to the customer 'you don't need an API, we'll just add a new representation'? That would be bad for business, as (a) adding a new representation is less work and (b) the customer will likely have more trust in another company that does what he says. There is often a major gap between what the customer thinks he needs, what the customer actually needs, and how the IT company delivers that need. In this example, the actual need is *machine-based access*, and the way that is most cost-effective and technically superior is to implement another representation, not an entirely new API. Remember that maintenance is always the highest cost for any application, so the more APIs there are, the higher that cost will be.

However, like pretty much any web API, REST APIs inherit one design characteristic from the governing design of the web's architecture that might not always be beneficial: unidirectionality. Web links only go one way, so if a page on my site links to yours, my visitors can get to your site but your visitors cannot automatically reach my site before you add a link back. This is also the root cause of broken links, which we are all too familiar with. Yet it was a fundamental departure from earlier hypermedia systems that allowed the web to scale globally, as bidirectional linking involved a tight connection of multiple parties. Unidirectionality has its consequences for the hypermedia constraint, which requires that the server gives the client the links it needs. These links will always be limited, as the server is unaware of all incoming links that might also interest the client. One way around unidirectionality is a SPARQL endpoint, which lets us query triples in both directions. You can query in the regular forward direction (e.g. `<myResource> :relatesTo ?other`) as easily as in the backward direction (e.g. `?other :relatesTo <myResource>`). For now, SPARQL endpoints are still expensive to maintain, so the more pragmatic option might be to accept unidirectionality until better solutions come up. These solutions might involve indexes such as Sindice, which offers access to data from different sources in one interface.

Using the technical background this chapter has provided you with, never settle for less than a REST API. Libraries, museums and archives are forced to think on a long-term scale when it comes to preserving items in their collection. It doesn't make sense to think in the short term when it comes to the digital equivalent of that collection. Technology *will* change, machines *will* access content in a different representation, within a few years' time. Therefore, any solution must be based on the content, which will eventually outlive the technology. REST satisfies this criterion on the web, whose building blocks will always be URLs and resources.

5.2 Piecing together the publication puzzle

This chapter started with URL design and representation design, which were then brought together as part of the first two constraints of REST's uniform interface. We could just leave it at that and say the puzzle fits nicely together, considering REST the end-goal of our publication endeavour. That would mean that REST is simply the Nirvana of online publishing because of its nice technical properties. However, as long as there are no tangible benefits from it, nobody but technology purists cares about the beauty of a technical solution (and seeing the limited adoption of REST, those purists are vastly outnumbered).

Interestingly, REST itself is just a piece of a larger puzzle that encompasses everything in this book so far. You will recall that our main goal is the sustainable publication of linked data. Let's now review what we've done in the previous chapters, and see how this fits in with data publication through a REST interface.

Chapter 2 featured different models of data publication, ranging from tabular and relational data over meta-markup languages to linked data formats. The REST architecture means that you don't have to make a definite choice. The conceptual resources of your collection exist independently of their representations, and there need not be a direct link from your internal format to the external format(s) you offer. As technology progresses, both the internal and external formats will change, but neither change has to affect the other. Furthermore, by using URLs to identify resources instead of concrete representations, we can ensure that the URL identifying a particular collection object today will continue to identify this object for eternity, while concrete representations are allowed to change at any time. The fact that each representation format is only a mapping from a resource, means that the cleaning techniques of Chapter 3 will propagate to all representations. You only need to clean the internal representation of the resource in order to obtain this result in all representations.

Chapters 4 and 5 studied the addition of links to structured and non-structured fields, respectively. Here, it is of utmost importance that the obtained URLs are stable, and this can only be the case if they identify resources rather than concrete representations, since representations will inevitably change. Unfortunately, you depend on the technical decisions of third parties: only if they have chosen to publish their data in a REST architecture can you benefit from the effects. Fortunately, large sources such as DBpedia have made the right decision, as we will see in the case study.

That said, if you want your data to be re-used flexibly, choosing to publish it in the REST way enables others to access and interact with it easily, which is what linked data is all about. And this is the final piece of the puzzle that makes everything come together. Let's compare the difference between integrating data from a non-REST and a REST source. Suppose we linked a record about a painting by Pablo Picasso to respectively http://nonrest-example.org/getDetails.

php?type=person&id=6748 and http://rest-example.org/people/pablo-picasso, either through reconciliation or named-entity extraction. We now want to incorporate data from the external sources in our web application. In the non-REST case, these are the steps we have to take:

1 Manually go to http://nonrest-example.org/ to find out how their JSON API works, figuring out the mapping between the HTML URL and how JSON is accessed.
2 Probably obtain a key for this API (even though access is free).
3 Hire a developer to write the interaction code between our web application and the JSON API.
4 Repeat this process for every different website you link to, as all APIs are different.
5 Pray that the APIs, the URLs and their representation formats do not change, as you will have to start all over again.

In contrast, the REST case involves the following step:

1 Get the URL asking for JSON.

No praying is necessary, as there is only one API and it's the same one the entire web uses. So in fact, REST ensures that both parties save on development costs: the other publisher does not need to pay for a JSON API, and you don't have to pay for the development of a specific API client. Furthermore, the process is repeatable for all different REST data sources, as they all implement the same uniform API. Now if we repeat the same steps but use RDF instead of JSON, we don't even have to parse different JSON representations any more, as the RDF data model is the same everywhere.

This is how REST's uniform interface makes linking between different collections easy, as it hides the underlying details. All that matters is stable URLs for resources, and flexible underlying representations that can evolve as demands change over time. There is no good reason why anybody should ever want an API on the web other than HTTP's URLs and resources.

6 CASE STUDY: Cooper-Hewitt National Design Museum

The Cooper-Hewitt National Design Museum, New York was founded at the end of the 19th century and harbours a collection of historical and contemporary design. In 2011, the museum closed for a three-year-long renovation, rethinking the collection in terms of different narratives for different visitor groups. A major part of this transformation is to remain true to its mandate to be there for every one: both the expert and the general public. This is translated into a technical challenge: the collection and its metadata must be offered in flexible ways inside and outside the museum. Not only is the agility to rapidly fulfil emerging user demands a requirement, it is also the ambition of the museum to promote the discovery of new unforeseen requirements.

Over the years, Cooper-Hewitt has used The Museum System (TMS) as a collection management software in combination with eMuseum to drive the public front-end of the collection.[3] This software environment does not offer any of the flexibility necessary for the information flow and agility described above. The museum needs to move faster than allowed by the internal architecture of TMS and the dictates of eMuseum's pricing model. As a generic software solution marketed towards a broad range of cultural heritage institutions, TMS is designed to be very flexible towards individual exceptions in the data model, at the cost of a rather complex relational database design. The problem is that this makes the data non-transparent and thus difficult to approach from outside TMS.

Despite all of its shortcomings, a pragmatic choice was made to keep TMS for the curatorial tasks it has been performing over the years and by doing so the database continues to serve as the system responsible for metadata creation and management. However, in order to address the agility concerns and to have maximum flexibility on the front-end website, eMuseum has been abandoned. Data is exported from TMS into a more flexible environment which can be perpetually in an alpha release. The first goal therefore was to generate automatically a CSV (comma-separated value) export from TMS. The export is then ingested in a PHP web-application framework which gives the freedom to rapidly build interfaces and indexes tailored to needs which can evolve rapidly.

This agile approach allowed the museum to bypass the complexities of data modelling. One conceptual requirement which became paramount, however, is the issuing of persistent identifiers and making almost everything a first-class resource on the web. In other words, as many facets as possible of the collection should be expressed as URLs. For example http://collection.cooperhewitt.org/countries/france and http://collection.cooperhewitt.org/objects/colors/ff1493/ respectively give access to all objects manufactured in France or which have deep pink (represented by the colour code ff1493) as their dominant colour palette.

Persistent identifiers under the form of URLs also are fundamental if Cooper-Hewitt wants to realize its vision of holding hands with as many partners as possible on the web. The museum has been actively reconciling its metadata with authorities such as VIAF (Virtual Authority Files) but also with knowledge bases such as Wikipedia and Freebase. For example, the museum does not have a biography of the American designer Ray Eames, but it provides through the reconciliation process a link to his Wikipedia page. Other cultural heritage institutions, such as the MoMA (Museum of Modern Art), are also actively reconciling their metadata with the same knowledge bases and authorities. This approach makes it then feasible at a second stage to make explicit what artists, places, etc., are shared across institutions.

The Cooper-Hewitt has made its entire metadata set available on https://github.com/cooperhewitt/collection. It is upon this data that we will build an application in this case study. However, we will first explore data access from other APIs, starting with the DBpedia API, and continuing with the Europeana and the DPLA APIs.

6.1 REST access to linked data

Arguably the most famous linked data source, DBpedia, is an excellent example to explore. Furthermore, we've already explored DBpedia's SPARQL endpoint in the case study of Chapter 2, so it is interesting to compare this to DBpedia's API. If you are familiar with DBpedia, you might be surprised to hear that there is something like a 'DBpedia API'. After all, this is not mentioned on their home page, and a quick search only refers to the Spotlight API we used in the previous chapter. So where is the DBpedia API?

The answer has been lying right in front of us the whole time: it is the DBpedia website itself. Even after half a chapter about REST, this might still surprise you, but the DBpedia dataset has only one API and it's the website itself. Since DBpedia uses representations to serve resources in HTML, JSON and RDF formats, different clients can access them through the *same* API. So the API you use in your browser is exactly what machine clients use as well.

Therefore, let's start with the DBpedia API in our browser by visiting the URL for Arthur Rimbaud, namely http://dbpedia.org/resource/Arthur_Rimbaud. By doing so, we are actually *dereferencing* this URL – manually. When you do this, you note something interesting: the browser automatically moves from http://dbpedia.org/**resource** /Arthur_Rimbaud to http://dbpedia.org/**page**/ Arthur_Rimbaud. Why would DBpedia use two kinds of URLs that seemingly are about the same thing? Actually, they're not the same: as we've discussed in Chapter 5, it is important to distinguish between the *thing itself* and *a document about that thing*. Even though both are 'resources' in the REST terminology, they are distinct resources and thus require different URLs. The first identifies Arthur Rimbaud, the poet himself, who cannot possibly be represented in HTML. The second identifies a document *about* Rimbaud, which can be represented in HTML; it's that representation the browser shows on your screen.

Now, what if we would like to see representations for machines? We can't directly go to their URLs, because the RDF and HTML representations of a

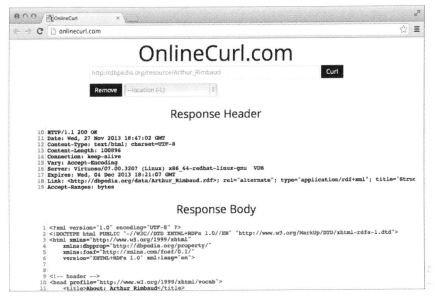

Figure 6.3 OnlineCurl showing the headers and body for the DBpedia page about Arthur Rimbaud

resource share the same URL. However, using a specialized browser, we can *pretend* to be a machine client and hence ask for representations other than HTML. This is possible with the *cURL* browser.[4] However, cURL is a command-line application and hence difficult to use if you are not familiar with this type of interaction. Therefore, we will use an online variant of cURL at http://onlinecurl.com/.

Let's first simply try things the regular way by entering the URL http://dbpedia.org/resource/Arthur_Rimbaud. However, remembering the automatic redirect your browser did from the person to the document, we need to tell cURL it is allowed to do the same. Click the **Add Option** button and choose the −location (-L) option that permits cURL to change the original location, then click the **Curl** button. You'll receive a response consisting of two parts: the response headers and the response body, as shown in Figure 6.3. The body is the HTML code of the page you just viewed in your browser, the headers are technical details that explain to your browser how to deal with the content. One header in particular is important:

```
Content-Type: text/html; charset=UTF-8
```

It tells the browser (or any other client) that the current representation is formatted as HTML. So for now, we did the same thing twice in different ways. First, we retrieved HTML through a regular browser, which displayed it in a graphical way; second, we retrieved HTML through the cURL browser, which displayed the HTML source code instead:

```
...
<head profile="http://www.w3.org/1999/xhtml/vocab">
    <title>About: Arthur Rimbaud</title>
...
```

But cURL can do something your browser cannot: request other representations. For instance, we can say to the server that we want to see the RDF/Turtle representation. To do this, we have to explicitly indicate our media type preferences by sending an extra header to the DBpedia server. Enter the same URL, http://dbpedia.org/page/Arthur_Rimbaud, together with the –location (-L) option, but now click the **Add Option** one more time. We need to set a header that says we want to retrieve Turtle. From the list of options, choose the –header (-H) option and enter the following value in the text field:

```
Accept: text/turtle
```

This will tell the DBpedia server that we accept Turtle representations, which are identified by the string text/turtle.[5] If you now click the **Curl** button, you will see quite similar response headers, except for:

```
Content-Type: text/turtle; charset=UTF-8
```

This server thus indicates here that its response will be formatted as Turtle. And indeed, the body is Turtle:

```
...
dbpedia:Arthur_Rimbaud rdf:type yago:Communicator109610660,
                                 yago:SymbolistPoets,
                                 dbpedia-owl:Writer,
                                 dbpedia-owl:Artist,
                                 dbpedia-owl:Person,
...
```

So adding an Accept header allows us to simulate what other clients see. DBpedia supports other content types as well, so be sure to try setting OnlineCurl's Accept header value to any of the following:

```
Accept: application/json
```

```
Accept: application/rdf+xml
Accept: application/ld+json
```

This will give you different representations of the same resource.

Note the importance of using the single URL in all these examples: the same URL allows us to retrieve different representations of the same resource. This enables two totally different systems (your browser and cURL) to both use the same API. This API consists of the HTTP protocol and the URL as unique identifier, regardless of the underlying content type. This allows those different systems to exchange and discuss the same pieces of content through the same URL, establishing system-independent identification.

Let's take a moment to reflect on how the browser and cURL illustrate the principles of the REST uniform interface exhibited by DBpedia.

- **Identification of resources:** URLs have been used to identify two different types of resource: the person Rimbaud and the DBpedia document about Rimbaud. DBpedia treats them correctly as separate resources; and since the person cannot be meaningfully represented, the browser automatically redirects to the document. The URLs of Rimbaud and the document remain unchanged, regardless of which client (browser or cURL) is used.
- **Resource manipulation through representations:** As resources are conceptual entities, the document is not transferred as such. Instead, a representation is served, which depends on the client's preferences. We've seen an HTML and a Turtle representation, but DBpedia supports others as well.
- **Self-descriptive messages:** The server only needed a single message to reply to the request, without knowing any other information about the client. When the server sent a response, the media type was indicated, so the message explained how to interpret its body contents.
- **Hypermedia as the engine of application state:** The HTML representation allows other pages to be found by following links; inside the Turtle representation are URLs of other entities that can be dereferenced in turn.

6.2 Exploring other APIs

To show the difference with APIs that do not follow the REST principles, we will briefly discuss the Europeana and Digital Public Library of America APIs, which have been designed in an ad hoc manner. The fact that the world's two largest digital library projects have chosen a more complicated API design shows that knowledge about REST APIs is not widespread in all sectors yet. It raises the question of whether their development will prove cost-effective in the years to come, given that REST APIs demand less development effort on both the provider and the consumer side.

6.2.1 Europeana

The Europeana website provides access to metadata from various institutions across Europe. We first visit an object on the Europeana website to familiarize ourselves with the way things work. We chose an object from the Dutch Rijksmuseum depicting Confucius, located at http://www.europeana.eu/portal/ record/90402/collectie_RP_P_1958_434.html. Your browser shows an image as well as associated metadata. Have a look around to see how the pages are structured and what data you can find on them.

If this were a REST API, we could use the same URL and retrieve a JSON representation as well. Let's try that with cURL. Enter the URL in OnlineCurl and add a header option with Accept: application/json, then click the **Curl** button. Unfortunately, we get an error message instead of a JSON response. This means that we will need to use a different mechanism to access the collection.

The documentation page (http://www.europeana.eu/portal/api-introduction. html) confirms that Europeana was implemented using a custom API mechanism. The very existence of documentation mostly indicates this: with REST APIs, the public website we use in our browser *is* the API, and websites mostly don't need documentation. Europeana has instead opted to offer separate APIs for human and automated use. The first thing we note is that access requires an API key. By filling out your e-mail address, you receive an API key and a private key; it's the former you will need to use in the following examples.

After browsing the documentation for some time, we find the following URL template:

```
http://europeana.eu/api/v2/record/[recordID].json
```

This means we will need the record ID to access the object. However, on the HTML page, there is no mention of such an ID. It turns out that this has to be taken from the URL: 90402/collectie_RP_P_1958_434 is the identifier for our object. When we substitute this in the template, adding our key, we get:

```
http://europeana.eu/api/v2/record/90402/collectie_RP_P_1958_434.
json?wskey=xxxxxxx
```

We can now try this with cURL (don't forget to add your own API key at the end). The response indeed shows a JSON version of the object.

While the entire procedure might seem manageable in the end, remember that we listed a precise instruction on how to use the API. This required studying the documentation, which is different for each API. Furthermore, it still involves manual work: registering for an API key, extracting the identifier, replacing it in the URL template, and adding the API key.

6.2.2 Digital Public Library of America (DPLA)

The Digital Public Library of America provides metadata of collection items all over the USA. As usual, we start on the human-accessible part of the site, for example, from a photo depicting the Apollo 11 launch at http://dp.la/item/ecdafcf9b06be6efed042e40b3923e57. When opening the HTML version in our browser, we see an image of the launching pad and associated metadata. We can try to see whether OnlineCurl is able to access the JSON version on this same URL. While no error occurs, we receive the HTML version, even though we specifically asked for JSON. This indicates that DPLA does not support the resources/representations approach of the REST architectural style.

Therefore, we head over to the API documentation at http://dp.la/info/developers/codex/. As with Europeana, we must first register for an API key through e-mail. We then need to wade through the documentation to find out how to retrieve a JSON representation. The URL template for this is listed as:

```
http://api.dp.la/v2/items/[id]?api_key=[key]
```

The ID of the Apollo photograph is not visible in the HTML version. It turns out that we have to extract it from the URL:

```
ecdafcf9b06be6efed042e40b3923e57.
```

Substituting this in the template, we can retrieve the JSON representation at:

```
http://api.dp.la/v2/items/ecdafcf9b06be6efed042e40b3923e57?api_key=
    xxxxxx
```

Even though the principles in this case are similar to those of the Europeana API, the details are different: knowledge about one API does not help when consuming another. Furthermore, even the basic principles might be quite different with a third API, because no architectural design governs these APIs. This contrasts with REST web APIs, which use an interface that has already been agreed upon (HTTP), and a single URL is sufficient to traverse the entire API without documentation.

6.2.3 Comparison to REST APIs

When comparing the steps we had to undertake with Europeana and DPLA to those for REST APIs such as DBpedia, the enormous burden that custom APIs bring becomes apparent:

- Different URLs are used to access representations of the same resource. As such, different systems end up with other identifiers for the same concept, making interoperability difficult.
- Since URLs serve to identify representations instead of resources, we need rules to construct the URL for each other representation. These rules differ for each API and have to be interpreted manually.
- HTML access to the API is open, but JSON access requires an API key. Not only does this make use more complex, it also poses a problem when you want to use the JSON API in web applications. You have to find a way to keep your key hidden from users, and this is in most cases not possible (not to mention that this does not add any security to the underlying data, as the HTML pages containing the same content can still be accessed freely).
- The JSON URL includes sensitive information (your personal API key); as such, it cannot be exchanged with other parties. For instance, in this book, I cannot list the URL to any JSON representation, as that would expose my private key. This is a consequence of the decision to use URL not as resource identifiers, but as a programming instruction ('do this using these parameters'). Such instructions change rapidly over time, as evidenced by the 'v2' in both APIs, while identifiers can be long-lived.
- Using the API requires studying the documentation, as we cannot simply use the web's URL-based interface.
- Representations do not contain links to other resources. Therefore, even if we successfully retrieved one item from the API, we have to start the process over again to retrieve another.

These problems indicate that REST is not only a nice conceptual framework, but a necessity for simple and uniform access to data for humans and machines alike. Especially in the long term, the resource-based approach guarantees stability. If DBpedia is still around in ten years' time, the same resource URLs will correspond to the same concepts: there is no need to change them, even though technology will evolve. In contrast, we are quite sure that the Europeana and DPLA APIs will change sooner than that, because their implementation is tightly bound to a particular way of programming that will become obsolete long before the data does. So when reading this book in a not too distant future, you will be able to verify whether our prediction was accurate.

6.3 Inside a REST Web application

6.3.1 About the application

The limited adoption rate of REST applications, and the observation that two major players in cultural heritage have not adopted them, might make you sceptical about their feasibility. Is it so hard to set up a REST web application?

To reassure you that this is not hard at all, we have created a basic open-source data publication platform on top of the Cooper-Hewitt National Design Museum's collection. In the next sections, we will study how this application makes the metadata available as HTML, JSON and RDF. First, we will explore the API through a regular browser, as people usually do, and then look at the same API through the eyes of an automated application. Finally, we will show a high-level overview of the application's source code. The goal is not to turn you into a programmer. Instead, you will see how the REST principles result in a simple design.

Now simplicity in itself is not a goal, but it strongly correlates with:

- lower development costs for the application
- lower maintenance costs for the application – (and maintenance is typically more expensive than initial development)
- lower development and maintenance costs for clients, which facilitates adoption.

Therefore, it is important to recognize simplicity in an information system, even though you are not a developer yourself. If you still doubt whether to choose one single web API such as DBpedia or adopt a multi-API approach such as DPLA and Europeana, this final hands-on experience with REST will convince you.

6.3.2 Using the application through the browser

The application is freely available online at http://dataplatform.freeyourmetadata. org/. Figure 6.4 shows a metadata document on this site. When you open the home page in your browser, you are greeted by a basic overview of the Cooper-Hewitt metadata. It has been divided into the different metadata categories of the dataset:

- departments (*/departments*)
- exhibitions (*/exhibitions*)
- objects (*/objects*)
- periods (*/periods*)
- persons (*/persons*)
- roles (*/roles*)
- types (*/types*).

We can click through each of these categories to see (part of) the items they contain. This is of course basic hypermedia navigation, yet it is the crucial way for people to browse a site. Most importantly, it is this aspect that makes us able to use the site without reading a manual first. When you browse the page, try to pay close attention to the elements that are there, as they will be reflected in other representations later on. For instance, the JSON representation will need its own way of representing these basic links, if we want automated clients to use the application as easily as we can.

Note on the bottom of the page that we have explicitly mentioned the 'permanent URL of the resource'; we will do this on every page to emphasize (a) the resource-based addressing, which allows you to share identifiers between different systems, and (b) the fact that the identifiers are 'Cool URIs' that do not change (Berners-Lee, 1998). Be sure to inspect the URL design in the application as you go along: it has been carefully set up so that the URLs can be maintained for as long as the dataplatform.freeyourmetadata.org application exists.

Next, choose a category you want to explore, for instance, **objects**. As expected, we receive a list of links to objects. As trivial as this might seem, take a mental note of the things that are different to the previous page, and those that remained the same. They will influence the template design,

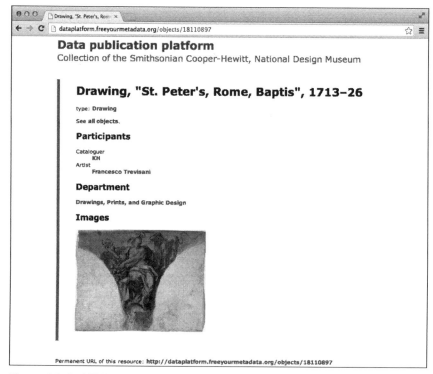

Figure 6.4 An HTML representation of the metadata of a Trevisani drawing

which we will discuss later on. Also note the presence of a link that brings us back to all categories: even though we might just click the **Back** button of our browser now, this doesn't work if you started the navigation on the current page (e.g., through a link somebody shared with you). Such a link is also important for machine clients, which are generally unaware of the resource's context.

Pick any object you like to have a look at its metadata. Figure 6.4 shows the metadata for a drawing by Francesco Trevisani (*/objects/18110897*). Especially note the links to related metadata entities. The link to *Francesco Trevisani* (*/persons/18042573*) leads us to more information about this artist, but at the same time, it also *identifies* the artist's metadata through its URL. The same holds for other links. The choice for URLs based on a numeric identifier rather than other attributes allows the evolution of the metadata. For example, we see that the cataloguer of the object is indicated as '*KH*', whose metadata is identified by */persons/18047487*. It might be possible that '*KH*' is later improved to contain the full name of this person; however, the URL can remain constant.

Interestingly, our pages can link to external APIs. If we have used reconciliation (Chapter 4) or named-entity recognition (Chapter 5) to find external identifiers, they can be incorporated here. Possibilities include Wikipedia, Freebase, VIAF and others. Furthermore, if those external APIs follow the REST principles, then these links are valid across different representations.

6.3.3 Using the application as an automated client

With the steps still fresh in our mind, let's now pretend we are an automated client and attempt to perform the same navigation path through JSON representations. The rules are that we should start from the same URL, and we should never craft URLs ourselves, i.e. each URL we follow should be given by the server. Additionally, the URL for each resource should be the *same* as if we were browsing HTML. That way, we can switch back to HTML (and back to JSON) anytime we like.

Go to http://onlinecurl.com/ and enter the URL http://dataplatform. freeyourmetadata.org/. When we ask the server for a document, it must know that we are interested in the JSON representation and not HTML. Therefore, we indicate that we want JSON by clicking the **Add Option** button and setting –header (-H) to Accept: application/json. After clicking **Curl**, you see the response appear. The first thing to notice is that the response headers indicate the content type is application/json, meaning we got the representation we asked for. Inside this representation, you will see a document we've encountered before, but this time it has been formatted as JSON:

```
{
  "title": "Categories",
  "kind": "categories",
  "categories": [
    {
      "title": "departments",
      "url":
"http://dataplatform.freeyourmetadata.org/departments"
    },
    {
      "title": "exhibitions",
      "url":
"http://dataplatform.freeyourmetadata.org/exhibitions"
    },
    {
      "title": "objects",
      "url": "http://dataplatform.freeyourmetadata.org/objects"
    },
    ...
  ],
  "url": "http://dataplatform.freeyourmetadata.org/"
}
```

As this representation contains URLs, we can continue to retrieve other resources. In fact, they are the same URLs we used when navigating in our regular browser. Copy the **objects** URL and paste it into the OnlineCurl field. Make sure the **header** option is still set to retrieve JSON and click **Curl**. We now see the list of objects in JSON format. Note in particular the back link we also had in the HTML representation:

```
...
  "parent": {
    "title": "Categories",
    "url": "http://dataplatform.freeyourmetadata.org/"
  }
...
```

From the list, pick again any object you like; we chose the same drawing (http://dataplatform.freeyourmetadata.org/objects/18110897). OnlineCurl will retrieve the JSON representation, which contains similar metadata and links as its HTML counterpart:

```
{
  "accession_number": "1901-39-1699",
  "title": "Drawing, \"St. Peter's, Rome, Baptis\", 1713–26",
...
  "participants": [
    {
      "person_name": "KH",
      "role_name": "Cataloguer",
      "person_url":
"http://dataplatform.freeyourmetadata.org/persons/18047487",
      "role_url":
"http://dataplatform.freeyourmetadata.org/roles/35352245"
    },
    {
      "person_name": "Francesco Trevisani",
      "role_name": "Artist",
      "person_url":
"http://dataplatform.freeyourmetadata.org/persons/18042573",
      "role_url":
"http://dataplatform.freeyourmetadata.org/roles/35236565"
    }
  ],
...
}
```

As you would expect, we can continue to navigate this representation through links. None of the rules we set were broken: we got from each point to another by following URLs (not crafting them ourselves), and each URL can be used to retrieve HTML as well.

Reflecting on the short HTML and JSON navigation sessions we did, we can see how the REST uniform interface constraints manifest themselves:

- **Identification of resources:** Each metadata document is identified by a URL, regardless of its representation.
- **Resource manipulation through representations:** Each document can be retrieved in multiple formats, depending on the client's indicated preferences.
- **Self-descriptive messages:** Each message contains all details needed to interpret it: we made the client send along its content preferences with every request, so the server doesn't have to remember them. The fact that the server indicates the content type on every message is also self-describing.
- **Hypermedia as the engine of application state:** Each representation

contains URLs to go to the next steps, so we never have to manually construct URLs or read documentation.

Concretely, it shows that retrieving JSON is just as easy as retrieving HTML, except that we just used another browser (OnlineCurl) to pretend we were an automated client. This means that if you want to use this API on your website, for instance to show related objects, all your developers have to do is retrieve the object the same way you would do in a browser. No studying of any documentation is required, allowing fast and easy development.

6.3.4 Supporting linked data clients

Before we look under the hood, we will briefly show how the application also offers Turtle representations to support clients needing linked data. Unsurprisingly, the same steps we used for HTML and JSON can be repeated with Turtle as well. Open OnlineCurl and use the http://dataplatform.freeyourmetadata.org/ start page, but now add a header with value `Accept: text/turtle`. You can now navigate in a similar way by using URLs indicated inside the Turtle representations.

One interesting peculiarity of the linked data variant is the need to distinguish between the resource and the document about the resource. For instance, the document about the drawing (*/objects/18110897*) is not the same as the drawing itself. To make the difference, the server uses hash fragments. This can be seen inside the drawing document's representation:

```
<http://dataplatform.freeyourmetadata.org/objects/18110897>
    foaf:primaryTopic
<http://dataplatform.freeyourmetadata.org/objects/18110897#
    concept>.
<http://dataplatform.freeyourmetadata.org/objects/18110897#
    concept> rdfs:label "Drawing, \"St. Peter's, Rome, Baptis\",
    1713–26"@en.
```

So /objects/18110897 is the URL of the *document*, whereas /objects/18110897#concept identifies the drawing itself. Therefore, the label property is attached to the drawing, not the document. Usage of the #concept fragment is purely a convention of this particular server. Hence, we need to make this relation explicit, which is done by the foaf:primaryTopic relation. The above fragment thus says that the document has the drawing as its primary topic, and this drawing has a certain label. As discussed in Chapter 5, distinguishing between the document and its topic allows to make different statements about both: the metadata document clearly has a different age from that of the drawing itself.

This mechanism is the same as used by DBpedia, which had resource and page

URLs. The difference is that opening the concept /objects/18110897#concept automatically shows you the associated document /objects/18110897, whereas DBpedia uses a direction from the resource to the page.

6.3.5 The application's architecture

Finally, we will look at how the application is built on the inside, and how this delivers the functionality we've just used. The main purpose of this section is to show how the REST architectural style simplifies an application's design, not to turn you into an API programmer. At the end, you will know how to recognize simple API design and see that implementing a REST API involves significantly less work than creating a full additional API just for machine access.

Before we go any deeper, let's understand the application you've just been browsing from a bird's-eye view. The Cooper-Hewitt is the base of the application. It consists of thousands of small JSON files that contain the metadata of an individual item. For example, the file 18110897.json contains the metadata for the Trevisani drawing. However, this is an *internal* version of the resource that may not be exposed to the public. Instead, this resource is *represented* as either HTML, (public) JSON, or Turtle. We expect thus to see a component responsible for reading the internal data source, and components that generate each of the representations. In addition, there will be a main component that orchestrates the others.

The application's source code is available on the online code sharing platform GitHub at https://github.com/RubenVerborgh/DataPublicationPlatform. There is no need to download the source code, as we can simply navigate it online. As you can see, the application is organized into five main folders:

- data: This folder contains the Cooper-Hewitt metadata, organized in subfolders. Each subfolder eventually consists of JSON files that correspond to individual items.
- templates: This folder contains the templates that will be used to represent the items as HTML documents.
- assets: This folder contains static resources, such as CSS stylesheets; in other words, auxiliary resources that are not part of the metadata.
- lib: The actual source code of the various components is organized in different subfolders of the lib folder.
- bin: This folder contains the executable file to start up the server. Basically, it simply runs the components from the lib folder.

We will discuss the contents of the data, lib and templates folders in more detail.

All individual metadata items of the collection have their own internal JSON file somewhere in the `data` subfolder, which is organized in a hierarchical way. While the internal JSON file has many things in common with its public counterpart, it is important to understand that they are different. The fact that the internal data source uses JSON is a mere coincidence; it might have as well been a MySQL database or CollectiveAccess. Because Cooper-Hewitt has chosen to use JSON as internal representation, this is what the application uses. The difference can be seen already at the top of an internal JSON file:

```
{
  "id":"18110897",
  "tms:id":"8229",
  "accession_number":"1901-39-1699",
  "title":"Drawing, \"St. Peter's, Rome, Baptis\",
1713\u201326",
  ...
}
```

Note how the internal identifiers `id` and `tms:id` are not present in the public JSON representation we obtained from http://dataplatform.freeyourmetadata. org/objects/18110897. Instead, the public representation contains the URL as the public identifier. However, the data storage does not need to be aware of that: internally, we can use our proprietary identifiers, but towards the external world, we only use URLs. As such, our public API does not depend on internal identifiers (that might change), only on URLs that we can keep unchanged even if the internal data storage evolves.

Next, the `lib` folder reveals the actual source code. We will have a high-level look at it. If you open the `lib` folder, you see the entire application consists of only five source files, organized in two subfolders:

- `datasource`
  - `JsonDataSource.js`
- `representers`
  - `HtmlRepresenter.js`
  - `JsonRepresenter.js`
  - `TurtleRepresenter.js`
- `Server.js`

The task of `JsonDataSource.js` is to read the JSON metadata files. The three files in the `representers` folder are responsible for generating the three possible representation formats HTML, JSON and Turtle. Finally, the main component `Server.js` connects the others together through the HTTP interface. Its task is to receive an HTTP request, fetch the correct resource from the data source, pass it to the correct representation generator, and send it back to the client.

If you want to have a look inside, you'll notice that each component has under 100 lines of source code. Admittedly, the application is very basic, but this is already sufficient to offer a REST API over the Cooper-Hewitt metadata. Keep in mind that all pages you have browsed so far on this application were generated using only those five small files. Even if we are not able to understand the actual source code, these metrics tell us that providing a REST API is not all that difficult. Moreover, the source code illustrates how easily an API can be made machine-readable. The traditional multi-API approach is to implement a whole new API just to provide access for another type of client. In contrast, the REST approach only requires adding one representation generator, and updating the wiring in Server.js.

Finally, the templates folder gives us an insight into how HTML representations can be built easily. Each of the different resource types (index, object, person . . .) has its own template. For example, here is the template to generate the main page:

```
<% inherits('main') %>
<h1>Overview</h1>
<p>
   The metadata of the Cooper-Hewitt spans the following
categories:
</p>
<ul class="categories">
<% categories.forEach(function (category) { %>
   <li><a href="<%= category.url %>"><%= category.title %></a></li>
<% }) %>
</ul>
```

As you can see, it contains a mix of regular HTML with code that loads the actual categories you see on the front page. The texts inside this template can be edited easily.

6.4 Concluding remarks

This case study compared the two main approaches to publish metadata for human and machine consumption. The traditional approach is to build and maintain an additional API that is distinct from the website you offer to people. The REST approach instead extends the same website with representations for machines, resulting in one API instead of multiple. You've interacted with both kinds of APIs, both as a regular visitor through a browser and by pretending to be a machine client through cURL/OnlineCurl. At the end, we demonstrated an implementation of a REST application on top of an existing dataset to show how this can be done in practice.

The main point is that REST APIs just work like any website you visit. As such, they are simple for developers to use, as no time should be spent reading the documentation on how one specific API provider happens to have designed its secondary interface.

If you want to offer machine access to your data, the immediate cost benefits are twofold:

- Your development costs will be lower, as instead of building and maintaining a second API, only an extension of your primary API (your website) is necessary. Maintenance of a single API is also less complicated, as changes are more localized.
- Developing applications that use your API becomes cheaper, as developers don't have to study the documentation of a secondary API. Instead, they can simply use the same resources they encounter when browsing your website (and hopefully, they don't need documentation for that).

The long-term benefit is stability: technology will continue to change often, but REST APIs are based on content, not technology. The only contract between your server and clients are based on URLs that identify your data items, and you can design them so that they don't require change.

As far as practice is concerned, things are slowly changing. The example application of this chapter was built on top of the Cooper-Hewitt metadata, but the museum actually offers a full REST API on its impressive collection website http://collection.cooperhewitt.org/. Actually, the main reason why we chose to show you our demo application and not the real thing, is because we wanted to take it easy by focusing on the basic elements of REST APIs. The official Cooper-Hewitt website takes the experience to a whole new level by providing intuitive and pleasant browsing for people and machines – thanks to the REST architectural principles.

Probably you will never implement an API yourself, but instead hire skilled developers for that job. Yet, it is important to understand the conceptual and practical benefits of REST because in the end, it all comes down to asking the right question. If you ask developers to build an API, they *will* build an API, and you end up in a DPLA or Europeana situation. They offer complex APIs that cost a lot to develop and maintain but are very hard to use in practice – and thus remain underused. Instead, ask developers to provide machine-access through your existing API: your website. (The source code of the application we discussed in this chapter could serve as an example.) By embracing the resource-oriented nature of the web, we can expose our data in a sustainable way that outlives technological hypes.

Notes

1 http://www.w3.org/TR/rdfa-in-html/.
2 http://json-ld.org/.
3 The description of the Cooper-Hewitt case study is based on an article for the
   Journal of Documentation (forthcoming) which the authors of this book co-wrote
   with Sebastian Chan and Aaron Straup Cope of the Cooper-Hewitt Museum
   (Verborgh et al. 2014).
4 cURL is freely available for download at http://curl.haxx.se/.
5 ww.w3.org/TR/turtle/#sec-mime.

References

Berners-Lee, T. (1998) *Cool URIs Don't Change*,
   http://www.w3.org/Provider/Style/URI.html.
Bizer, C., Eckert, K., Meusel, R., Mühleisen, H., Schuhmacher, M. and Völker, J.
   (2013) Deployment of RDFa, Microdata, and Microformats on the Web – a
   Quantitative Analysis. In *Proceedings of the 12th International Semantic Web
   Conference*, 21–25 October, Sydney. Lecture Notes in Computer Science, Springer
   Berlin Heidelberg, **8219**, 17–32.
Fielding, R. T. (2000) *Architectural Styles and the Design of Network-based Software
   Architectures*, PhD thesis, University of California, Irvine, CA.
Fielding, R. T. (2008) *REST APIs Must be Hypertext-driven*,
   http://roy.gbiv.com/untangled/2008/rest-apis-must-be-hypertext-driven.
Sporny, M. (2013) *The Downward Spiral of Microdata*,
   http://manu.sporny.org/2013/microdata-downward-spiral/.
Verborgh, R., van Hooland, S., Cope, A. S., Chan, S., Mannens, E. and Van de Walle, R.
   (2014) The Fallacy of the Multi-API Culture: conceptual and practical benefits of
   representational stat transfer, *Journal of Documentation* (forthcoming).

7

Conclusions

Within this handbook we have focused on practical steps (modelling, cleaning, reconciliation, enriching and publishing) that allow you to understand how to benefit your institution and your users when adding metadata to the global pool of linked data. A lot of ground was covered in the five core chapters, and we necessarily had to sidestep some important global issues. In these conclusions, we want to take a step back from the operational side of linked data and reflect on the bigger picture.

Even the fiercest critic of linked data must acknowledge that the structured publication and consumption of data is increasingly affecting our day-to-day use of the web. Just launch a Google query with the name of a well known individual, a country or a product name, and you will see an information box with structured data from Freebase appearing alongside the traditional search results. Over the years to come, not only your search engine queries but also mobile phone, car navigation system or even fridge will be consuming linked data.

Now that you understand the conceptual and technological underpinnings of linked data, let us think critically about its global impact. Everyone agrees that search engines like Google have revolutionized how we access information on the web. Even if the advantages are tremendous, we cannot ignore some of the dangerous side-effects. Increasingly, we are confronted with personalized information, limiting our access to types of content that search engines and social networks know we have accessed before and therefore like. Through these funnelling practices, we are more and more confirmed in the views we already have and rarely confronted with information that might oblige us to question our beliefs. The initial ideal of the web as a promoter of the 'global village', in which the free flow of information stimulates understanding and dialogue, has been severely discredited by phenomena such as spamming, targeted marketing and cyber-balkanization.

As we have explained in Chapter 2, linked data theoretically holds the promise of creating a 'global database'. By unleashing structured data from the confines of local databases, the linked data approach stimulates a better communication and re-use of structured data in a transparent manner. During his TED talk *The Next Web*, Tim Berners-Lee (2009) made an engaging plea for more access to raw data. If we consider this as a milestone in the promotion and uptake of linked data, what are the important evolutions which have taken place since then? More particularly, what are the trends and issues that are specifically relevant for cultural heritage institutions?

To limit and guide this discussion, we have identified three problematic areas:

- the tension between the practical need to rely on statistics and probability to make sense of linked data and the research tradition of the humanities
- the presence of market forces that remain opaque for the end-user
- the current ambiguities with regard to the use of URLs.

We are convinced that the way in which these issues will be tackled (or not) will determine to a large extent the shape and nature of linked data at large, but particularly in our libraries, archives and museums.

1 Statistics, probability and the humanities

> History isn't what happened. History is just what historians tell us.
>
> Barnes, 1989, 86

Keep this Julian Barnes quotation in the back of your mind next time you consult linked data from the cultural heritage sector. Within the linked data cloud, anyone can theoretically say anything about anything. From a practical point of view, SPARQL endpoints often need to impose severe limits on the amount of triples sent back as a response to a query which could potentially contain millions of triples and causing an instant failure of the server. Even seemingly simple queries sometimes require processing large amounts of data, which can cause endpoints to break down. Try for example to ask DBpedia how many different topics it describes: `SELECT COUNT(DISTINCT ?s) WHERE { ?s ?p ?o }`. The chances are quite high you will not get an answer.

Just as Google's algorithm decides for us which of the millions of results corresponding to a query are put on the first pages and which ones are put in the back and remain in obscurity, choices have to be made in order to give priority to certain triples. The use of statistics and probability are necessary to keep us from drowning in the sea of triples.

The problem we would like to highlight here is that these methods often give priority to popular values, hiding the outliers and exceptional cases from sight. However, scholars in the humanities are sometimes interested exactly in the long tail of minority values which actually move away from the norms and standards. Within the humanities, there has always been a tension between searchers of generally applicable laws, such as Chomsky with his formalized generative grammar or the processual archaeology of Willey and Phillips, and the hermeneutical tradition with its focus on the subjective and the singular. According to Dilthey, considered the founding father of hermeneutics, scholars in the human sciences should interpret and understand (*'Verstehen'*) the world instead of explaining it (*'Erklären'*), which is the role of the natural sciences (Bod, 2013). Interpreting and understanding within the humanities often consists of a continuous process of going back and forth between individual observations and the larger context in which the observations can be framed. The detection of exceptions and outliers allows one to question and adapt the unifying and sense-making horizon offered by hermeneutics (Boydens, 1999; Boydens and van Hooland, 2011). Drucker eloquently formulates the tension between this hermeneutical tradition and the usage of methods based on statistics and probability:

> We use tools from disciplines whose epistemological foundations are at odds with, or even hostile to, the humanities. Positivistic, quantitative and reductive, these techniques preclude humanistic methods because of the very assumptions on which they are designed: that objects of knowledge can be understood as ahistorical and autonomous.. . . Probability is not the same as ambiguity or multivalent possibility within the field of humanistic inquiry. The task of calculating norms, medians, means and averages will never be the same as the task of engaging with anomalies and taking their details as the basis of an argument.
>
> Drucker, 2012, 86, 90

Drucker's critique on the assumption of knowledge as an autonomous given can be related to the work of Manovich which we cited in Chapter 2 on data modelling. As you might recall, Manovich uses the terms *databases* and *narrativity* as metaphors for two very distinct ways to organize information: 'As a cultural form, a database represents the world as a list of items and it refuses to order this list. In contrast, a narrative creates a cause-and-effect trajectory of seemingly unordered items' (Manovich, 2001, 231). The atomization of metadata in RDF triples could be considered as a radical implementation of the database as a cultural form of expression. Within a triple store, statements are packed together and can be accessed randomly. If you have already opened an RDF file, you might have noticed how difficult it can be to find your way around and to make sense of the data.

Let us illustrate this with a short example. Based on the text string 'Henry IV', the NER services which we used in Chapter 5 send us back URLs from three knowledge bases which allow us to learn more about this historical figure. We know that Henry IV of France had a fascinating but complex life: baptized as a Catholic, he was raised as a Protestant. After leading the Protestant forces against the royal Catholic army during the religious wars, he took hold of the throne of France in 1589. In order to keep the Catholics at ease, he abjured his Calvinist faith, but gave religious liberties to Protestants with the Edict of Nantes in 1598. Despite (or perhaps because of) his pragmatic skills, he was assassinated by a fanatical Catholic. What type of information do RDF triples, provided by knowledge bases, give us about the religious convictions of Henry IV?

- **DBpedia** offers the following triples, which we express here in Turtle:

```
dbpedia:Henry_IV_of_France
    dbpprop:religion dbpedia:Catholic_Church,
                     "previously Huguenot";
    dcterms:subject category:Roman_Catholic_monarchs,
    category:Converts_to_Roman_Catholicism_from_Calvinism,
    People_excommunicated_by_the_Roman_Catholic_Church;
    rdf:type yago:Convert109962414.
```

By reading the Turtle representation (go back to Chapter 2, section 5.5 if you do not recall how the syntax is structured), we understand that different predicates give us information regarding the religious beliefs of Henry IV. There is the explicit predicate dbpprop:religion which proposes two objects: dbpedia:Catholic_Church and the literal value 'previously Huguenot'. If we look more in detail, we see that the more generic applicable predicate dcterms:subject also offers information regarding Henry's religious beliefs, including the categories category:Roman_Catholic_monarchs category:Converts_to_Roman_Catholicism_from_Calvinism and category:People_excommunicated_by_the_Roman_Catholic_Church.

- **Freebase**, the commercial competitor of DBpedia, offers the following triple with regard to the religion of Henry IV:

```
ns:m.0fw6r ns:people.person.religion ns:m.0c8wxp.
```

- **Yago** is a knowledge base developed at the Max Planck Institute for Computer Science in Saarbrücken and is built up by content extracted from Wikipedia and other sources. Yago offers the following triple:

```
yago:Henry_IV_of_France rdf:type
yago:wikicategory_Converts_to_Roman_Catholicism_from_Calvinism.
```

What do we learn from this example? The power of the RDF open-world assumption, based on the premise that anyone can say anything about anything, allows diverging or even seemingly contradictory statements to co-exist harmoniously. For example, Freebase simply mentions that Henry IV was a Catholic. DBpedia confirms this statement but adds the facts that he converted from being a Huguenot, which can be considered as a subclass of Calvinists. Yago both puts Henry IV in the general class of converts, but also re-uses the predicate of DBpedia which indicates he converted to Roman Catholicism from Calvinism. It does take some time to manually understand these subtle differences and to distinguish original, redundant and conflicting information.

Through the (ab)use of the predicate `owl:sameAs`, different descriptions of the same concept can be reconciled across knowledge bases, bringing together predicates and objects which either duplicate, complement or contradict one another. In order to bring in some extra chaos, people use a multitude of different predicates to express the same (or almost the same) as `owl:sameAs`. A small selection includes `rdfs:seeAlso`, `owl:equivalentClass`, `ore:similarTo` and the whole army of SKOS predicates (`skos:closeMatch`, `skos:exactMatch`, `skos:broadMatch`, `skos:narrowMatch`, `skos:relatedMatch`). All of these predicates were originally designed and issued to express subtle differences. Unfortunately, the people who use these predicates very often do not understand or interpret them in a consistent manner.

Inevitably, practical ways are needed to select only subsets of this ever-expanding universe of triples. For this, we again have to rely on probability and statistics, based on for example how often a URL is referred to. So even if everything can be said and the most diverse or alternative statements can be made, the most popular statements will unavoidably attract the most visibility. Before starting to apply linked data principles on a large scale, the humanities community needs to be fully aware of these issues. The practical need to use statistics and probability to make sense of linked data conflicts with the reluctance of many approaches within the humanities to rely upon such methods.

2 Market forces

Aside from the probabilistic nature of querying triples or a technique such as NER, we should also remain vigilant regarding the economic forces and market shifts of knowledge bases and metadata schemas. This aspect remains by and large opaque to the general public, but also to researchers. Within the next years, the competition between knowledge bases (DBpedia, representing an open-source approach, versus Freebase, which has been acquired by Google) and metadata schemes (Schema.org, an initiative of Google, Bing, and Yahoo! versus the Open Graph Protocol, a Facebook initiative) will rise as linked data principles are applied. Whether we like it or not, a small number of competing players are currently imposing their way of rendering semantics explicit within the linked data cloud. Again, anyone can create an ontology to express their unique worldview and make it available as linked data on a web server, but if no one is using or referring to it, it is bound to remain in obscurity.

If we are not careful, monopolies will form, as there are 'mechanisms of positive feedback that operate – within markets, businesses, and industries to reinforce that which gains success or aggravate that which suffers loss' (Arthur, 1996). As a community, the digital humanities remain for the most part ignorant of these issues, as we are busy writing up grant proposals to hook up our data into the linked data cloud. Instead of this hype-driven and opportunistic behaviour, the LIS and DH communities should use their unique potential to stand up and launch a debate on these matters. Through their historical interest in exceptional values and outliers, the humanities can and should collaborate with engineers on how to facilitate and safeguard the access to the long tail of values which traditionally are disregarded in a probabilistic approach.

3 Use of URLs

Real estate professionals often say there are three important qualities to take into account when investing in a house: the location, the location and the location. We could not agree more: URLs are the cornerstone of your linked data real estate. The analogy with the housing market does not stop there. Just as you permanently need to invest in a house (from minor maintenance such as polishing wooden floors to major renovation of the roof, for example), the investment in a URL does not stop at acquiring a domain name. Commercial parties are very much aware of the future importance of URLs, illustrated by practices such as the domain name aftermarket where URLs are bought and sold by commercial parties. Unfortunately, the cultural heritage sector remains mostly ignorant of the importance of issuing URLs. It is the core business of libraries, archives and museums to preserve and give access to collections. Maintaining solid URLs should therefore be a priority.

If we leave aside for a moment the issue of maintaining URLs, we should also think about their affordance: what do we actually use URLs for? Do they identify a resource or a document about that resource? The clarification of the role of URLs we introduced in Chapter 5 will only become increasingly urgent as linked data principles are being used as building blocks within humanities projects. This issue also confronts us with a fundamental characteristic of metadata: they are ever-extendible. Every representation can be documented by another resource, that can have representations of its own (Boydens, 1999). Distinguishing between information and non-information resources is therefore context-dependent. If we stick our heads in the sand and do not explicitly address this issue, we are bound to encounter problems in the long run.

4 Engage

As you see, there are enough exciting and challenging topics to address in the years to come. Technology has profoundly influenced the humanities, but we can also leave our marks on technology. Let us hope that the application of linked data principles in our cultural heritage institutions invites people from the humanities and the sciences to pick up the gloves, step into the intellectual boxing ring and engage in a challenging sparring round. As anyone who has done some boxing training knows, sparring is the best and the quickest way to improve your skills: you are forcefully confronted with the strengths and the weaknesses of yourself and your opponent. Since the 19th century, we have made progress in regard to how both *Verstehen* and *Erklären*[1] can help us to make sense of the world. But there is still a lot we can learn from one another. This handbook is the outcome of an intense but rewarding sparring session between a historian and an engineer. We have come out smarter, and hope you, dear reader, do too.

Note

1. Loosely, 'interpretative understanding' and 'causal explanation'.

References

Arthur, W. (1996) Increasing Returns and the New World of Business, *Harvard Business Review*, **74** (4), 100–9.

Barnes, J. (1989) *A History of the World in Ten and a Half Chapters*, Picador.

Berners-Lee, T. (2009) *The Next Web*, http://www.ted.com/talks/tim_berners_lee_on_the_next_web.

Bod, R. (2013) *A New History of the Humanities: the search for principles and patterns from antiquity to the present*, Oxford University Press.

Boydens, I. (1999) *Informatique, Normes et Temps*, Bruylant.

Boydens, I. and van Hooland, S. (2011) Hermeneutics Applied to the Quality of Empirical Databases, *Journal of Documentation*, **67** (2), 279–89.

Drucker, J. (2012) Humanistic Theory and Digital Scholarship. In Gold, M. (ed.) *Debates in the Digital Humanities*, Minnesota Press, 85–95.

Manovich, L. (2001) *The Language of New Media*, MIT press.

Index